ETHICS AND LAW FOR
NEUROSCIENCES CLINICIANS

ETHICS AND LAW FOR NEUROSCIENCES CLINICIANS

Foundations and Evolving Challenges

JAMES E. SZALADOS

RUTGERS UNIVERSITY PRESS
New Brunswick, Camden, and Newark, New Jersey, and London

Library of Congress Cataloging-in-Publication Data

Names: Szalados, James E., author.
Title: Ethics and law for neurosciences clinicians : foundations and evolving challenges / by James E. Szalados.
Description: New Brunswick : Rutgers University Press, [2019] | Includes bibliographical references and index.
Identifiers: LCCN 2018006047 | ISBN 9780813593883 (pbk.) | ISBN 9780813595993 (epub) | ISBN 9780813593906 (Web PDF)
Subjects: | MESH: Neurosciences—ethics | Neurosciences—legislation & jurisprudence | Clinical Medicine | Ethics, Clinical
Classification: LCC QP360 | NLM WL 21 | DDC 174.2/968—dc23
LC record available at https://lccn.loc.gov/2018006047

A British Cataloging-in-Publication record for this book is available from the British Library.

Copyright © 2019 by James E. Szalados

All rights reserved

No part of this book may be reproduced or utilized in any form or by any means, electronic or mechanical, or by any information storage and retrieval system, without written permission from the publisher. Please contact Rutgers University Press, 106 Somerset Street, New Brunswick, NJ 08901. The only exception to this prohibition is "fair use" as defined by U.S. copyright law.

⊖ The paper used in this publication meets the requirements of the American National Standard for Information Sciences—Permanence of Paper for Printed Library Materials, ANSI Z39.48-1992.

www.rutgersuniversitypress.org

Manufactured in the United States of America

This could not have been possible without my lovely supportive family. For my dad, who taught me that personal fortitude and a gentle spirit can co-exist and prevail; for my mom, who taught me to win by never quitting and never giving up; for my sister Liz, who taught me that there is magic in this world and that we just need to keep believing; and, finally but not lastly, for my love, my wife, and my life companion, Doris, who shares the credit for all I have accomplished because she has been with me every moment and on every step of our journey and she has never stopped encouraging and supporting my dreams.

CONTENTS

	Preface	ix
	Author's Note	xi
1	Morality, Ethics, and the Law: An Overview of the Foundations of Contemporary Clinical Ethical Analysis	1
2	Case Studies: Ethical and Legal Challenges in the Care of the Neurologically Injured Critically Ill Patient	27
3	Civil Law and Liability: The Law of Medical Malpractice	42
4	Legal Reasoning, Legal Process, Legal Proof, and Why It Is Confusing to Clinician Scientists	62
5	Regulatory Law and the Clinical Practice of the Neurosciences	81
6	Digital Medicine and the Data Revolution: Managing Digital Distraction and Electronic Medical Record Liability While Leveraging Opportunities in Teleneurology and Telecritical Care	104
7	Developing and Leading a Sustainable High-Reliability, High-Performing Unit: Theories of Quality, Teamwork, Medical Error, and Patient Safety	116
8	Neurolaw and the Integration of Neuroscience, Ethics, and the Law: The New Frontiers	130
9	Afterword	143
	Acknowledgments	145
	Notes	147
	Index	171

PREFACE

The practices of medicine and its allied professions are among the most highly regulated of public services and economic activities. There is little doubt that health care providers, by and large, chose health care as a profession to help their fellow human beings through illness and personal medical catastrophes. Thus, almost uniformly, health care providers are persons with strong internal moral and ethical compasses, driven to their respective fields because of a sense of caring, work ethic, diligence, and intellectual need. My fellow health care workers are truly special. In contrast to almost all other professions, health care entails enormous commitment and personal sacrifice and also is not devoid of personal risks. In their day-to-day and moment-to-moment hectic worlds, health care practitioners tend to be so focused on the care of each individual patient, tending to each successive urgency and emergency, and completing paperwork requirements, that they seldom stand back to look at the legal and regulatory complexity of the health care system; that is, until they find themselves, their work, or practices under scrutiny.

The purposes of this book are both to provide a concise practical review of the ethical, legal, and regulatory foundations that affect our complex practices, and to explore new and evolving areas of neuroscience practice, in which many will find new opportunities and challenges, as well as legal and ethical risks and conundrums.

Neurosciences represent what is arguably the final frontier of medicine. Research, diagnostic tools, therapeutic interventions, and delivery of care models in neuroscience are evolving rapidly, largely because of digital imaging and processing technologies that allow us to see what we have never seen before. Throughout this revolution in medical sciences, we must ensure that technology does not distract us from our ethics and morality.

Technology is rarely created by legislation, regulations, or laws; instead, technological innovation forces the development of laws and regulations to harmonize technological innovation with existing public policy. However, health care providers are typically scientists, whereas regulators and politicians are instead typically social scientists with disparate but not necessarily irreconcilable views. Thus, it is imperative that providers participate fully in organizations that represent patient and provider interests to help those who formulate public policy, rules, regulations, and even standards understand the intricacies of clinical care.

To the extent possible, we must take steps to understand and shape the environments in which we practice, and we can only accomplish that goal through active involvement and engagement. I hope this book helps us all start that dialogue by presenting an overview of the most critical ethical, legal, and regulatory issues facing us now and into the future.

—JES

AUTHOR'S NOTE

The material presented here is intended to provide readers with an academic overview of legal and ethical principles for educational purposes only and to convey general information.

The material and perspective herein deal primarily with the laws and the legal system in the United States and may not represent a worldwide subject view.

The material herein in not intended and must not be construed in any way to provide legal advice in any form. This book in no way implies the existence of an attorney-client relationship. The information presented herein may not reflect new and evolving legal developments. No actions should be taken in reliance on the information contained here, and the author disclaims all liability in respect to actions taken or not taken based on any or all of the contents of this material to the fullest extent permitted by law.

Please consult with a qualified attorney regarding specific legal advice on your specific legal issues.

The opinions expressed are the opinions of the individual author and may not reflect the opinions of any institutions or firms with which the author previously has been or is currently affiliated with.

ETHICS AND LAW FOR NEUROSCIENCES CLINICIANS

1 · MORALITY, ETHICS, AND THE LAW

An Overview of the Foundations of Contemporary Clinical Ethical Analysis

THE DELICATE INTERPLAY BETWEEN MORALITY AND THE LAW

The laws of a nation are inextricably linked to the culture of the people who govern. Therefore, laws vary greatly between nations because of shared cultural values, which, in turn, are reflected in governmental structures and the method of governance of any particular nation. Discussions of fracture and morality presuppose a shared cultural definition of socially acceptable and socially unacceptable behaviors. Cultural definitions of behavioral norms are largely rooted within tradition and religion. Culture creates a shared ethical system. Although any one person may reflect and discover his or her internal sense of what is good, right, and meaningful, the course of human history is punctuated by diverse groups and cultures unifying around unique sets of values, purposes, and principles. Laws evolve from the ethical system when the culture forms a government. Each society in some fashion defines its own government, and, in doing so, entitles the government with the authorities of oversight, compulsion, and control over its people. Laws are created and put into practice through societal processes. Therefore, notions of legal versus illegal activities are defined in the context of shared cultural values, delegated authority, and social context. People of common morality traditionally have joined together in forming communities. A society cannot survive without limits of toleration and standards for conformity, and each society has the right to preserve its own existence and therefore to sanction and punish. Morality refers to a set of deeply held, widely shared, and relatively stable values within a given society. Society imposes moral standards by enforcing conformity because a society cannot survive without such laws.[1] Laws that are written but do not conform to the values shared by the majority within a society will likely be resisted unless the people governed are powerless to effect change.

In general, there are two types of freedoms: the first is the freedom to pursue one's own individuality and personal goals and interests; the second type of freedom is from the encroachment upon one's rights by others. Just laws must be carefully crafted in such a way as to delicately balance personal freedoms against societal interests. Laws exist to reconcile "principles of conformity and individual initiative, group living and private freedom of choice, social regulation and personal autonomy."[2] Thus, "to individuality should belong the part of life in which it is chiefly the individual that is interested; to society, the part which chiefly interests society . . . everyone who receives the protection of society owes a return for the benefit, and the fact of living in society renders it indispensable that each should to observe a certain conduct towards the rest."[3] To a large extent then, laws are arguably utilitarian in the sense that the standard for morality is determined by the laws' usefulness to a specific society, or, as Mill would argue, "the greatest good for the greatest number."

The concept of justice is therefore not uniformly normative but instead defined as conformity with existing laws. Legal order implies that decisions will be made not arbitrarily but rather in accordance with rules, which are neither good nor bad in themselves but rather designed to accomplish a specific purpose.[4] Thus, laws are teleological in that they are designed to achieve a specific end or goal, that of societal harmony. Justice presupposes that laws are enforced uniformly and that people can expect equal and impartial treatment in the eyes of the law. In the United States, the Constitution represents the foundational legal principles from which laws are derived. The Preamble to the Constitution articulates its guiding principles to be unity, domestic tranquility, and general welfare.

> We the People of the United States, in Order to form a more perfect Union, establish Justice, insure domestic Tranquility, provide for the common defence, promote the general Welfare, and secure the Blessings of Liberty to ourselves and our Posterity, do ordain and establish this Constitution for the United States of America.[5]

THE RELATIONSHIP OF ETHICS TO LAW

Although morality strongly informs the basis of laws, that morality represents shared societal values that demand enforcement to promote societal harmony, ethics more properly addresses a person's internal and more personal moral compass. Thus, as violations of moral norms are likely to carry a punishment enforced through a system of justice, ethical violations are less likely to be enforceable. Traditionally, ethical violations were considered unenforceable; however, some ethical norms, such as the failure to obtain informed consent prior to treatment, have become enforceable and punishable by both legal and regulatory bodies.

Regulations and laws often incorporate ethical principles to which the majority within a society subscribes. The Greek philosopher Plato is credited with the statement that "ethics belongs to the *body polis*," referring to the political body and the community; what a society decides to be ethical or unethical is ultimately determined through the courts and through legislation.

Also known as moral philosophy, normative ethics is a branch of philosophy that has its foundations in philosophy and focuses on the generally accepted standards of values regarding right and wrong and the consequent assignment of quasi-legal rights and obligations. Actions are ethically justified on the basis of such shared values. Internalized values, ethical principles, and a sense of purpose define our sense of goodness—of right and wrong—and they give meaning to our lives while defining our choices and actions. Classically, western ethics are derived from Judaic-Christian principles and the subsequent teachings of Aristotle (virtue ethics), Kant (duty-based ethics), and Bentham and Mill (utilitarian and consequentialist ethics). Eastern ethical principles are derived from diverse sources including those that are Buddhist, Taoist, Confucian, Hindu, and the Islamic Hadith. Arguably, western ethics are more concerned with the exploration of universal truths, whereas eastern ethical principles are more concerned with protocol and respect; however, it is evident that there are in fact recognizable and indistinct universally shared ethical principles.[6]

Ethical duties frequently have legal ramifications. Laws delineate concrete duties that are thus necessary to maintain equality and social order and to provide a predictable and uniformly applied framework for preventing and resolving disputes.

OF OATHS AND CODES

In a manner similar to societies at large, which share common values, professions represent a culturally heterogeneous group of individuals who share a common training and who are bound together by values specific to their profession, even as these professionals practice within a larger society with potentially conflicting values. Nonetheless, codes of conduct are one hallmark of professionals that address the fiduciary nature of the relationship between the professional and the client. Professional codes hold members to a higher standard than the law imposes, and some societies have enforceable codes that predicate membership upon ethical behaviors. Values derived from statements of normative ethics act as behavioral guidelines for professionals within segments of the professional medical fraternity.

The general guiding ethical principles for the medical profession are contained within oaths, sworn to ritualistically by medical graduates, which embody the ethics of "good" medicine. Oaths outline the ethical elements of patient and physician relationships but have their greatest meaning when they are taken in a free and heartfelt fashion. Oaths represent promises, aspirational statements, of idealized ethics. Many traditional oaths are criticized for their potential lack of applicability in a modern world; however, such criticisms likely lose sight of the importance of aspirational statements in codes of ethics. It has been argued that oaths are characterized by "greater moral weight compared with promises because of their public character, their validation by transcendent appeal, the involvement of the personhood of the swearer, the prescription of consequences for failure to uphold their contents, the generality of the scope of their contents, the prolonged time frame of the commitment, the fact that their moral force remains binding in spite of failures on the part of those to whom the swearer makes the commitment, and the fact that interpersonal fidelity is the moral hallmark of the commitment of the swearer."[7] The most well-known is the Hippocratic Oath, in either its classical version[8] or its modern version,[9,10] written in 1964 by Louis Lasagna, the Academic Dean of the School of Medicine at Tufts University at that time. The modern version[11] states:

> I swear to fulfill, to the best of my ability and judgment, this covenant:
> I will respect the hard-won scientific gains of those physicians in whose steps I walk, and gladly share such knowledge as is mine with those who are to follow.
> I will apply, for the benefit of the sick, all measures [that] are required, avoiding those twin traps of overtreatment and therapeutic nihilism.
> I will remember that there is art to medicine as well as science, and that warmth, sympathy, and understanding may outweigh the surgeon's knife or the chemist's drug.
> I will not be ashamed to say "I know not," nor will I fail to call in my colleagues when the skills of another are needed for a patient's recovery.
> I will respect the privacy of my patients, for their problems are not disclosed to me that the world may know. Most especially must I tread with care in matters of life and death. If it is given me to save a life, all thanks. But it may also be within my power to take a life; this awesome responsibility must be faced with great humbleness and awareness of my own frailty. Above all, I must not play at God.
> I will remember that I do not treat a fever chart, a cancerous growth, but a sick human being, whose illness may affect the person's family and economic stability. My responsibility includes these related problems, if I am to care adequately for the sick.
> I will prevent disease whenever I can, for prevention is preferable to cure.
> I will remember that I remain a member of society, with special obligations to all my fellow human beings, those sound of mind and body as well as the infirm.
> If I do not violate this oath, may I enjoy life and art, respected while I live and remembered with affection thereafter. May I always act so as to preserve the finest traditions of my calling and may I long experience the joy of healing those who seek my help.

Other less widely known oaths of medical conduct include the Oath of Maimonides attributed to Maimonides (circa 1145–1204), a Jewish theologian and physician born in Cordova, Spain, and the Physician's Oath developed by the World Medical Association in Geneva, Switzerland in 1948 and subsequently amended, most recently in 1983. Similar to the Nuremberg Code, which addresses research on human subjects, the Physician's Oath was written in response to atrocities committed in Nazi Germany during World War II and reads:

> I solemnly pledge myself to consecrate my life to the service of humanity;
> I will give my teachers the respect and gratitude which is their due;
> I will practice my profession with conscience and dignity;
> The health of my patient will be my first consideration;
> I will respect the secrets which are confided in me, even after the patient has died;
> I will maintain by all the means in my power, the honor and the noble traditions of the medical profession;
> My colleagues will be my brothers;
> I will not permit considerations of religion, nationality, race, party politics or social standing to intervene between my duty and my patient;
> I will maintain the utmost respect for human life from its beginning even under threat and I will not use my medical knowledge contrary to the laws of humanity;
> I make these promises solemnly, freely and upon my honor.[12]

Professional associations, boards, and organizations have also authored codes of ethics. Standards of conduct in any profession reflect the shared values of that profession and define behaviors by its members that are considered either mandatory or proscribed. Violations can lead to revocations of licenses, suspensions of rights to practice, censures, or other sanctions or penalties.[13] Thomas Percival, an English physician and philosopher, in 1803 published a version of the Code of Medical Ethics generally outlining professional duties and ideal behaviors for providers and hospitals.[14] Percival's Code is credited with forming the basis for the American Medical Association's (AMA) Code of Ethics, enacted at the initial meeting of the AMA in Philadelphia, PA in 1847. The AMA Code of Ethics adopted at that meeting drew heavily on Percival's Medical Ethics. The AMA Principles of Medical Ethics and the Opinions of the AMA Council on Ethical & Judicial Affairs compose the AMA Code of Medical Ethics.[15] The AMA's Council on Ethical and Judicial Affairs (CEJA) publishes an annual report chronicling each year's adjudications of the complaints presented before it.[16]

The Neurocritical Care Society has published a code of professional conduct[17] developed by the society's ethics committee and ratified by the society's board of directors, the preamble of which states that "[t]he medical profession has long subscribed to a body of ethical statements developed primarily for the benefit of the patient. As a member of this profession, neurocritical care personnel must recognize responsibility to patients first and foremost, as well as to society, to other health professionals, and to self. The following Principles adopted by the Neurocritical Care Society are not laws, but standards of conduct which define the essentials of honorable behavior for our members. As members, all are expected to exhibit the highest standards of honesty and integrity."[18] Similarly, the American Academy of Neurology codified its own code of professional conduct[19] and the American Association of Neurological Surgeons (AANS) published a code of ethics[20] that is "a statement of ideals, commitments, and responsibilities of neurological surgeons to patients, other health professionals, society and themselves." In contrast to the AMA's CEJA, which rarely, if ever, imposes sanctions on its members for ethics violations, the AANS has received considerable attention and publicity, and it has even been the target of litigation because it has chosen to enforce its code of ethics with respect to member neurosurgeons' reports and testimonies[21] that were provided in professional liability litigation.[22] Over the years of 2004 to 2009, the AANS investigated twenty-two complaints of alleged improper expert witness testimony of its members.[23]

It is notable that such codes of conduct or codes of ethics are not unique to the medical profession; for example, the American Bar Association has a similar code,[24] which is very much enforced among practicing attorneys, and violations of which can result in harsh disciplinary action. The legal profession places great weight on ethics as part of law school education and as a fact of day-to-day law practice. In fact, an ethics examination represents a separate component of the multistate bar examination process and yearly continuing legal educations in ethics in mandatory for state bar membership and licensure.

BIOMEDICAL ETHICS

Applied ethics develop the practical framework by which professionals approach problems that arise in the daily practice of a profession such as medicine or law. Biomedical ethics, or bioethics, are concerned with health policy, biomedical sciences and research, and medical practice. Beauchamp and Childress articulated four guiding principles that have come to be accepted as the core values of modern bioethical theory: (1) the principle of respect for autonomy; (2) the principle of nonmaleficence; (3) the principle of beneficence; and, (4) the principle of justice.[25]

Hospital ethics committees are advisory groups, usually composed of a variety of members such as providers, nurses, social workers, bioethicists, lay persons, and attorneys who review, on request, ethical or moral questions that may arise during inpatient care. Although ethics committees had been informally established since at least the 1960s,[26] it was the New Jersey Supreme Court which, in its opinion, suggested that ethics committees might play an advisory role in such cases as an alternative to the courts.[27]

Hurst and colleagues identified the main reasons for ethics consultations:

To obtain needed help in deciding what to do
To identify a practical way of doing what had already been decided should be done
To implement a practical solution
To obtain reassurance that the correct decision was being made
To better to face people who might otherwise think that the decision was inappropriate
To seek consensus.[28]

THE PRINCIPLE OF RESPECT FOR AUTONOMY: CONSENT AND RIGHT TO DIE

The principle of respect for autonomy addresses personal autonomy and assumes that rational persons have the right to make uncoerced, informed, and voluntary decisions regarding their personhood and their bodies. The antithesis of autonomy is that of paternalism whereby individual choice is subjugated to the choices of a superior father-like figure. The respect for autonomy within the medical decision-making process is exemplified by the principles of informed consent and informed refusal. Informed consent is fundamental to the patient-provider relationship and can only be waived under very specific circumstances. Consent is permission and is a legal defense to the legal charges of both civil and criminal assault and battery, which relate to unpermitted bodily contact. The notion of "informed" as it relates to both consent and refusal presupposes that there has been a full disclosure of the indications for, and the risks, benefits, and alternatives to a proposed medical therapy; therein is a critical process of communication including an opportunity to ask questions and to finally decide for oneself. The ability to make an informed choice also presupposes that the patient has a legal capacity to make decisions for himself or herself and can include both situational capacity, such as intoxication, and also more permanent issues relating to mental illness, age, or acute or chronic neurological injuries that may impair a patient's ability to understand the potential consequences of his or her decision. The issue of a potential lack of capacity underlies the legal remedies of healthcare proxies or legal guardians who are empowered to make substituted judgments on behalf of the patient based on an understanding of the patient's needs or preferences, as the patient would choose if he or she had the capacity to do so. Finally, the principle of informed consent implies voluntariness and a right to freely exercise independent decision making in the absence of coercion, manipulation, conflict of interest, misrepresentation, or undue influence. Just as patients may give their informed consent, they may also withhold consent or actively refuse treatment through informed refusal. The principle of informed refusal forms the legal basis for the rights to refuse blood transfusions, feeding tubes, or resuscitation.

There is a strong line of legal precedent in the United States supporting the principle of autonomy in the medical context. In 1914, Supreme Court Justice Benjamin Cardozo wrote:

> Every human being of adult years and sound mind has a right to determine what shall be done with his own body; and a surgeon who performs an operation without his patient's consent commits an assault for which he is liable in damages. This is true except in cases of emergency.[29]

The concept of informed refusal of medical treatment dates to a prior decision by the U.S. Supreme Court.[30] In *Cruzan v. Director, Missouri Department of Health*, the U.S. Supreme Court opined "that the Constitution granted competent persons a constitutionally protected right to refuse lifesaving hydration and nutrition."[31] The *Cruzan* case was seminal in that in 1990, *Cruzan* was the first "right to die" case to be deliberated by the U.S. Supreme Court. The *Cruzan* case addressed the right of a surrogate to discontinue life-sustaining medical care; 26-year-old Nancy lost control of her vehicle and landed face-down in a water-filled ditch, where paramedics and physicians resuscitated her; she subsequently fell into a persistent vegetative state (PVS) when a feeding tube was inserted for her long-term care. After five years in a PVS, Cruzan's parents requested the medical team to remove the feeding tube and allow her to die. The legal question faced by the Supreme Court was whether the state of Missouri had the right to require "clear and convincing evidence" regarding Nancy Cruzan's wishes in order to discontinue life support, and whether the state of Missouri was in violation of the Due Process Clause of the Fourteenth Amendment in its refusal to limit life sustaining therapy. In the majority opinion, Chief Justice Rehnquist opined that competent individuals have the right to refuse medical treatment under the Due Process Clause, which states that "[N]or shall any State deprive any person of life, liberty, or property, without due process of law."[32] The right to refuse life sustaining treatment has now been codified into federal and state laws.

In 1990 Congress enacted The Patient Self-Determination Act (PSDA), a federal law that requires providers to inform all adult patients about their rights to accept or refuse medical or surgical treatment and the right to execute an advance directive.[33] An advance directive is a written instruction such as a living will or durable power of attorney for health care recognized under state law relating to the provision of health care when the individual is incapacitated.[34] It is important to understand that terms such as "capacity to make health-care decisions," "health-care agent," "health-care proxy," and "surrogate" are legal terms of art; providers should consult their state laws in any situation in which there are questions regarding ambiguity. States have also enacted regulations regarding surrogacy hierarchy whereby the legally-defined succession to decision-making rights is clearly stipulated; these hierarchies are not always intuitively obvious, and providers are advised to consult their state-specific laws when determining which family member has the right to speak on behalf of an incapacitated patient.

Federal law does not require individuals to complete any form of an advance directive (nor do state laws), and it expressly forbids requiring an advance directive as a requisite for treatment. State laws, generally codified in regulations regarding the practice of medicine and generally enforced through State Departments of Health (or their surrogate branches), also require providers to adhere to the principle of autonomy via the processes of informed consent and the respect for advance directives; violations are actionable through disciplinary hearings that result in sanctions upon or revocations of state medical licensure.[35]

From a regulatory point of view, the U.S. Centers for Medicare and Medicaid Services (CMS) has incorporated the right to informed decision-making and the right to refuse care in the Hospital Conditions of Participation (CoP),[36] the U.S. Health Care Financing Administration (HCFA),[37] and the Joint Commission, which accredits hospitals in the United States. CMS specifically requires hospital policies to be in place regarding uniform application of the informed consent process[38] and policies on advance directives.[39]

Thus, the principle of respect for autonomy is one example in which an ethical principle has become so well acknowledged and respected that it has been adopted through federal and state laws and is also implicated in the regulatory rules and regulations of multiple regulatory and oversight bodies in the United States.

THE PRINCIPLE OF RESPECT FOR AUTONOMY AS IT APPLIES TO BIOMEDICAL RESEARCH

The landmark ethical codes to address the ethical standards as they apply to biomedical research are the Nuremberg Code and the Declaration of Helsinki. The Nuremberg Code articulated principles regarding research on human subjects and was developed in May 1947, during the "Doctors' Trial" of the Nuremberg trials, during which Nazi physicians were held responsible for conducting unethical medical procedures on human war prisoners. The ten elements of the "Nuremberg Code" articulate the elements of voluntary informed consent and absence of coercion, properly formulated scientific method, and beneficence:

1. The voluntary consent of the human subject is absolutely essential. This means that the person involved should have legal capacity to give consent;

should be so situated as to be able to exercise free power of choice, without the intervention of any element of force, fraud, deceit, duress, over-reaching, or other ulterior form of constraint or coercion; and should have sufficient knowledge and comprehension of the elements of the subject matter involved, as to enable him to make an understanding and enlightened decision. This latter element requires that, before the acceptance of an affirmative decision by the experimental subject, there should be made known to him the nature, duration, and purpose of the experiment; the method and means by which it is to be conducted; all inconveniences and hazards reasonably to be expected; and the effects upon his health or person, which may possibly come from his participation in the experiment. The duty and responsibility for ascertaining the quality of the consent rests upon each individual who initiates, directs or engages in the experiment. It is a personal duty and responsibility which may not be delegated to another with impunity.

2. The experiment should be such as to yield fruitful results for the good of society, unprocurable by other methods or means of study, and not random and unnecessary in nature.

3. The experiment should be so designed and based on the results of animal experimentation and a knowledge of the natural history of the disease or other problem under study, that the anticipated results will justify the performance of the experiment.

4. The experiment should be so conducted as to avoid all unnecessary physical and mental suffering and injury.

5. No experiment should be conducted, where there is an a priori reason to believe that death or disabling injury will occur; except, perhaps, in those experiments where the experimental physicians also serve as subjects.

6. The degree of risk to be taken should never exceed that determined by the humanitarian importance of the problem to be solved by the experiment.

7. Proper preparations should be made and adequate facilities provided to protect the experimental subject against even remote possibilities of injury, disability, or death.

8. The experiment should be conducted only by scientifically qualified persons. The highest degree of skill and care should be required through all stages of the experiment of those who conduct or engage in the experiment.

9. During the course of the experiment, the human subject should be at liberty to bring the experiment to an end, if he has reached the physical or mental state, where continuation of the experiment seemed to him to be impossible.

10. During the course of the experiment, the scientist in charge must be prepared to terminate the experiment at any stage, if he has probable cause to believe, in the exercise of the good faith, superior skill and careful judgement required of him, that a continuation of the experiment is likely to result in injury, disability, or death to the experimental subject.[40]

The key contribution of Nuremberg was to merge Hippocratic ethics and the protection of human rights into a single code. The Nuremberg judges believed that Hippocratic ethics alone were insufficient to guarantee the rights of human research subjects since, even when supplemented with informed consent, researchers might be motivated to subsume a subject's autonomy into a paternalistic risk-benefit calculus. Within the scope of Hippocratic ethics the subject would rely upon the physician-researcher to determine when to withdraw a subject from a study, whereas a Nuremberg Code-based approach would allocate equal power to both the researcher and the subject regarding withdrawal from the study. Informed consent, the core of the Nuremberg Code, has become the fundamental pronouncement regarding the protection of the rights of human subjects within the scope of biomedical research.[41] Although the Nuremberg Code has not been codified into law by any nation, it is almost uniformly relied upon by the human subjects review boards and ethics committees of developed nations.[42]

The Declaration of Helsinki represents the second and equally important statement regarding the ethics of research on human subjects and is so named because it was adopted by the 18th World Medical Association General Assembly in Helsinki, Finland in June 1964. The declaration is significantly more ambitious in its detail and reach; it is composed of a preamble and thirty-seven elements divided into sections: General Principles, Risks, Burdens and Benefits, Vulnerable Groups and Individuals, Scientific Requirements and Research Protocols, Research Ethics Committees, Privacy and Confidentiality, Informed Consent, Use of Placebo, and Post-Trial Provisions.[43] Since its first writing in 1962, the declaration has been revised five times, but its most recent revision in 2013 has generated controversy with respect to ethical requirements surrounding placebo-controlled trials and the issue of responsibilities to research participants at the conclusion of the research study.[44] Early revisions of the declaration (pre-2000) divided research into two categories: therapeutic (potentially of direct benefit to the subject) and nontherapeutic research. In its most recent renditions, a new category of "Medical Research Combined with Medical Care" is recognized as a subset of "all medical research involving human subjects" and the declaration no longer addresses "nontherapeutic" research or "healthy volunteer" research.[45] Nonetheless, the declaration retains its pivotal place alongside the Nuremberg Code as the foundation of human subject research ethics. The Council for the International Organizations of Medical Sciences (CIOMS) includes the full text of the Declaration of Helsinki in the appendix of its guidelines on research ethics. The International Bioethics Committee (IBC) of UNESCO (United Nations Educational, Scientific, and Cultural Organization) is composed of thirty-six members from diverse countries and advocates for a universal respect for human dignity and human rights.

THE LEGAL CODIFICATION OF ETHICAL PRINCIPLES REGARDING HUMAN SUBJECTS RESEARCH REGULATIONS

Although the Nuremberg Code and the Declaration of Helsinki impressed the need for the ethical treatment of human research subjects, they in themselves do not rise to the level of enforceable laws. In the United States, the translation of ethics into law occurred via the National Research Act, 42 U.S.C. § 201 in 1974 and The Belmont Report of the U.S. Department of Health and Human Services (DHHS) in 1979; subsequently, in 1981, DHHS published the Common Rule.[46] Research that involves the clinical testing of investigational drugs or medical devices is additionally subject to regulations promulgated by the U.S. Food and Drug Administration (FDA).[47]

The goals of biomedical research are twofold: (1) to generate data through carefully designed and controlled studies from which generalizable conclusions might be drawn that further the state of scientific medicine and (2) to potentially improve the future care of similar individuals. Therefore, although biomedical research is conducted under the rubric of medical science, it differs from clinical medicine in that the research interventions are not clearly known to be diagnostic or therapeutic, and that they may involve a risk of harm. Thus, although the ethical principles of biomedical research and clinical medicine are the same, the context in which they are applied differs in a fundamental way. U.S. legislative doctrine articulates three core ethical principles as they apply to the protection of human research subjects: (1) the respect for persons, (2) beneficence, and (3) justice. The notion of "respect for persons" addresses respect for bodily integrity and individual self-determination via voluntary participation and informed consent, which are especially important to the protection of potential subjects who may situationally have a diminished or loss of autonomy, such as prisoners. The regulatory provisions that address informed consent in research are clearly a codification and extension of the U.S. legal doctrine addressing the requirement for informed consent within the therapeutic context. The privacy of data obtained via clinical research[48] is now also subject to the law via the privacy provisions of the Health Insurance Portability and Accountability Act (HIPPA).[49] The notion of beneficence in research requires that research be designed in a way as to minimize the risk of physical and emotional harm to research subjects and to design research protocols to maximize the potential for useable data that may advance the state of medical science. Finally, the notion of justice in biomedical research addresses fair selection of research subjects so as to minimize the inclusion of vulnerable populations and to fairly allocate participants into the various arms of the research protocol.

One area in which laws and regulations remain unclear is the collection of human tissue specimens for potential future research, an issue recently brought into the public forum by a bestseller that addressed the use of perpetuated tissue cultures, the HeLa cell line, obtained from Henrietta Lacks, a patient with cervical cancer.[50] Allegedly, a physician obtained two blocks of tissue, one cancerous and one healthy, from Lacks's cervix without informed consent and then passed the tissue to a researcher who had previously been unsuccessful in establishing a continuous cell line for use in cancer research. The issue of cell line research and the use of pathology tissue specimens in biomedical research have become increasingly controversial because the patient is no longer within the scope of the research per se, and therefore the applicability of biomedical ethical principles becomes less persuasive.[51] The National Bioethics Advisory Commission addressed this issue in a 1999 report[52] that attempted to harmonize the evolving field of tissue research with the Common Rule.[53] The informed consent requirements of the Common Rule delegate to institutional review board (IRB) requirements, which, *inter alia*, state:

> Informed consent will be obtained, including at least the following items being communicated to potential participants or their authorised surrogates: purposes of the research, its expected duration, and the nature of any interventions/experiments; anticipated risks and benefits of participation and the reasonable alternatives to participation in the research protocol; confidentiality provisions relating to the research records; any compensation and/or treatment available for research related injuries; the right to not participate and to discontinue participation at any time without penalty.

Nonetheless, as of this writing, the collection of tissue specimens intended for use in present or future research does not fall under the Common Rule regulations and therefore is not subject to IRB review, and this type of collection is exempt from the informed consent requirements of the Common Rule, with the caveat that the specimens are not personally identifiable.[54] The issue of identifiability will likely continue to evolve as genetic mapping becomes more commonplace. The use of tissue for research purposes is also addressed by the 2006 revision of the Uniform Anatomical Gift Act (UAGA) of 1968, which expressly allowed tissue donation for the purposes of transplantation, therapy, research, or education.[55]

Specifically within the area of neurosciences research, the use of neural tissues and preserved brains is increasingly important to the study of diseases of the nervous system. For example, The Brain and Body Donation Program (BBDP) at the Banner Sun Health Research Institute was organized in 1987 with brain-only donations; it has banked more than 1600 brains and published under the rubric of the Arizona Study of Aging and Neurodegenerative Disorders (AZSAND).[56] Through its analysis of brain banked biospecimens, the program intends to further clinicopathological correlation studies and to provide pathologically characterized control and diseased tissue to basic scientists, enabling them to discover the underlying molecular mechanisms specific to each disease (a reported 82% of tissue renders useable RNA) and to design appropriate therapeutic interventions.[57] A similar program in Denmark is also focused on the neuroscience applications of donated brain specimens.[58] Significant progress is being made with respect to the elucidation of the molecular biology of neurodegenerative disorders that share the common pathology of Lewy bodies and, hence, are based in the regulation of the expression of the *SNCA* gene. These diseases, which include familial and non-familial Parkinson's disease, are expected to facilitate the development of genetic biomarkers and potential therapeutic targets.[59] Brain banking is also being used in neurobiological studies of psychiatric illness such as the study of brain-specific isoforms and molecules; centers involved in such research include the National Institute of Mental Health Brain Collection (NIMH), the Harvard Brain Tissue Resource Center (HBTRC), and the Mount Sinai School of Medicine Brain Bank (MSSM-BB).[60] In the absence of legislative regulation or internationally accepted ethical principles regarding the conduct of tissue and organ banks in support of biomedical research, codes of conduct have been developed by responsible researchers as guiding documents; one such document is the Model Code of Ethics,[61] although standard operating procedures[62] have also helped fill the void in oversight.

Both the Common Rule and FDA regulations require that proposed protocols that involve research on human subjects be a priori reviewed and approved by an IRB that has been recognized by the U.S. Federal Office of Human Research Protections (OHRP), which reports to the Office of the Secretary of the DHHS. Although the law specifically requires that "all research funded by the federal government and involving human subjects [must] be overseen by an IRB," in reality, the law has been held to extend to all entities that receive federal funding.

As is almost universally the case with respect to federal laws and regulations involving healthcare, many individual states have enacted an additional layer of state statutory oversight that further reinforces the protection of human participants in biomedical research requiring some type of prior review and oversight.[63] Lastly, the courts have also enforced tort law standards of due care as they apply, for example, to contracts and medical negligence in which human subjects are harmed during the conduct of medical research.[64] Data safety monitoring boards (DSMBs)[65] and Data Monitoring Committees (DMCs)[66] and their individual members are also at risk for legal accountability under joint and several theories of liability. The primary purpose of data monitoring is to ensure that continued research under a specific clinical trial proceeds in accordance with its stated protocol, remains ethical, and accounts for both individual and collective ethics even though these responsibilities are potentially shared by research ethics committees, trial steering committees, and the investigators. In the area of clinical research involving brain imaging, an area of both evolving ethical and also legal risk involves the issue of incidental findings; both fiduciary duty and accepted standards of medical care have been held to apply.[67] In such research, it is reasonable that imaging should be conducted in accordance with good medical practice for reviewing the clinical status of the whole person, and that the informed consent process should disclose the possibility of incidental but clinically relevant findings and the potential consequences thereof.[68]

THE PRINCIPLE OF BENEFICENCE

Morality, ethics, and the law again merge within the principle of beneficence: an ethical duty shared by all professionals toward their clients. Beneficence is variably defined as an obligation to help others further their important and legitimate interests and also generally as charity, mercy, and kindness. Beneficence is strongly rooted within the fiduciary duty and the duty of care that is a tenet upon which the provider-patient relationship is based. A fiduciary relationship arises in professional relationships wherein there is an imbalance of education, training, and experience that results in a dependence and confidence extended by the client to the fiduciary.[69] Fiduciary actions always and without exception favor the well-being and interest of the client/patient; therefore, there is an inextricable interrelationship of between the principles of beneficence and nonmaleficence, which will be discussed in detail below. The concept of beneficence is rooted within the values expressed in the Hippocratic Oath. Medical beneficence exclusively addresses the end goal of healing and traditionally has not addressed collateral third party benefits. However, Beauchamp and Childress divide beneficence into two separate principles: (1) the provision of benefits, or positive beneficence; and (2) the balancing of benefits and harms, as a version of the principle of utility.[70] The complexity of beneficence within a clinical framework is that it can be at odds with the principle of autonomy because it removes the element of risk balancing from the patient and places that obligation within the responsibility of the provider.[71]

It is notable that the landmark court cases shaping professional and public moral judgment and ethics regarding limitation of medical care all involved patients with severe brain injury who developed a persistent vegetative state. There is no consensus among health-care professionals regarding well-defined boundaries of the legitimate practice of medicine. If utility is indeed subsumed under the concept of beneficence, then the range of benefits under consideration can expand significantly. The ethical goal of "doing good" on behalf of the patient then begins to encompass non-healing-directed goals such as cosmetic surgery, fertility and libido enhancement, end-of-life care planning, and even physician-hastened death at the request of the patient (probably inaptly referred to as "physician-assisted suicide"). The courts, in the cases of *Karen Ann Quinlan* (1976) and *Cruzan* (1990), helped build legal, medical, and public consensus around the notion that refusal to withhold or withdraw a validly refused treatment, even if the patient's death was thereby hastened, could not be held to be morally wrong and that the said provider's cooperation could be rightly viewed as merciful and benevolent.

Traditionally, viable state interests include the following: (1) preserving life, (2) preventing suicide, (3) protecting innocent third parties, and (4) maintaining the ethical standards of the medical profession, including supporting the right of physicians to effectively render necessary and appropriate medical services.

Neurosciences clinicians are frequently faced with the issue of prognostication—not so much regarding survival, but rather a prognostication regarding future quality of life. These analyses frequently represent both a respect for autonomy and beneficence because providers are often in the unique position to understand not only the implications of the neurologic injuries but also to consider the course of care through both inpatient hospitalization and subsequent rehabilitation and convalescence. Although acute care providers frequently emphasize the short-term prognosis, the implications of devastating neurologic injury and the associated complications, such as pneumonia and decubitus ulcers, are frequently unapparent to patients and surrogates/family members. In the 1986 California case of *Bouvia v. Superior Court*,[72] a 26-year-old mentally competent, quadriplegic woman who suffered from cerebral palsy expressed a desire to end her life by self-starvation in a California public hospital. Bouvia was completely bedridden and completely dependent on others to perform all her activities of daily living. When Ms. Bouvia could no longer be spoon-fed without nausea and vomiting, hospital staff inserted a feeding tube against her will. Ms. Bouvia subsequently sued the hospital and its staff, seeking a court order to have the feeding tube removed and to stop all medical measures to which she did not consent. The trial court denied Ms. Bouvia's request, stating that her prognosis justified the state's interest in preserving her life. The appellate court acknowledged that a competent adult has the fundamental right to consent or refuse medical treatment, even if it may save or prolong his or her life. Importantly, the appellate court emphasized that the trial court's focus on the potential additional years of life was in itself insufficient and that a consideration to the quality of life represented an equal, if not more significant, consideration to be weighed by the court; in its decision, the court stated its opinion that "[i]n Ms. Bouvia's view, her quality of life has been diminished to the point of hopelessness, uselessness, unenjoyability, and frustration. She, as the patient, lying helplessly in bed, unable to care for herself, may consider her existence meaningless."[73] The court in *Bouvia* echoed the opinion of the Supreme Court in the *Quinlan* decision regarding the importance of quality of life. The subsequent case of *Cruzan* (1990) became the first right-to-die case to be heard at the level of the U.S. Supreme Court, although the questions of beneficence and right to die were again tested in the case of Schiavo, which generated significant medical, legal, and ethical controversy but again reaffirmed the paramount importance of a patient's best interests. In 1993, in the California case of

Barber, the Superior Court of California was prohibited from prosecuting two physicians for murder when, at the request of the family, they disconnected life-support from a patient diagnosed to be in a persistent vegetative state.[74]

In the Supreme Court case of *Glucksberg*,[75] physicians, terminally-ill patients, and the Compassion in Dying organization challenged Washington State's existing ban against assisted suicide in the Natural Death Act of 1979, asserting that assisted suicide was a liberty interest protected by the Due Process Clause of the Fourteenth Amendment to the United States Constitution. The Court in *Glucksberg* held that assisted suicide was not a fundamental liberty interest and was therefore not constitutionally protected, and it drew a clear line between assisting suicide and the withdrawing or permitting the refusal of unwanted life-sustaining medical treatment. The Supreme Court reaffirmed its position in *Vacco v. Quill*[76] in reaching a unanimous opinion that states have a legitimate interest in outlawing assisted suicide and that there is no violation of the Equal Protection Clause when a state criminalizes assisted suicide.

Nonetheless, soon after the Supreme Court handed down its decisions in the physician-assisted suicide cases, Oregon voters reaffirmed their support for assisted suicide. It is important to note that physician-assisted suicide differs from euthanasia. Physician-assisted suicide presupposes that the patient affirmatively requests medication for the purpose of ending his or her life (autonomy); euthanasia more implies a provider-driven administration of a lethal drug in the patient's best interest (beneficence). Here the balancing between autonomy and beneficence becomes more complex, even as both assisted suicide and euthanasia run against the Hippocratic Oath.

The Oregon Death with Dignity Act (DWDA) was a citizen's initiative first approved by Oregon voters in November 1994 and subsequently reaffirmed (as Measure 51, Oregon House Bill 2954) by voters in 1997. Physician-assisted suicide was legalized in Oregon in October 1997 under the Oregon Death with Dignity Act. Under Oregon law, any competent adult Oregon resident with a medical diagnosis of a terminal illness and an expected life expectancy of less than six months could make a written request to a physician for a lethal dose of medication prescribed for the purpose of ending that resident's life. In 2001, United States Attorney General Ashcroft sought and received a memorandum from the Office of Legal Counsel concluding that physician-assisted suicide violates the U.S. Controlled Substances Act (CSA) and thereupon concluded that physician-assisted suicide was not a legitimate medical purpose, and that any physician administering federally controlled drugs for that purpose would be in violation of the CSA.[77] In October 2005, the U.S. Supreme Court heard the case of *Gonzales v. Oregon*[78] and in 2006 ruled that the federal CSA did not give the attorney general the power to interfere with physicians obeying the state law. Notably, Justice Scalia dissented stating that "[i]f the term "legitimate medical purpose" has any meaning, it surely excludes the prescription of drugs to produce death."[79] In 2008, the state of

Washington passed Initiative 1000, the state's Death with Dignity Act, which became law on March 5, 2009; subsequently Vermont (Patient Choice and Control at the End of Life Act; 2013), California (End of Life Option Act; 2016), Colorado (End of Life Options Act; 2016), and the District of Columbia (Death with Dignity Act; 2017) followed with similar versions of physician-assisted dying or aid-in-dying laws. Under an ethical analysis, such laws support both a respect for patient autonomy and also beneficence by supporting a physician's ability to diagnose a terminal illness, prognosticate with the patient's interest at heart, and render a compassionate response to a patient with loss of dignity due to continued suffering at the end of life.

Parenthetically, advances in neurosciences may again change the parameters under which such cases evolve going forward.[80] What if there were a way to communicate with patients in a "minimally conscious" or persistent vegetative state to determine their wishes? Neuroscientists argue that as the ability to correlate conscious states with patterns of neural processing advances, the brain might contribute to more precise definitions of what it means to be human; such technological advances are likely to not only provide a richer understanding of human ethical and existential functioning[81] but are likely to again challenge and shape the law.[82]

Social beneficence, wherein the concept of beneficence moves toward the utilitarian point of view, is highlighted by the routine retrieval of organs and tissues. Under this form of organ procurement, a community could rightly harvest organs from potential organ donors unless a previously registered refusal was in effect, a notion similar to that of implied consent. Under such a theory, it could be argued that implied consent for organ donation would represent a communal effort to advance the good of all society; however, simultaneously, the counter-argument would once again return to the principles of "freedom to versus freedom from" and the rights of the individual under the principle of autonomy against the rights of the collective.

Within the field of neurosurgery, it has been argued that because patients may lack the capacity to understand the implications of their decisions and therefore lack the capacity to exercise the autonomous decision-making required for informed consent, neurosurgeons are often faced with a need to explore the moral beliefs, personal values, and social structures that characterize each individual patient and support the patient in weighing possible benefits and harms in making a decision of substantial autonomy.[83]

The principle of beneficence is at the root of the doctrine of implied consent whereby the ethical and legal requirements for informed consent are waived because of exigent circumstances, in the absence of a surrogate decision-maker, and where it could be supposed that a person would have consented to medical care if he or she were capable of doing so. Nonetheless, the potential benefits of any intervention must outweigh the risks in order for the intervention to be considered ethical. The principle of beneficence is relevant to bioethics in that it furthers the aims of preservation of life, maximizing patients' wellness, and the utilitarian societal goals of cost avoidance and risk reduction; however, beneficence may not be universally applicable to all biomedical scenarios.[84]

The legal doctrine of *parens patriae* authorizes the state to protect individuals who are determined to be legally unable to act on their own behalf. *Parens patriae* is a Latin term meaning "parent of his country" and dates to the King's Bench of England; the term was first introduced in 1608 and was intended for parents that were seen as *non compos mentis* adults ("not legally competent") and therefore not capable of caring for their children. The doctrine of *parens patriae* has extended or been translated in the United States and grants the attorney general of a state the authority to assume care for and protection of children, mentally ill persons, and other individuals who have been deemed legally incompetent to handle their affairs, and even to initiate litigation on behalf of these state residents. The doctrine grants sovereign power of guardianship over persons with disabilities. In the Supreme Court case of *Heller v. Doe*,[85] Justice Kennedy observed that "the State has a legitimate interest under its *parens patriae* powers in providing care to its citizens who are unable to care for themselves." Thus, the doctrine is interwoven into legislation and common law with a primary focus or obligation of courts to protect the best interest of a person or persons but is limited by the doctrine of parental liberty, which is a constitutional doctrine intended to prevent state encroachment on individual civil rights via potentially unjustified governmental intervention. When applying the doctrine, the law applies a two-pronged test that functions as a guide to help the court to reach a reasoned and justifiable conclusion: (1) the "Best Interests" test requires the Court to ascertain the course of action that would serve the person alone and not consider the interests of the stakeholders such as guardians or society in general; and (2) the "Substituted Judgment" test requires the court to step into the shoes of a person who is considered to be mentally incapable and attempt to make the decision that the person would have made if he or she were competent to do so. Once again, the state of the doctrine in U.S. law illustrates the balancing test which attempts to maximize autonomy and minimize paternalism but also recognizes the situational need for beneficent oversight and intervention. The doctrine of *parens patriae* is an excellent illustration of the application of ethical principles and analysis that are then translated into a legal doctrine and applied by the courts, a situation parallel to the complexity of clinical biomedical ethics.

One evolving area of ethical analysis involves the disclosure of medical errors as a moral obligation of providers[86] and also a patient right under the ethical principle of beneficence. Arguably, through the act of non-disclosure of a medical error, the provider conspicuously chooses to place his or her own interests above that of the patient to the detriment of the patient. When providers chose not to disclose medical errors to patients, subsequent discovery creates an environment wherein the public trust in the profession of medicine may be undermined because of potential intentional deception and providers become suspect for choosing to preserve their own professional interests over the welfare of patients. Where the welfare of a patient may be discretionarily compromised, a situation is created that is at odds with the principle of beneficence. This failure can be seen as a breach of trust, fiduciary duty, and professional ethics—a lapse in the commitment to act solely for the patient's best interests. Arguably, the disclosure of medical errors and adverse events to patients has relevance to issues of both patient safety[87] and medical ethics.[88,89] Ethical standards articulated by the American College of Physicians, the American Medical Association, and the Joint Commission[90] require the disclosure of medical errors and unanticipated outcomes. State laws variably also encourage hospitals or physicians to disclose adverse events to patients.[91] In the Canadian legal case of *Stamos v. Davies*, a pulmonologist biopsied a patient's spleen instead of the lung and subsequently avoided honestly answering questions posed by the patient regarding the results of the biopsy; the Canadian court found that the pulmonologist had breached a duty of disclosure owed to the patient "as a matter of professional relations."[92] U.S. court cases tend to focus more on the admissibility of apology and disclosure into evidence rather than failure to disclose.

THE PRINCIPLE OF NONMALEFICENCE

The principle of nonmaleficence requires the avoidance of harm; the principle of primum non nocere—or—"above all (or alternatively "first") do no harm"; therefore, the term has evolved to have substantial legal and regulatory significance. There is a subtle linguistic twist since malfeasance connotes a person doing something wrong, whereas maleficence suggests an intrinsic predisposition to causing harm—the antonym of beneficence. Indeed, ethical writings frequently use the terms interchangeably; however, we will adopt the Beauchamp and Childress terminology herein. Beneficence and nonmaleficence are closely interrelated and both principles are highly contextual requiring a balancing of respect for individual autonomy, explorations of personal values, and utilitarianism. The Hippocratic Oath enjoins the principles of beneficence and nonmaleficence: "I will use treatment to help the sick according to my ability and judgment, but I will never use it to injure or wrong them." Therefore, in cases of conflict between beneficence and nonmaleficence, nonmaleficence will normally override beneficence.

Arguably, the duty not to harm has greater ethical weight than our duty to provide benefit. Furthermore, it is axiomatic that in the clinical context in which harm in unavoidable, clinicians are ethically obligated to minimize the harm done; therefore, where risks and benefits are poorly defined, beneficence must be balanced against nonmaleficence through clinical judgement or practical wisdom. In the application of chemotherapy or the decision to resect a brain tumor, side effects and functional compromise may be inevitable; however, the analysis must focus on the probabilities of functional recovery against the probabilities of devastating handicap. Additionally, from a medical-legal point of view, harm is likely to be more easily discernible than is benefit. Harm to the patient may be created through either acts of commission or omission; since errors of commission are more obvious, they alone formed the basis for the landmark Institute of Medicine (IOM) report "To Err is Human."[93] The IOM defined error as "the failure of a planned action to be completed as intended or the use of a wrong plan to achieve an aim." Furthermore, since harm is more easily quantifiable, it forms the basis for health quality analysis and also for a damages-based tort system. Negligence can be defined as the foreseeable imposition of an unreasonable risk of harm upon another, and the occurrence of that harm causing quantifiable damages. The importance of avoiding harm affirms the need for medical competence. The inevitability of medical error is a fact of medical care; hence, *errare humanum est*: "to err is human." In fact, William Osler aptly surmised that "errors in judgment must occur in the practice of an art which consists largely of balancing probabilities."[94] Notwithstanding human fallibility, generations of providers have been conditioned to struggle with their fallibility because errors threaten the foundation of the patient-provider relationship, which is the trust bestowed on providers within the framework and duties of the fiduciary relationship.

The symbolic and practical importance of nonmaleficence is exemplified in the use of terminal or compassionate sedation during end-of-life care. Terminal sedation will undoubtedly hasten a patient's death, but the importance of compassion focused on human dignity negates the toxic effects while emphasizing the benefits. Compassionate sedation through the use of sedative and analgesic agents illustrates the principle of double effect, by which a beneficent intention (relief of suffering) is balanced against the unintended consequence (hastening death). The doctrine of double effect is based in the ethical principle of proportionality, attributed to Thomas Aquinas in the thirteenth century, who asserted that an action in the pursuit of a good outcome could be acceptable, even if it is achieved through means with an unintended but foreseeable negative outcome, if that negative outcome is outweighed by the good outcome.[95] Skillful administration of palliative therapeutics cannot be construed as either physician-assisted suicide or euthanasia when the appropriate ethical constructs are deliberated and appropriately documented. In *Washington v. Glucksberg*, the U.S. Supreme Court endorsed the right of informed patients to pursue relief of suffering, even if the treatment may unintentionally shorten life.

The important ethical issues pertinent to end-of-life care in the ICU at the point-of-life support discontinuation are (1) the distinction between allowing patients to die in accordance with their wishes and causing them die, (2) the fine line between respecting a patient's wish to die with dignity and control and the risk of subsequent allegations of euthanasia or physician-assisted suicide, and (3) the adjunctive use of medications that simultaneously provide comfort but also may hasten death.[96] Four requirements are generally applicable to the principle of double effect:

> The action itself must not be intrinsically wrong, it must be a good or neutral act.
> Only the good effect must be intended, not the bad effect, even though it is foreseen.
> The bad effect must not be the means of the good effect.
> The good effect must outweigh the evil that is permitted.[97]

Voluntary active euthanasia represents the injection of a lethal agent by a provider with the intention of causing a patient's death, which, as noted above, is distinct from the withdrawal of unwanted life-prolonging interventions.

Within the neurosciences, the balancing of the opportunity for beneficence against the risk of maleficence is important and obvious in a wide range of novel therapies and interventions, especially when such interventions remain within the realm of clinical research, where maturing but relatively novel therapies are supported by only limited evidence regarding either the benefits or the risks to patients. One example of such an intervention is deep brain stimulation (DBS). There are multiple attendant risks of craniotomy and foreign body placement into the brain parenchyma, such as hemorrhage, infection, fracture, misplacement, or migration of the lead, as well as the relative lack of long-term outcome data on which to base recommendations; therefore, surgical implantation of DBS electrodes has generally been employed as a treatment of last resort for patients who are refractory to other forms of therapy. Nonetheless, the potential harm due to complications must be balanced against the ongoing harm due to chronic debilitation. Technologies which may irreversibly alter neurologic function, cognition, and behavior highlight the importance of risk and unintended consequences. Cases are reported in which the placement of DBS successfully treated patients' motor deficits but exacerbated or precipitated cognitive problems, depression, or hypomania; in addition, at times, patients reported difficulties adapting to the expectations associated with being restored to a normal level of function.[98] Thus, unintended side effects must be considered and managed in all areas of medical therapy whether pharmaceutical or interventional; the important elements continue to be ethical and must be grounded in informed and shared decision-making. Controversial pharmaceutical neurointerventions include elective neuroenhancement—requests by patients for prescription drugs that were originally developed to improve executive function or memory in persons with disorders such as attention-deficit/hyperactivity disorder or Alzheimer's disease, for the purpose of enhancing memory, focus, or cognitive skills. Examples of such pharmaceuticals include stimulants such as methylphenidate to improve performance on academic tests or to learn new skills, and cholinesterase inhibitors such as donepezil to modulate normal age-related memory changes; there is some evidence to suggest that these medications may have desired effects in normal individuals, although the long terms side-effects are largely unknown in this population.[99] Proponents would draw a parallel to cosmetic surgery;[100] opponents argue the largely unknown risks associated with non-therapeutic prescribing.[101]

THE PRINCIPLE OF JUSTICE

Justice is a traditional central concern of philosophers; nonetheless, that same philosophical tradition forms the basis not only for ethics but also for our system of laws. There are many contexts in which the principle of justice applies. Distributive justice refers to the equitable allocation of assets in society, which presupposes resource scarcity and imposes the requirement of fairness in the distribution of those scarce resources. Retributive justice seeks to punish wrongdoers objectively and proportionately; this principle underlies the goal of the judicial system in general. Restorative justice refers to the goal of justly compensating those wronged—to "make whole" those injured; this principle underlies the goal of the tort law system. Procedural justice refers to structured and transparent decision-making based upon fair and unbiased processes that are uniformly applied.

The principle of distributive justice addresses the equitable distribution of benefits and burdens to individuals in society and how the rights of individuals are realized. Societal criteria for the employment of the principle of distributive justice may include the following:

To each person an equal share
To each person according to need
To each person according to effort
To each person according to contribution
To each person according to merit
To each person according to free-market exchanges
(Beauchamp & Childress, 1994, p. 330)

Justice in health care is usually defined as a form of fairness, traditionally and still arguably a notion of "equal shares for all." Later, Aristotle distinguished between justice as overall equality and instead construed justice in a narrower sense as it applied to equality of treatment. Philosophers Jeremy Bentham and John Stuart Mill advanced the theory of consequentialism, an approach that values the good of the collective over that of the individual. Indeed, many have observed that the one key issue that distinguishes public health ethics from clinical ethics is the justification of paternalism for the good of society as a rationale for overriding individual autonomy.

Thus, the inevitable question regarding justice is this: to whom is justice owed? If justice represents fair and equal treatment, then an individual has no greater rights than do those in society. This notion implies fair distribution of available resources. Entitlements imply unfair access to limited resources whereas discrimination implies unfair denial of access to limited resources. Justice can be appropriately considered only when criteria are similar and applied equally to all involved in the community's population. Such utilitarian issues, which pit the focus of low resource consumption against the needs of the individual patient, are at odds with the Hippocratic duty of doing everything possible for the individual patient and can create an internal dissonance. In such cases, the fiduciary obligation of the patient-provider relationship must, to a reasonable extent, trump the societal perspective. Medical providers have an obligation to treat all patients equally, fairly, and impartially.

Nondiscrimination implies not only equal treatment regardless of age, social status, race, culture, sexuality, and disability, but also with respect to cost and economics. In those instances in which persons lose their ability to exercise their autonomy, they may be denied access to their share of resources. This principle holds not only in the geopolitical arena but also to decision-making in health care. For example, healthcare providers may harbor biases against patients with dementia because of the cost of care balanced against the likelihood of successful outcome. Successful outcomes, however, can be difficult to define and may include the treatment of acute infections, a return to custodial care, or, in the extreme—a return to productive life in society. Since the last may be unlikely, the use of this outcome measure may bias against aggressive treatment of patients with dementia. Those least likely to benefit are most easily denied access. During World War I, the U.S adopted a triage algorithm, which prioritized access to medical care on the basis of the likelihood of successful and rapid return to the battlefield; those most likely to return to combat quickly were treated first in order to maintain the numbers of the fighting force.[102] Presently, there is no universal international consensus agreement regarding the ethics of triage. Both the Geneva Convention of 1864[103] and the Universal Declaration of Human Rights of 1948[104] underscore fundamental obligation to respect human rights.

The term "triage" is derived from the French word *trier*, which means "to sort." In general, three preconditions must co-exist in order for successful triage: (1) at least a modest scarcity of resources, (2) a designated and qualified triage officer assesses each patient's medical needs on the basis of examination; and (3) an established system or plan, usually based on an algorithm or a set of criteria, to determine a specific treatment or treatment priority for each patient.[105] Where resources are allocated on the basis of acute scarcity, such as in the event of triage, the algorithm upon which the decisions are based should be transparent and the circumstances documented for retrospective review.[106]

The fundamental purpose of triage, rationing of resources, demands that not everyone who needs a health-care intervention can readily gain access to it. Triage in health care is most often encountered in mass casualty scenarios and in the dilemma of the "last ICU (intensive care unit) bed." With respect to ICU triage, there are no randomized clinical trials that unequivocally demonstrate that patients treated in ICUs have better postoperative outcomes; however, there is in fact much published to support this contention in the form of observational studies. Nonetheless, if, for the sake of argument, ICU care did in fact reduce the risk of morbidity and mortality for hospitalized patients, there would nonetheless remain a resource limitation of bed availability. Although ICU admission guidelines have been published by a variety of professional organizations, these guidelines do not provide guidance regarding the triage of patients with similar acuities of illness. Indeed, the American Thoracic Society has recommended that the allocation of scarce ICU resources be based on a first-come, first-served basis. The Society of Critical Care Medicine 2016 ICU Admission, Triage, and Discharge Guidelines emphasize the individualization of triage decisions based on policies and protocols specific to the institution and clinical context:

> The decision to admit to the ICU can be very easy when resources are abundant or very difficult when limited. Scarce resources may threaten or impede the allocation of critical care services to patients; misusing these resources can aggravate the problem. The ICU should be reserved for critically ill patients who require life-supportive therapies from a trained team of health-care providers; however, we cannot ignore our responsibility outside the boundaries of these units. We need to further develop preventive strategies to reduce the burden of critical illness, educate our noncritical care colleagues about these interventions, and improve our outreach, developing early identification and intervention systems.[107]

CONCLUSIONS

Ethics is the cornerstone of professionals and is founded upon philosophical principles that also laid the foundation for moral construct and legal theory. The scope of philosophical deliberation is broad and continues to be debated. Applied (or clinical) ethics employs the four key ethical principles of autonomy, beneficence, nonmaleficence, and justice in the analysis of complex clinical situations as a framework for a structured analysis. In a sense, the application of structured analysis to clinical ethical decision making itself is an application of the principle of justice.

It is obvious that morality, and rules, are in themselves insufficient unless they are ingrained and followed, and perhaps even incentivized. On the other hand, there is an element of practical wisdom (Aristotle's concept of *phronesis*) that refers to the practical process of perceiving the relevant issues within the situation, recognizing the feelings provided by one's internal moral compass, carefully deliberating upon the choices, and ultimately acting appropriately. In his discourse on ethics, Aristotle argued that each of us needs to develop character traits such as self-control, love, generosity, gentleness, truthfulness, friendliness, and courage. Aristotle called these traits virtues (*arete*) and stated that such virtues provided a practical application of wisdom, because rules without wisdom are blind, and can, at best, only guarantee mediocrity. The wise and virtuous application of the rules of decision making is the goal of practical wisdom.[108] Therefore, ethical constructs are meaningless unless they are applied in the context of caring, and it is precisely that level of caring that defines the relationship between a professional and his or her client or patient. All too often, rules are construed in accordance with a deference to professional discretion while simultaneously ignoring the importance of professional dedication. Perhaps issues such as professional burnout and job dissatisfaction may be best addressed through a nurturing of qualities such as integrity, thoroughness, kindness, perseverance, and integrity, which, in turn, not only foster internal fortitude and resilience but also reinforce the internal moral compasses upon which our professions are based.

2 · CASE STUDIES
Ethical and Legal Challenges in the Care of the Neurologically Injured Critically Ill Patient

I. FEEDING TUBE PLACEMENT, SEVERE ACUTE NEUROLOGIC INJURY, OR ADVANCED NEUROLOGIC DEGENERATIVE DISEASE

Case Scenario
The patient in your intensive care unit (ICU) has severe and irreversible neurologic impairment. The family, including the proxy, requests that "everything be done."

Ethical and Legal Analysis
Patients with dementia present with a generally unrelenting and incurable disease manifested by impaired cognition and loss of decision-making capacity. Dementia is not one disease; rather, it is a clinical presentation shared by many diseases including Lewy body dementia, pre-senile Alzheimer type dementia, traumatic brain injury, and senile dementia. A number of clinical assessment scales have been developed that address cognition, function, quality of life, behavior, depression, and caregiver burden; these include, for example, the General Practitioner Assessment of Cognition,[1] the Alzheimer's Disease Assessment Scale,[2] and the Barthel Index.[3] Although the progression of dementia is not linear and can be variable between individuals, the later stages of the condition are marked by impaired mobility, loss of coordination, incontinence, dysphagia, and impaired cough. Quality of life is especially important to quantify, and specific grading scores have been developed to measure disease burden, including the EuroQol[4] measure and the Alzheimer's Disease-Related Quality of Life scale (QoL-AD).[5] The measure of global deterioration in functioning is important to quantify because there is no cure, the late stages are not well impacted by interventions, and the prolongation of life without an associated prospect for improved quality of life may not be

consistent with a patient's wishes; some have proposed that advanced dementia be considered a terminal disease for which there is a continuum of care that goes from palliative care with life-extending measures to symptomatic interventions only.[6] Others have reported good longer term outcomes despite advanced cognitive impairment.[7]

Careful and thoughtful consideration is important because similar analyses may be applicable for patients with progressive neurologic diseases such as ALS (amyotrophic lateral sclerosis), severely disabling strokes, or severe traumatic brain injury.[8,9] Generally, in healthy patients with progressive disease or severe acute neurologic injury, feeding tubes may prolong life significantly, whereas in those who were previously in poor health, feeding tubes are likely to have a relatively short-term benefit, although the outcome data have only a relatively high variable and are context dependent,[10] especially with technological and pharmaceutical advances. Thus, the notions of prognostication and futility are highly fluid, and when such ethical and medical concepts are interpreted in a legal sense, there is even more confusion; this is because medicine focuses largely on the individual and the law looks at the individual in the context of society and fairness.

An important application of clinical ethical analysis in medical care centers on the question of futility. Webster's dictionary defines "futile" as "serving no useful purpose, completely ineffective."[11] The Hippocratic corpus defined futility in a quantitative sense, stating that "Whenever the illness is too strong for the available remedies, the physician surely must not expect that it can be overcome by medicine. . . . To attempt futile treatment is to display an ignorance that is allied to madness."[12] The term "medical futility" has not been absolutely defined. In general, medical futility can be defined as the delivery of medical care and therapeutic interventions that are unlikely to produce any significant benefit for the patient. Because definitions of futile care are value laden, a universal consensus on the definition of futile care is unlikely to be achieved.[13] More specifically, discussions generally involve two kinds of medical futility, which are distinguished as follows: (1) quantitative futility, in which the likelihood that an intervention will benefit the patient is exceedingly poor, and (2) qualitative futility, in which the quality of the intervention's benefit is exceedingly poor.[14] In the application of clinical ethics, futility invokes the notions of autonomy, beneficence, nommaleficence, and, to some extent, distributive justice. Perhaps the two key issues in the application of a medical futility label to a particular case involve (1) the level of certainty in the prognosis, and (2) a situation in which there are expectations or demands for overtreatment. The ethical principle of nonmaleficence requires that providers uphold the fiduciary obligation to "first do no harm." Thus, providers are not ethically obligated to provide treatments they believe are ineffective or harmful to patients.[15] However, as long as futility retains an "I'll know it when I see it" definition, the application of futility in clinical decision making is likely to remain an area in which the law can differ from the ethical construct.

To date, only four states have provided legal definitions for the notion of medical futility. Maryland and Delaware statutes state that medical futility "means that, to a reasonable degree of medical certainty, a medical procedure will not: (1) Prevent or reduce the deterioration of the health of an individual; or (2) Prevent the impending death of an individual."[16,17] Alaska interprets futility to mean "[a treatment] that according to reasonable medical judgment cannot cure the patient's illness, cannot diminish its progressive course, and cannot alleviate severe discomfort and distress."[18] Finally, the New Mexico statute defines futile to mean "that the treatment would not offer the patient any significant benefit, as determined by the physician."[19]

Courts have ruled in favor of the patient's right to refuse treatment and the patient's surrogate's right to withhold treatment. Such decisions would be in line with notions of liberty interests and the respect for autonomy. Similarly, the courts have upheld the right of patients or their surrogates to request even those medical treatments from which physicians believed they would receive no medical benefit. The courts remain divided on this issue. For example, in the cases of *Wanglie*[20] in 1991 and *Baby K*[21] in 1994, courts upheld, respectively, the rights of surrogates to determine the level of care based upon a prior knowledge of the patient's wishes, the continuation of heroic interventions, such as mechanical ventilation on an anencephalic newborn, were "futile" or "medically and ethically inappropriate" and that they "would serve no therapeutic or palliative purpose."

On the other hand, in 1999, Texas legislation combined pre-existing laws regulating end-of-life treatment into a single law, the Texas Advance Directives Act,[22] which established a legally sanctioned extrajudicial process for resolving disputes about end-of-life decisions.[23] The Texas statute allows that either "(1) if the patient or the person responsible for the health care decisions of the patient is requesting life-sustaining treatment that the attending physician has decided and the ethics or medical committee has affirmed is medically inappropriate treatment, the patient shall be given available life-sustaining treatment pending transfer; or (2) [t]he attending physician, any other physician responsible for the care of the patient, and the health care facility are not obligated to provide life-sustaining treatment after the 10th day after both the written decision and the patient's medical record."[24] Thus, although a hospital in Texas must initially provide life-sustaining treatment after a procedures-driven determination of medical futility, pending transfer arrangements, the hospital has no obligation to continue the treatment after 10 days;[25] additionally, the family or surrogate may seek court intervention to extend the 10-day period, but the courts require a demonstration, to a preponderance of the evidence, that there is a reasonable expectation that the family or surrogate will find an accepting physician or facility in that time.[26] In addition, an Idaho statute specifically addresses futile care, stating in part, "[n]othing in this chapter shall be construed to require medical treatment that is medically inappropriate or futile."[27] A New Jersey statute states, in part, that "Life-sustaining treatment may be withheld or withdrawn from a patient in the following circumstances: (1) When the life-sustaining treatment is experimental and not a proven therapy, or is likely to be ineffective or futile in prolonging life, or is likely to merely prolong an imminent dying process."[28]

Because of the lack of a medical definition of futility and the lack of legal consensus regarding its application, medically futile care may be best approached through a process of shared decision-making.[29] Increasingly, a patient's pre-existing wishes regarding heroic interventions can be discovered in living wills or other advance directive documents. Where uncertainty or conflict regarding the goals of care arise, the institutional ethics committee can provide valuable, albeit non-binding, reassurance and advice. In addition, the importance of involving a multidisciplinary palliative care team cannot be over-emphasized, especially when the primary care or critical care teams have reached an impasse with family. Clinical issues such as those involving medical futility highlight the importance of multidisciplinary care.

II. BALANCING PALLIATIVE SEDATION AND DOUBLE EFFECT

Case Scenario
The family has requested that life supporting measures be withdrawn and are asking that the patient be "made comfortable" per end-of-life care; however, they are uncomfortable with the initiation of palliative sedation, feeling that it might hasten death.

Legal Analysis
The doctrine of double effect is applicable to end-of-life care as a rational justification for medications, in judicious doses, prescribed in order to minimize pain and anxiety while simultaneously potentially hastening the dying process. Although the goal of palliative sedation is to provide relief in an ethically acceptable way to the patient, some family or members of the care team may voice concerns about the necessity of palliative sedation and express concerns regarding a perceived similarity between palliative sedation and either physician-assisted suicide or euthanasia. Ethically, morally, and legally, the distinction between these precepts is in the underlying intent. Clearly, therefore, in order to invoke the notion of double effect of palliative sedation, there must be a situation legally and ethically justifying palliative care. Terminal sedation in an ambiguous end-of-life-care clinical scenario is more compatible with physician-assisted suicide or euthanasia. For example, if the patient has refused a feeding tube, mechanical ventilation, or other heroic interventions and is suffering through hunger, respiratory distress, or pain, compassionate care becomes a priority. Alternatively, it

may be that a patient is requesting the removal of life support and heroic measures, rather than refusing the initiation of life support and heroic measures, and it is anticipated that discontinuation of life support may produce a rapid but painful death. In both scenarios, palliative sedation is considered to be legally, ethically, and, morally justified. Relief of suffering through medications represents not only the compassion expected of health care professionals, but also represents a respect for humanness and human dignity. The relief of suffering is one of the key ethical tenets of medical care. The task of medicine, variably attributed to both Hippocrates and the French surgeon Ambroise Paré (1510–1590), "the task of medicine is to cure sometimes, to treat often, but to comfort always." Since the pharmaceutical agents used to treat anxiety and pain are controlled through professional licensing in medicine and its allied specialties, physicians and providers are tasked with the responsibility to exercise professional judgment regarding the use of opiates, benzodiazepines, and adjunctive medications for palliative sedation. If a balancing test analysis were used to legally determine whether the justification for the use of medications that would certainly relieve suffering but would hasten death was to be offset by the forbidden act of hastening death, relief of suffering would almost certainly prevail as the operative intention.

Once again, intent becomes operative in the mode in which medications are administered; the intent of palliative sedation is a relief of suffering and therefore implies a titration of medication to a desired effect rather than the administration of a large dose of medication, which would be expected to imminently cause death. Therefore, in a legal sense, documentation of the patient's wishes, medical circumstances, and evidence of the pain and suffering for which treatment is being administered is essential in the event of any legal retrospective review. Because of the subjective nature of assessing pain and suffering, in any such circumstance, a team approach, which includes all members of the care team, and, as always, solid supporting documentation, represents a best practice.

Ethical Analysis

Palliative sedation is justified by using the principles of autonomy and beneficence. Clearly, allowing a competent person to make health care decisions based on his or her own personal beliefs, values, and goals regarding potential heroic medical interventions represents personal choice and therefore autonomy. Similarly, since the ethical principle of beneficence imposes a duty to benefit patients, imposing needless suffering at the end of life, in a situation in which death is otherwise imminent, would be inconsistent with either moral principles or the ethical principle of beneficence. Health care providers are expected to extend caring to vulnerable populations, and patients who are suffering at the end of life are vulnerable.

III. NIHILISM, SELF-FULFILLING PROPHECY, AND PROGNOSTICATION: WHAT DO WE REALLY KNOW?

Case Scenario

You have been asked to render a prognosis regarding a 36-year-old patient in the ICU with a traumatic intraparenchymal hemorrhage. The ICU team is asking your opinion in order to help a family determine how they should make decisions regarding ongoing and future care.

Legal and Ethical Analysis

Merriam-Webster's dictionary defines prognosis as "the prospect of recovery as anticipated from the usual course of disease or peculiarities of the case."[30] Prognosis and prognostication remain within the purview of medical judgment. In general, physicians and health care providers are not obligated to provide care that they feel is medically futile or unreasonable. However, refusal of requested care has not been well resolved by either case law or legal statute.[31] Nonetheless, the likelihood of legal scrutiny of the care provided, wherein elements of care were refused, is greater. The fundamental legally operative principle at the basis of either initiation or non-initiation of a medical intervention is the issue of informed consent and its corollary, informed refusal. However, both informed consent and informed refusal decisions are influenced by the explicit and implicit biases of the provider leading the consent discussion. It is important to note that prior experience in medical decision-making is an important source of bias in future decision-making. Although it is unspoken, it is tacitly accepted in health care that the patient's family's decision will largely be based upon the way in which the information is presented. Thus, when a picture is painted optimistically, the instinct of hope will prevail, and patients and families are likely to consent to even heroic interventions; on the other hand, if the same picture is painted pessimistically, despair will prevail and patients and families are likely to consent to limitation or withdrawal of heroic interventions. Section analysis puts great emphasis on ethical conduct, recognition, minimization and disclosure of bias, and prudent medical judgment. Since medical judgment cannot be well scrutinized by the courts, the courts are generally reluctant to intervene or second-guess the intricacies of medical judgment. In the scrutiny of such circumstances, the legal system will look to the documentation within the medical record regarding the clinical presentation, scoring scales (if available), the assessment of other providers and consultants, and mitigating circumstances such as comorbidities. The documentation will form the evidentiary basis upon which medical judgment will be evaluated.

The state of medical knowledge, the state of pharmaceutical therapy, and elevations in technology continuously redefine the limits of medical care. Therefore, interventions that were futile 40 years ago may be commonplace today; for example, extracorporeal membrane oxygenation, advances in cardiopulmonary monitoring, and cerebral metabolic monitoring continue to evolve and redefine not only the limits but also the standards of medical care.

Furthermore, the latest advances in medical care are most likely to be available and used within tertiary care, generally in academic or medical centers. Decisions regarding the initial aggressiveness of care must often be made at the time of presentation, and perceived short- and long-term prognosis is an important element in the decision-making process. The use of early do-not-resuscitate (DNR) orders among patients with serious traumatic brain injuries is highly variable by individual hospital and hospital type. Objective severity of illness scores have been developed, but they may not be applicable to specific cases, especially in neurocritical care. The elements of prognostication are complex and involve a myriad of subjective factors, such as prior experience and training, the location or context, attendant clinical support and backup, and a general sense of the patient's resilience and reserve. Just as the providers of 40 years ago could not envision the cutting edge technology available today, practitioners in rural or community health care settings cannot access and perhaps cannot even envision the applicability of that cutting edge technology to patients presenting acutely under their care. Therefore, to a large extent, prognosis is contextually defined. Therefore, the notion of futility depends greatly on the location of care; case presentations that are considered futile in a rural community hospital may be seen as routine in a university trauma center setting. For example the presence of attending neurosciences clinicians and the availability of a neurocritical care unit have each been demonstrated to positively impact outcome. Also, a patient's prior medical history and comorbidities will likely impact a prognostication, weighing upon the likelihood of not only surviving the acute illness but also convalescence. Providers cannot be expected to offer treatments to which they have no reasonable access; barring a transfer between institutions, which may be unreasonable for a patient's medical status, providers can only offer those treatments immediately available under most circumstances. Once again, the legal standard is based on "a reasonable provider similarly situated"; therefore, the issue of medical judgment in a specific clinical circumstance, and hence prognosis within that circumstance, cannot be legally defined or evaluated.

Prognostication matters to outcome. Communication of a poor prognosis with subsequent limitation of heroic intervention will inevitably lead to a poor outcome; communication of a potential good outcome may still lead to a poor outcome, although the possibility of a good outcome would not be realized without offering a chance. Thus, decisions to limit treatment at the time of initial assessment are predicated on the assumption that the prognostication is sufficiently accurate and reliable to enable decision-making early after an acute neurological catastrophe; this assumption raises important concerns about how we prognosticate, how we use this information in individual patient decision-making in the emergency setting, and how we communicate this information to patients and their families.[32] Scoring systems may or may not be helpful with respect to prognosis. The Glasgow Coma Scale and the Intracerebral Hemorrhage (ICH) score both represent severity of illness grading scores that were initially developed as tools to communicate a patient's clinical status more reliably between providers but, subsequently became statistical prognostication tools. The ICH score is a severity of illness grading system that also assigns a mortality risk to the various grades of hemorrhage.[33] Moreover, the assignment of mortality values with each level of ICH score has generally remained static; therefore, these probabilities may not reflect the impact of new technologies and techniques. The outcome probabilities assigned to each level of ICH score have not been updated for some time and may represent an overly pessimistic prognostication in need of reassessment and potential re-evaluation.

A self-fulfilling prophecy represents the validation of a prior prediction based in a course of approach. For example, although it has been widely emphasized that a DNR order does not mean 'Do Not Treat,' it is widely recognized that patients with a DNR designation are less likely to receive aggressive care, even though it may potentially treat a reversible illness.[34,35] It is widely recognized that DNR patients are more likely to die in the hospital than are similar patients who do not have a DNR status. For example, "high-risk" DNR patients, compared with a matched cohort of "high-risk" non-DNR patients, independent of comorbidities and perioperative complications, had higher rates of "failure to rescue" and death.[36] The importance of such data fracture not only affects risk adjustment data, but also has ethical implications regarding the initiation of shared decision-making in challenging circumstances, especially when there is uncertain prognosis. Similarly, early care limitation in patients with ICH independently predicts mortality.[37,38] Thus, early decisions to limit treatment after acute neurologic illness or injury must be balanced with the avoidance of self-fulfilling prophecies of poor outcome due to clinical nihilism.[39] On the other hand, prognostication is also important to patients and their families; it is a vital communication wherein there is honest disclosure of the facts upon which informed consent or informed refusal can be predicated. Communication of prognosis places great importance upon a patient's right to choose—the principle of autonomy.

The impact of self-fulfilling prophecies due to a premature limitation of heroic intervention can, most likely, be best countered by the dissemination of education and knowledge regarding advances and capabilities within subspecialties. Since neurocritical care is a new specialty that continues to advance regularly and rapidly, it is incumbent on neuroscience professionals to reach out within their institutions, their communities, and the pertinent regional patient catchment areas to educate other providers with regard to the possibilities and capabilities that may be offered to patients and families. In addition, subjective nihilism could be offset by validated outcome data, which either would clearly support continued heroic intervention (or, alternatively, the early discontinuation of heroics) or provide an imperative for the development of new protocols, techniques, and interventions.

In the end, a conscientious care team, who are aware of the possibilities and limitations of the current state of medical care, through consensus and communication, are best situated to explore an individual patient's or family's wishes and expectations. It must be unbiased communications and the patient's or family's informed decision-making that must drive the plan of care.

IV. A PATIENT'S FAMILY REFUSES TO ACKNOWLEDGE A DIAGNOSIS OF BRAIN DEATH

Case Scenario

A 42-year-old previously healthy male has been involved in a high speed motor vehicle accident. He presents to you with a severe closed head injury; there are no data to support intoxication, and he is on cardiopulmonary life support. Your initial and subsequent examinations reveal fixed and dilated pupils, the absence of cough and gag with suctioning, and the absence of posturing. The family is present. What are the key considerations regarding the initiation of formal testing to establish a diagnosis of brain death?

Legal Analysis

Brain death was first described generally by Mollaret and Goulon[40] in 1959. The concept of brain death received more widespread attention in 1968 when Henry Beecher, through a Harvard ad hoc committee, proposed that a person could be diagnosed as dead when there was irreversible cessation of the function of the entire brain. In 1978, the Uniform Law Commissioners (ULC) created the Uniform Brain Death Act (UBDA), which established that the "irreversible cessation of all functioning of the brain, including the brain stem" is, in fact, death. The Uniform Determination of Death Act (UDDA)[41] was promulgated in 1981 jointly by the American Medical Association and the American Bar Association as model legislation (non-binding statutory text meant to serve as a guide for state lawmakers); it was later adopted nationwide in the United States, and provides some alignment between medical and legal concepts of brain death. The UDDA specified that "[a]n individual who has sustained either (1) irreversible cessation of circulatory and respiratory functions, or (2) irreversible cessation of all functions of the entire brain, including the brain stem, is dead." All states' definitions of death are based on the UDDA, although these laws vary among the states.

For example, the relevant state of Florida statute states in part that:

(1) For legal and medical purposes, where respiratory and circulatory functions are maintained by artificial means of support so as to preclude a determination that these functions have ceased, the occurrence of death may be determined where there is the irreversible cessation of the functioning of the entire brain, including the brain stem, determined in accordance with this section.

(2) Determination of death pursuant to this section shall be made in accordance with currently accepted reasonable medical standards by two physicians licensed under chapter 458 or chapter 459. One physician shall be the treating physician, and the other physician shall be a board-eligible or board-certified neurologist, neurosurgeon, internist, pediatrician, surgeon, or anesthesiologist.

(3) The next of kin of the patient shall be notified as soon as practicable of the procedures to determine death under this section. The medical records shall reflect such notice; if such notice has not been given, the medical records shall reflect the attempts to identify and notify the next of kin.[42]

The state of New York statute is similar:

(a) An individual who has sustained either:
  (1) irreversible cessation of circulatory and respiratory functions; or
  (2) irreversible cessation of all functions of the entire brain, including the brain stem, is dead.
(b) A determination of death must be made in accordance with accepted medical standards.
(c) Death, as determined in accordance with paragraph (a)(2) of this section, shall be deemed to have occurred as of the time of the completion of the determination of death.
(d) Prior to the completion of a determination of death of an individual in accordance with paragraph (a)(2) of this section, the hospital shall make reasonable efforts to notify the individual's next of kin or other person closest to the individual that such determination will soon be completed.
(e) Each hospital shall establish and implement a written policy regarding determinations of death in accordance with paragraph (a)(2) of this section. Such policy shall include:
  (1) a description of the tests to be employed in making the determination;
  (2) a procedure for the notification of the individual's next of kin or other person closest to the individual in accordance with subdivision (d) of this section; and
  (3) a procedure for the reasonable accommodation of the individual's religious or moral objection to the determination as expressed by the individual, or by the next of kin or other person closest to the individual.[43]

Although it is widely accepted, medically and legislatively, that a determination of death must be made in accordance with accepted medical standards, the UDDA, or state law in general, does not specify the elements of diagnosis. In 1995, the Quality Standards Subcommittee of the American Academy of Neurology (AAN) published practice parameters for determining brain death in adults;[44] these were then reviewed by the Royal College of Physicians.[45] The AAN guidelines were subsequently updated in 2010.[46] Nonetheless, there remains substantial variation[47,48,49,50] and there also remain ongoing gaps between written hospital parameters and the 2010 AAN update.[51] In 2017, the state of Nevada became the first state to impose legislative protocols on the medical determination of brain death, stating, in part:

1. Consent is not required to administer tests to determine brain death.
2. After brain death is determined, treatment must be withdrawn within 24 hours.
3. Brain death must be assessed in accord with the 2010 American Academy of Neurology guidelines.[52]

For the purposes of medical malpractice, with rare exceptions, references to the standard of care refer to national standard of care. The Locality Rule[53] generally states that health care providers are expected to conform to the standard of care prevalent among other similarly situated professionals in the same community. In *Pederson v. Dumouchel*, the Locality Rule was liberalized on the basis that "[t]he fact that several careless practitioners might settle in the same place cannot affect the standard of care . . . [n]egligence cannot be excused on the ground that others in the same locality practice the same kind of negligence."[54] *Pederson*, coupled with the fact that board certification now occurs on a national level, supports a national standard of care. Variability in practice, and certainly variability in diagnostic procedure and criteria, can potentially create confusion regarding the validity of a diagnosis. The importance of uniform procedures and criteria for a diagnosis are especially important given public confusion regarding the superficially similar medical conditions of coma, persistent vegetative state, and brain death.[55,56] New York law mandates a period of reasonable accommodation after a declaration of brain death.[57] Thus, the practical and legal meanings of reasonable accommodation are subject to individual interpretation and likely vary across New York hospitals. Religious exception[58] to a declaration of death determined by neurological criteria (DDNC) may be accommodated on the basis of state-specific statutes. For example, the state of New Jersey requires that

> Death not declared in violation of individual's religious beliefs. The death of an individual shall not be declared upon the basis of neurological criteria pursuant to sections 3 and 4 of this act when the licensed physician authorized to declare death, has reason to believe, on the basis of information in the individual's available

medical records, or information provided by a member of the individual's family or any other person knowledgeable about the individual's personal religious beliefs that such a declaration would violate the personal religious beliefs of the individual. In these cases, death shall be declared, and the time of death fixed, solely upon the basis of cardio-respiratory criteria.[59]

Where the law is clear, the diagnosis of brain death remains a medical one. However, in the absence of clear statutory protections, medical providers face substantial legal risk when making a diagnosis of DDNC.

In the Virginia case of *Miranda Lawson*, the patient's parents objected to the performance of an apnea test to confirm brain death;[60] however, during motion practice and pending final judicial resolution, the patient died of a cardiopulmonary arrest. In the case of *Allen Callaway*, the Montana courts upheld the right of a family to refuse to consent to an apnea test (prohibited providers from performing an apnea test to formally declare brain death) in part because (1) although the Montana legislature adopted UDDA in 1983 as a means to determine legal death in the event of irreversible cessation of all brain functions, including those of the brainstem, UDDA did not mandate or otherwise grant a right to physicians to conduct a brain death examination and (2) because an individual's right to choose or refuse medical treatment is protected under the personal autonomy guarantees of the Montana Constitution.[61] Restraining orders have been imposed by the courts against providers seeking to declare DDNC, as in the California cases of *Pierce*,[62] *Fonseca*,[63] and *Stinson*,[64] and in the Nevada case of *Hailu*.[65]

Legal cases challenging the diagnosis of brain death potentially limit physicians' authority to pronounce death, encourage patients' families to challenge and seek injunctions to continue organ support after brain death, and force providers to allocate valuable resources to dead patients in lieu of patients with reparable illnesses or injuries.[66] In the absence of definitive policies, clinicians remain confused regarding their legal and ethical duties when families object to the withdrawal of physiological support after DDNC.

Ethical Analysis

The traditional cardiopulmonary determination of death is subject to universally accepted criteria such as the absence of breathing and heartbeat; DDNC can be much more difficult to rationalize, because in the presence of artificial cardiorespiratory support, the patient does not meet traditionally perceived criteria for death. The legal cases above illustrate that the ethical construct of autonomy in cases of brains death can have mixed interpretation; the classic application of the principle of autonomy, whereby providers may not impose treatment without the individual's consent, can also be inverted—if patients or their surrogates can decline treatment, then surely they can also affirmatively demand treatment—even if treatment is not clinically indicated or cost-effective.[67]

Extracorporeal membrane oxygenation (ECMO) especially can make determination of brain death challenging because of both the complex nature of the technology and issues with apnea demonstration.[68,69] After resuscitation and therapeutic hypothermia, neurologic prognostication can be confounded by drugs because of delayed clearance. Thus, clinical criteria for brain death are not absolute. Families can also become confused, and potentially suspicious, when the opportunity for organ donation is discussed while a person's heartbeat continues.[70] The "Dead Donor Rule" (DDR) represents a formalization of the ethical norm that it is wrong to facilitate the death of one person in order to save the life of another, leading to the inevitable conclusion that a person should be dead before vital organs are removed, an act which would certainly kill them.[71] The act of facilitating death through organ recovery abuts the ethical principles of nonmaleficence and the moral obligation of respect for persons. When organ donation has already been defined by a person's pre-existing directives, the respect for autonomy represents a valid competing interest that may in fact outweigh the principle nonmaleficence in that context. Nonetheless, the forum for organ donation discussions must be chosen with great care since hasty and uncompassionate conversations can fuel suspicions regarding ulterior motives for a declaration of brain death.

A clinical declaration of brain death can be confirmed through the use of radiologic studies that demonstrate unequivocally the absence of cerebral blood flow. Although it is well-established that a diagnosis of brain death is a clinical one, the demonstrated absence of cerebral blood flow can have tremendous persuasive importance in the event of an objection to the diagnosis of brain death.[72]

The timing of death in a case of brain death also remains unsettled, especially when the "declaration of death" has been made on the basis of brain death criteria but the patient continues to demonstrate cardiopulmonary function on life support. States vary in their interpretation of the time of death; New York statutorily defines death as the time of brain death determination, whereas other states require cessation of cardiopulmonary function. The act of a declaration of death triggers ethical, medical, and legal issues such as the following: (1) how is the family informed?; (2) what is the time of death as reflected in the death certificate; (3) what are the obligations of the providers to continue medications that provide cardiopulmonary as well as compassionate effects?; and (4) who will bear the ongoing costs of care after death has been documented? Health insurance policies do not ordinarily cover care provided after the determination of death, a principle consistent with the ethics of distributive justice and fair allocation of scarce resources.

The ethical, legal, and medical controversies surrounding brain death remain far from settled. In the words of Gostin:

At one level, the outcome of these cases seems so clear—both individuals have died and they have a right to a dignified burial; and the physician's ethical responsibilities to treat are finished. At another level, the sheer symbolism of a beating heart, together with the human emotions of a loving parent or spouse, suggest that these kinds of cases at the intersection of law, ethics, and medicine will continue.[73]

V. TRIAGE AND THE DILEMMA OF THE LAST ICU BED

Case Scenario

You are the provider faced simultaneously with two potential competing admissions and you have only one ICU bed, without other reasonable options, and must make a decision on which of the patients will be admitted to the bed. The first patient is a 32-year-old who has overdosed on drugs; this patient has severe hypoxic brain injury, is in a comatose state, has a tracheostomy and a percutaneous endoscopic gastrostomy tube, is septic and hypotensive from an unknown source, and is in need of mechanical ventilation and vasopressor support. The second patient is an 83-year-old who has a perforated sigmoid diverticulum; has acute generalized peritonitis; is profoundly hypotensive; and is in emergent need of very aggressive fluid resuscitation, vasopressor support, and urgent operative intervention. The surgical team can be ready in 1 hour.

Legal Analysis

The duty to treat arises from the patient-provider relationship. Classically, a physician or other health care provider does not have a duty to anyone except a patient in that provider's practice or under that provider's care. However, in hospitals, providers have an implicit duty to treat patients who may fall under their scope of care regardless of whether a pre-existing relationship exists or not. Thus, an ICU physician or provider may be called upon to emergently assume the care of a patient who unexpectedly or acutely becomes unstable and is in need of ICU services. Within the institutional sense, the duty to treat, especially by employed providers, is significantly broader than in the office-based setting. Nonetheless, the duty to treat the patient who is not yet admitted under the care of the ICU is somewhat superseded by the pre-existing relationship of the provider with the patients already in the ICU. Triage presupposes the rationing of scarce resources on the basis of a transparent process of prioritization. Therefore, where ICU triage must occur, a well-defined and generally accepted algorithm of prioritization may be material if triage decisions are scrutinized retrospectively. Certainly, assuming *arguendo* that all the existing patients in the ICU and the two potential admissions in this particular circumstance all have a similar severity of illness and all came be seen have an equal right to ICU care, the choice as to which patient is admitted to the last bed will become, legally and ethically, a matter of clinical judgment. Clinical judgment is justified on the basis of careful analysis of the data and a logically derived conclusion that are documented within the body of the medical record. In this particular case, in a legal sense, admission could either be reasonably justified or reasonably denied. Therefore, the documentation of the reasoning that underlies the final decision is critical. The source of the preordained reasoning, such as an algorithm, must be referenced. In the event that there is no available or applicable algorithm, unbiased transparent medical judgment must prevail. Although the provider should discuss his or her decision with the care team, and a team consensus is an optimal outcome, the final decision will remain at the discretion of the provider in charge.

Ethical Analysis

In contradistinction to the notion of futility, the notion of rationing specifically acknowledges that although a potential treatment or intervention does offer a potential benefit, the question relates to the fair allocation of scare resources; the fair allocation of scarce resources is addressed by the ethical principle of distributive justice.

Distributive justice requires that when allocation decisions regarding limited resources are made, such decisions are made fairly and with a fair distribution of benefits and burdens. Distributive justice does not require that individuals receive their share of the available resources; rather, distributive justice requires that access be allocated fairly on the basis of reasonable principles and criteria. Distributive justice embodies certain presumptions: (1) equality—that all persons are of equal worth and therefore must be afforded an equal chance to access the scarce resources and (2) utility—that decisions must be based on the likelihood of producing the greatest potential benefit. Therefore, assuming that the two potential ICU candidates have equal status in that, for example, neither has exercised autonomy so as to limit ICU intervention, either candidate could be reasonably chosen for ICU admission. In addition however, the principle of utility must be introduced so as to help decide which patient might benefit most from ICU admission. Here, value judgments have no place in the decision-making process and a prognostication must be made regarding the probability of achieving a good outcome in either case. However, a "good outcome" is highly subjective and therefore there is no clear answer as to which patient should be prioritized for admission. Good outcome, in this particular case, will be a matter of provider judgment. Thus, although an ethical analysis provides a useful framework, it does not supply an answer in this case.

3 · CIVIL LAW AND LIABILITY
The Law of Medical Malpractice

CIVIL NEGLIGENCE IN GENERAL

The concept of negligence developed from English Common Law. Negligence is a specific form of tort and is governed by tort law. *Tort* is the Old French word for "wrong." Torts are heavily based in ethics and morality and are also based in normative concepts such as justice, rights, and duties. A tort is an act or omission that causes an injury or harm to another; it is a civil wrong for which courts impose liability and a duty of compensation by the wrongdoer to the harmed. The intent of tort laws is to provide relief to injured parties. Torts are generally classified as (1) intentional torts, (2) negligent torts, and (3) strict liability torts such as product liability. There are many tort causes of action that include, for example, trespass, defamation, invasion of privacy, assault, battery, negligence, product liability, and negligent or intentional infliction of emotional distress. Torts are distinguished from crimes and are therefore governed by civil statutes rather than criminal ones. The goal of the judicial process in torts is to provide a remedy to the injured and thus requires that the plaintiff demonstrate and claim a compensable harm. Judicial awards in torts compensate the plaintiff financially in an attempt to "make the injured party whole" through a formal redress of wrongs. Since patients who have been injured either through a medical mishap or medical error may have lifelong impairment, the goal of the justice system is to provide reasonable compensation for injuries suffered through negligent acts.

Negligence is a tort that is generally defined as either (1) the failure to exercise the degree of care toward others that a reasonable or prudent person would do in the circumstances or (2) taking an action that a reasonable person would not. An allegation of another's negligence requires that the injured party (the plaintiff) prove (1) that the party alleged to be negligent had a duty to the injured party; (2) that the defendant's action, or failure to act, was unreasonable; (3) that the damages were proximately caused by that unreasonable act; and (4) that the injuries were "reasonably foreseeable" at the time of the alleged action. Thus, negligence requires a reasonable person standard; a person may be found to have acted negligently if he or she departed from the conduct expected of a reasonably prudent person acting under similar circumstances. Under the law, which requires an objective standard for adjudication, the reasonable person is not simply an average person but is instead a composite of the community; in a sense, the reasonable person is a societal moral construct regarding a norm of behavior. Once again, the operative elements within the tort of negligence are (1) reasonableness and (2) foreseeability.

In the interest of fairness, the law considers a variety of factors in determining whether a person has acted in accordance with the reasonable person standard: knowledge, experience, and perception. For example, a child's conduct is measured against the conduct expected of a child of similar age, intelligence, and experience; likewise, a person's conduct in an emergency is evaluated in light of whether it was reasonable under the circumstances. In a lawsuit alleging negligence, the plaintiff bears the burden of proof to show that the defendant did not act as a reasonable person would have acted under the circumstances. The plaintiff may introduce a statutory law, submit evidence regarding the usual and customary conduct or practices prevalent in the relevant community under similar circumstances, introduce expert testimony, or argue through the introduction of circumstantial evidence (see the Doctrine of *Res Ipsa Loquitur* section further in this chapter). With respect to civil torts occurring outside the realm of professional malpractice, the jury is empowered with the responsibility of determining whether or not a defendant's conduct was in fact reasonable; however, with respect to professional malpractice, the standard for reasonable conduct must be determined through testimony of experts and to the introduction of accepted standards of practice.

PROFESSIONAL NEGLIGENCE AND THE LAW OF MALPRACTICE

The concept that every person who enters into a learned profession undertakes to practice with a reasonable degree of care and skill dates back to the laws of ancient times. Professional negligence is a breach of the standards of care between professionals and their clients. Thus, all learned professionals, including physicians, nurses, pharmacists, other health care providers, lawyers, engineers, and accountants, are subject to liability under the professional negligence doctrine. Professionals are expected to adhere to a higher standard of reasonable conduct than the ordinary person; therefore, professional negligence compares one's conduct to that of other professionals similarly situated, whereas ordinary negligence simply relies on the reasonable person standard. Professionals are held to a strict duty of care. Typically, professional negligence is not a willful or intentional act, but rather an inadvertent act or act of omission. For example, an attorney may be liable to his or her client in legal malpractice if he or she employs questionable legal strategy or technique or makes critical errors that no "reasonable attorney" should make. In the United States, the laws governing professional malpractice have traditionally been delegated by the federal government to the authority of the individual states; thus, individual state statutes govern definitions, procedure, and case law and should be consulted in each specific circumstance.

The plaintiff in professional negligence can be the client or patient or the patient's estate in the event of death. In the event that the malpractice claim involves the federal government acting through, for example, a federally funded clinic or a Veterans Administration facility, then the malpractice action is filed in a federal district court; additional rules of law, such as the Federal Tort Claims Act, may become relevant. Each state has at least one such federal district court. Federal courts may also be appropriate for filing malpractice claims in which a diversity of state citizenship exists. Examples of this include cases in which the parties to the litigation are from different states or a federal question is invoked, such as the violation of a fundamental constitutional right during the allegedly negligent conduct. In the United States, the right to a jury trial is regarded as a fundamental constitutional right; however, most civil causes of action are settled prior to formal litigation.

THE ELEMENTS OF MEDICAL MALPRACTICE

Medical malpractice is professional negligence committed by a medical professional. Medical malpractice is defined as any act or omission by a physician, hospital, or other licensed health care professional that deviates from the accepted norms of practice during care of a patient and results in an injury to the patient. In any cause of action, the law defines the specific elements, each of which must be established and proven, in order to achieve the requisite standard of proof. Negligence and medical malpractice both require that the plaintiff prove each of four elements: (1) duty, (2) breach, (3) causation, and (4) damages. Specifically in the United States, a plaintiff who alleges medical malpractice must generally prove four elements for a *prima facie* case: (1) the existence of a legal duty on the part of the provider to the patient; (2) a breach of this duty through a failure of the treating provider to adhere to the standards of care, within the circumstances, as defined by the profession; (3) a causal relationship that established the breach of duty as the proximate or actual cause of the harms suffered by the plaintiff; and (4) the proof of existence of compensable damages. If a plaintiff meets the burden of proof by establishing each of these elements, then he or she has established a *prima facie* ("at first look" or "on its face") case. A *prima facie* case meets the evidentiary hurdles for the establishment of a legal argument and thus creates a required rebuttable presumption of proof; the case remains rebuttable until the defense has been accorded the opportunity to answer. The standard of proof in a civil action is that of preponderance of the evidence ("more probable than not").

In order to be liable for medical malpractice, a physician or other health care provider must owe a duty of care to the plaintiff. The duty of care arises from the provider-patient relationship and is, in part, a fiduciary duty. The practice of medicine as a profession is governed by complex implicit and explicit rules and regulations that share their bases both in ethical theory and in principles of morality (see chapter 1). The principles of good medical care, as articulated within the Hippocratic Oath, define that physicians both uphold the interests of the patient and also endeavor to "do no harm." Inherent in the professional obligations of physicians is the ethics-based fiduciary duty to act in the best interests of their patients.

Fiduciary duties arise whenever there is an imbalance of knowledge, training, or experience that puts one party at a relative disadvantage when seeking aid. In a fiduciary relationship, the client justifiably vests confidence, good faith, reliance, and trust in the fiduciary. The provider-patient relationship is ordinarily a consensual one, based in informed consent and requiring the assent of both parties. Absent special circumstances, individual providers are not obligated to accept all comers under their care. Borrowing from the principles of contract law, the mutual assent of both parties is required to create a treatment relationship. Nonetheless, a duty might be imputed in a variety of ways including, for example, proximity and foreseeability, especially for hospital-based emergencies invoking the principle of justifiable reliance; ethical arguments; through public policy considerations; and in certain jurisdictions, through legislation. Thus, the existence of a provider-patient relationship is fundamental to the creation of a duty, and therefore the very existence of this special relation is frequently a point of contention during litigation.

Proof of breach of duty requires a demonstration of the relevant standard of care. In a general sense, the standard of care is the care that would have been provided by a reasonable, similarly situated professional, in good standing, under the same or similar circumstances. The principal types of allegations regarding breach of duty in medical negligence claims include (1) failure to diagnose, (2) failure to treat, (3) inadequate or inappropriate treatment, (4) inadequate supervision or monitoring, and (5) complications or side effects of treatment. The law acknowledges that there are certain medical standards that are recognized by the profession as being acceptable medical treatment by reasonably prudent health care professionals under like or similar circumstances. Since the layperson jury cannot be expected to understand the specific issues inherent in medical diagnosis and treatment, the standard of care, or its breach, these issues must be established through expert testimony. After weighing the testimonies of experts at trial, the issue of whether a defendant has breached a duty of care is decided by a judge or jury as a question of fact. Breaches in the standard of care are not actionable unless they cause harm.

Causation requires a showing that the breach in the duty of care was the proximate cause of the injuries sustained or claimed by the plaintiff. Causation of a particular event is insufficient in itself to create legal liability; the other elements of the cause of action must also be established. Proof of causation seeks to establish a direct relationship between the alleged act or omission and the subsequent injury. Causation includes an analysis of both actual and proximate causation; however, the proximate causation is the legally requisite level of proof. Causation in fact is usually established through the "but for test," which means that "but for the negligent act or omission, would the injuries to the plaintiff have occurred"? However, causation, which passes the "but for" test, may, nonetheless, not be compensable because the relationship between the cause and the effect is too remote or tenuous. Thus, the plaintiff must also prove that he or she sustained an injury that would not have occurred in the absence of negligence. The next question centers on proximate causation, which establishes the legally liable cause. Under the substantial factor test, if several potential causes could each have caused the harm, then any cause that was a substantial factor is held to be liable. Legal causation is also expressed as a question of "foreseeability," since actors cannot be responsible for injuries that are not foreseeable.

Proof of damages is an essential element to the tort of negligence. Damages describe the actual ascertainable loss or harm suffered by the plaintiff. Damages include compensatory damages and punitive damages. Compensatory damages include economic expenses that are quantifiable as a direct result of care required to manage and treat the patient's injuries, such as medical bills; domestic services costs; lost wages; loss of earning capacity; and costs associated with past, present, and future rehabilitation or custodial care. Compensatory damages also include noneconomic damages such as pain and suffering, disfigurement, loss of enjoyment of life, and loss of consortium. Loss of consortium refers to the interference with the spousal relationship and encompasses a variety of tangible and intangible relations that exist between spouses living together in marriage, such as affection, society, companionship, and sexual relations. Punitive damages are intended to punish wrongful conduct and can only be sought when there are aggravating factors, such as willful or wanton conduct; the use of such terminology in a complaint will often suggest that the plaintiff is seeking punitive damages. Caps on damages are established through state-specific tort-reform legislation that limits the amount of monetary compensation that a plaintiff can receive in a medical malpractice case.

The monetary compensation for pain as damages will depend greatly upon the context; factors that influence damages include testimony by economic experts regarding future care needs at a loss of income, expert testimony by rehabilitation experts and psychologists regarding the potential for recovery and/or lasting psychological impairment, pre-existing level of functioning, family circumstances, the perceived or actual egregiousness of the alleged malpractice, damages assessed in similar cases within the area, and the jury. Nonetheless, despite a jury allocation of damages, the judge can modify the damages. In the event of catastrophic damages, which exceed the limits of the liability policy, providers may be at personal financial risk. Most, but not all, of large value medical malpractice claims are shouldered jointly between multiple providers and the institution. Nonetheless, providers should consider financial planning in the event that a catastrophic malpractice verdict may implicate their personal finances. Moreover, the importance of negotiation during the pretrial settlement, and even during the trial itself, can help mitigate the financial impact of damages. Therefore, attorneys representing medical malpractice clients must be skilled not only in litigation but also negotiation. Finally, providers should consult with their attorneys and financial planners prior to litigation.

THE MEDICAL JUDGMENT RULE AND THE RESPECTABLE MINORITY RULE

Independent medical judgment is a vague term that is defined by the facts of the given situation. The right to exercise independent medical judgment is a right of medical professionals by virtue of extensive education and specialized training. Clinical judgement is developed through practice, experience, knowledge, and continuous critical analysis.[1] Some would argue that clinical judgement is considered the nonobjective part of medicine, allowed to pursue a merciful existence "in the darkness of the doctor-patient relationship and that individual clinical judgement and clinical expertise have remained a blind spot in modern medicine."[2]

The "professional judgment" rule is intended to shield medical providers from liability simply because a prescribed course of treatment later was found to prove ineffective. In order to invoke the Medical Judgment Rule, a two-fold test is applied: (1) did the provider conduct a proper examination and evaluation of the patient and the facts and (2) did the provider elect a course of treatment that fell within a range of medically accepted choices? Physicians must understand that a bad outcome does not equate with medical malpractice. Physicians and providers cannot guarantee outcomes or cures. Complications occur and not everyone can be cured, so sound judgement may lead to erroneous conclusions in the clinical context. A provider is generally not liable in negligence for errors in judgment; rather, liability can only legitimately be inferred where the treatment rendered clearly falls outside the recognized standards of good medical practice.

The medical literature is replete with controversy and new medications and technologies, and there is great variation between patients. Medicine rarely prescribes a single treatment for a disease or condition. In claims of professional malpractice, the "two schools of thought doctrine" may be a successful defense.[3] In *Jones v. Chidester*, the Pennsylvania Supreme Court stated that:

> Where competent medical authority is divided, a physician will not be held responsible if in the exercise of his judgment he followed a course of treatment advocated by a considerable number of recognized and respected professionals in his given area of expertise.[4]

A number of states also recognize the Respectable Minority Rule as a defense to alleged medical malpractice in which the defendant acted in accordance with at least a "respectable minority," or recognized subgroup, of the relevant profession, even though his or her actions were at odds with mainstream professional practice.[5] In *Helling v. Carey*, a Washington court opined that reasonable prudence, not customary professional practice, should be determinative in setting legal standards for medical care.[6] The trier of fact is not legally bound to accept only the majority standard of care.

The relevance of the Medical Judgment Rule lies in the importance of documentation relating to the diagnostic and treatment considerations employed by the provider when formulating a diagnosis and treatment plan. Providers commonly make the details of their decision-making process in an implicit rather than explicit manner. Thus, the justification of a diagnosis through careful consideration of a differential diagnosis and the formulation of a treatment plan based upon each patient's unique medical attributes represent medical judgment. The importance of careful documentation therefore, cannot be overestimated.

THE DOCTRINE OF *RES IPSA LOQUITUR*

Res ipsa loquitur (*res ipsa*) is translated from Latin as "the thing speaks for itself." It is a doctrine that allows the facts in a lawsuit to be proven through the introduction of circumstantial evidence and is most often invoked in instances in which there is no direct evidence of the defendant's negligence.[7] *Res ipsa* is a rule of evidence and not a rule of law.[8] The legal effect of *res ipsa* loquitur is to create a *prima facie* case ("valid on its face") of negligence.[9] The doctrine of *res ipsa* introduces a rebuttable presumption of negligence, upon the preconditions that (1) the instrumentality or condition causing the injury was in the defendant's exclusive control, (2) the injury was of a kind that ordinarily does not occur in the absence of negligence (the inference of negligence), and (3) that the plaintiff could not have contributed to the circumstances of the injury (absence of contributory negligence). Examples of *res ipsa* claims include retained instruments or fragments after procedures, dental injuries during airway management, positioning injuries, burns, awareness,[10] or injuries sustained by patients while sedated or chemically paralyzed under anesthesia.[11]

THE EGGSHELL PLAINTIFF

The Eggshell Plaintiff Rule, also known as the Thin Skull Rule, states that the unknown frailty or vulnerability of an injured person is not a valid defense to their consequent injury.[12] However, if the plaintiff has pre-existing health conditions that are aggravated by the injuries caused by the defendant, the defendant is subsequently liable to the plaintiff for full damages.[13] Although the plaintiff is not entitled to recover damages for the pre-existing conditions themselves, the plaintiff is entitled to recover the portion of damages for the pain and suffering attributable to the aggravation of the pre-existing conditions.

The Eggshell Plaintiff Rule is extremely relevant to situations such as emergency care, acute care interventions including surgery, and critical care. Most patients present to the acute health care environment with pre-existing comorbidities that will impact the patient's ability to respond to acute care. While such comorbidities do in fact impact the ratios of observed to predicted mortality, they do not, by themselves, protect providers from additional liability. A careful consideration and documentation of comorbidities may be the most relevant factors in determining statistical probabilities of alternate outcomes.

THE LOSS OF CHANCE DOCTRINE

In medical malpractice actions, it is the plaintiff's burden to demonstrate that (1) the defendant-physician was negligent by deviating from the standard of care, and (2) the injuries were "more likely than not" a direct result of that negligence. "More likely than not" defines the "preponderance of the evidence" standard necessary to prove liability in a civil case; in order for the plaintiff to succeed, the demonstrated probability of negligence must be greater than 50 percent; if such cannot be inferred on basis of the weight of the evidence, the plaintiff loses and recovers nothing. The key ruling on the loss of chance doctrine is often attributed to the analysis in *Hicks*[14]:

> When a defendant's negligent action or inaction has effectively terminated a person's chance of survival it does not lie in the defendant's mouth to raise conjectures as to the measure of the chances that he has put beyond the possibility of realization. If there was any substantial possibility of survival and the defendant has destroyed it he is answerable. Rarely is it possible to demonstrate to an absolute certainty what would have happened in circumstances that the wrongdoer did not allow to come to pass. The law does not in the existing circumstances require the plaintiff to show to a certainty that the patient would have lived had she been hospitalized and operated on promptly.

Thus, under the LOCD or the "loss of chance doctrine," a plaintiff who cannot meet the traditional "more likely than not" burden may still prevail and recover compensation. The doctrine compensates plaintiffs for injuries related to the likelihood that the outcome would have been better had some act or omission of medical care not occurred. A testifying medical plaintiff's expert need only suggest that a potential for a better outcome was lost because of the delay. LOCD is highly speculative, but the conclusion ultimately rests with the trier of fact—the judge or jury. This theory essentially allows for a judgment to be handed down regardless of whether proximate cause can be established. LOCD is limited to a factual causation analysis only: 'but for' the act or omission, the chance of cure would theoretically have been greater.

LOCD raises the risk of liability in medical cases involving a delay in the diagnosis of cancer or a progressive degenerative condition. Under the doctrine, the plaintiff would argue that the disease or condition, and its attendant pain and suffering, were compromised because of a delay in diagnosis and/or treatment. One example is the treatment of ischemic stroke with tissue plasminogen activator (tPA): if we accept that tPA is associated with a 70 percent failure rate and a 7 percent risk of adverse events, such as hemorrhages, failure to timely administer tPA may jeopardize the remaining 30 percent chance of a favorable outcome.

Damages under the LOCD are awarded on the basis of the extent to which the defendant's tortious conduct reduced the plaintiff's likelihood of receiving a better outcome. Damages may be calculated in one of three ways and based upon one of the following: (1) an estimate of a loss assuming full recovery; (2) an estimate of loss assuming the patient's pre-existing probability of recovery; or (3) an estimate of loss assuming an incremental change in the patient's probability of recovery.

A WORD ON DOCUMENTATION IN THE MEDICAL RECORD

Good documentation generally reflects good medical care. Although good medical care can and does occur in the absence of good documentation, parties who review the quality of care provided will usually rely primarily on the documentation in their assessments. Documentation in the medical record of a specific patient serves numerous equally important purposes: (1) the creation of a record memorializing a specific encounter between the patient and physician/provider; (2) the creation and perpetuation of a patient's medical history for future reference; (3) the facilitation of a formal line of communication among various members of the health care team; (4) the contemporaneous memorialization and explanation of medical decision-making that occurs during a specific therapeutic encounter; (5) the creation of a foundation for potential peer-review and quality-assurance activities; (6) the justification of the nature, type, and acuity level of professional and/or hospital charges submitted to third-party payers; (7) the provision of data for medical research; and (8) compliance with administrative and regulatory requirements. Medical records also constitute legal documents that are potentially admitted as evidence in courts of law. The most effective way for providers to minimize the exposure attendant with a poor medical outcome is to ensure that the data and reasoning pertinent to a patient's medical care have been entered into that patient's chart. Thorough and accurate documentation induces a reader to infer that the documenter is careful, caring, considerate, and thoughtful. Documentation should not reflect biases and should not be defensive or adversarial. Experts would argue that in the event of a malpractice lawsuit, defendants and counsel will rarely feel that there has been too much documented in the records, especially as it pertains to differential diagnosis, decision-making, and patient counseling. Good medical record documentation is essential to a strong legal defense.

A WORD ON INFORMED CONSENT

Informed consent in the health care context reflects a patient's assent to medical treatment. As we have previously discussed, the principle of informed consent is rooted in respecting a person's dignity and autonomy; therefore, informed consent represents a respect for autonomy and shared decision-making. "Informed" typically means that consent is based upon a full disclosure of the facts, implications, and consequences of an action and is given after careful consideration by a person with the capacity to understand and judge the alternatives. Thus, valid informed consent has three prerequisites: (1) disclosure, (2) capacity, and (3) voluntariness. The legal disclosure requirements for informed consent are discussion of the risks of, benefits of, and alternatives to a proposed treatment plan.

The legal standard for disclosure has largely shifted to from the prudent practitioner (disclosure of the elements that a similar prudent practitioner would have disclosed under similar circumstances), to the more patient-centric reasonable patient standard (disclosure of the elements that a reasonable person would want to know). The reasonable patient standard is also more objectively ascertainable in a court of law since juries can judge for themselves the elements that they themselves would have wanted to know in order to reach a conclusion regarding consent.

Capacity is defined as legal decision-making power and may include age, legal custody through guardianship, or neurologic impairment; however, capacity may also be contextual, such as in the case of acute intoxication or acute head injury. Voluntariness refers to the subject's right to freely exercise his or her decision making without being subjected to external pressure such as coercion, misrepresentation, manipulation, or undue influence. The legal requirements for informed consent are parallel to the requisites for contract formation; therefore, informed consent might be considered a contract for medical care.

Failure to obtain informed consent is a basis for medical malpractice; however, few medical malpractice allegations are actually predicated on the absence of informed consent. Rather, if there is an allegation of medical malpractice, and it is subsequently determined that there was no informed consent, the defensibility of that legal case will be greatly compromised. However, failure to obtain informed consent may also implicate potentially the more serious allegations of civil and criminal charges of battery and state-specific definitions of professional misconduct.

IMPLICATIONS OF SETTLEMENT OR GUILTY VERDICT IN MEDICAL MALPRACTICE LITIGATION

At various times during the litigation process, the parties might chose to settle, attempt alternative dispute resolution such as mediation or arbitration, proffer motions for either summary judgment or dismissal, or voluntarily discontinue the action.

It has been estimated that over 90 percent of medical malpractice cases are settled out of court;[15] the reasons for settlement include (1) the time and cost associated with a jury trial, (2) judicial efficiency, (3) the uncertainties inherent the jury process, and (4) the risk of catastrophic verdicts. The average court settlement is about $425,000; the average jury award exceeds $1 million.[16] The majority of medical malpractice lawsuits result in defense verdicts. Once a civil case goes to court, the legal costs rise exponentially. Sound trial strategy probably as much involves negotiation skills as it does litigation technique.

Nonetheless, settlements against providers are reportable to the same extent as are adverse judgments.[17] The National Practitioner Data Bank (NPDB) is a federal data bank that was created to serve as a repository of quality of care information about health care providers in the United States through the Medicare and Medicaid Patient and Program Protection Act of 1987. The intent of the NPDB is to support professional peer review by encouraging hospitals, state licensing boards, professional societies, and other health care entities to identify and discipline health care practitioners who engage in unprofessional conduct. The NPDB contains information about health care practitioners' malpractice payments, adverse licensure actions, restrictions on professional membership, and negative privileging actions by hospitals. Actions reportable to the NPDB are listed in Table 3.1. The Health Insurance Portability and Accountability Act of 1996 led to the creation of the Healthcare Integrity and Protection Data Bank (HIPDB). The HIPDB was created to combat fraud and abuse in health insurance and health care delivery but actually contains information regarding all civil judgments, criminal convictions, or actions by federal or state licensing agencies against a health care provider, supplier, or practitioner related to the delivery of a health care item or service.

Reporting to the NPDB may have adverse consequences to providers, even if the report resulted from a minor out of court settlement. A NPDB report must be queried when providers request hospital privileges, licensure, and admission to professional societies. The NPDB report may create a presumption of potential competence or professional misconduct issues.

Failure to report is punishable by sanctions such as the following: (1) malpractice carriers who fail to report medical malpractice payments are subject to a civil money penalty of up to $11,000 for each payment; (2) a hospital or other health care entity that fails substantially to report adverse actions will have its name published in the Federal Register, and the organization will lose its immunity from liability under Title IV with respect to professional review activities for a period of 3 years, commencing 30 days from the date of publication in the Federal Register; (3) a professional society that fails substantially to report adverse membership actions can lose immunity protections provided under Title IV for 3 years.

LEGAL RISKS FROM STATE BOARDS OF MEDICINE

Individual states have the authority to regulate the practice of medicine within their state boundaries through police powers conferred upon them in the Constitution. State laws and regulations regarding the practice of medicine vary significantly, and it is imperative that physicians and other health care providers familiarize themselves with the regulations specific to the state in which they practice. State enforcement of regulations related to medical practice is usually delegated to the State Board of Medicine, the State Department of Health, the Office of Professions, or a similar state agency. The primary responsibilities of State Boards of Medicine are (1) the issuance of licenses to practice medicine, (2) the investigation of complaints against licensees, and (3) disciplinary actions. In general, state licensure boards discipline physicians for conduct that is either potentially harmful to public health or conduct involving moral turpitude. Physicians convicted of crimes are uniformly subject to loss of licensure.

Most providers have not heard of the investigatory and enforcement branch of their state Department of Health (DOH) until they are faced with answering a complaint. Complaints typically reach the DOH from patients, although investigations can be triggered by practice patterns, misdemeanors, peer-review findings, or complaints filed by colleagues. Providers uniformly do not understand and do not sufficiently appreciate the scope of authority and the powers vested in State Boards of Medicine. An investigation by the DOH can jeopardize one's career and livelihood.

The definition of professional misconduct encompasses a wide range of activities and is specific to individual states. Providers are prosecuted by the DOH for professional misconduct, not malpractice per se. In the state of New York, the disciplinary arm of the DOH is known as the Office of Professional Medical

TABLE 3.1. Actions Reportable to the National Practitioner Data Bank

Who Reports?	What Information Is Reported?
Medical malpractice payers, including self-insured hospitals and other health care entities	Medical malpractice payments made for the benefit of a health care practitioner resulting from a written claim or judgment
State medical and dental boards	Certain adverse licensure actions related to professional competence or conduct
Hospitals, other health care entities with formal peer review	Professional review actions, based on reasons related to professional competence or conduct, adversely affecting clinical privileges for a period longer than 30 days; voluntary surrender or restriction of clinical privileges while under, or to avoid, an investigation
Professional societies with formal peer review	Professional review actions, based on reasons relating to professional competence or conduct, adversely affecting membership
Drug Enforcement Administration (DEA)	DEA controlled substance registration actions
Department of Health and Human Services (HHS) Office of Inspector General	Exclusions from participation in Medicare, Medicaid, and other federal health care programs
Peer review organizations	Negative actions or findings by peer review organizations
Private accreditation organizations	Negative actions or findings by private accreditation organizations
State licensing and certification authorities	State licensure and certification actions (resulting from formal proceedings) • Adverse actions (including but not limited to revocation, suspension, reprimand, censure, and probation) • Any dismissal or closure of the proceedings by reason of surrendering the license, certification agreement, or contract for participation in a government health care program or by reason of leaving the state or jurisdiction • Any other loss of—or loss of the right to apply for or renew—a license or certification agreement or contract for participation in a government health care program • Any publicly available negative action or finding
State law enforcement agencies	Exclusions from participation in a state health care program

Who Reports?	What Information Is Reported?
State Medicaid fraud control units	Health care-related civil judgments in state court
State agencies administering or supervising the administration of a state health care program	Health care-related state criminal convictions
	Other adjudicated actions or decisions related to the payment, provision, or delivery of a health care item or service
Federal government agencies	Federal licensure and certification actions:
Health plans	• Formal or official actions including, but not limited to, revocation, suspension, reprimand, censure, or probation
	• Any dismissal or closure of the proceedings by reason of surrendering the license, certification agreement, or contract for participation in a government health care program or by reason of leaving the state or jurisdiction
	• Any other loss of—or loss of the right to apply for or renew—a license, certification agreement, or contract for participation in a government health care program
	• Any publicly available negative action or finding
	Health care-related civil judgments in federal or state court
	Health care-related criminal convictions in federal or state court
	Exclusions from participation in a federal health care program
	Other adjudicated actions or decisions related to the payment, provision, or delivery of a health care item or service

SOURCE: Adapted from the U.S. Department of Health & Human Services, National Practitioner Data Bank (undated). Accessed November 20, 2018. https://www.npdb.hrsa.gov/hcorg/whatYouMustReportToTheDataBank.jsp.

Conduct. The definitions of professional misconduct as they apply to medical licensees in the state of New York[18] are found in Table 3.2. Although the definitions that are specific to New York may not apply to the reader's practice, readers should be aware of the breadth of reach of the DOH and the variety of behaviors that may be considered to constitute professional misconduct.

Providers commonly believe that an allegation of medical malpractice is their greatest risk to financial and professional integrity, when in fact, it is actually the

DOH. The threat from the DOH is greater because although malpractice lawsuits may find a provider liable for a plaintiff's damages, they are unlikely to result in loss of licensure. On the other hand, state boards of medicine can discipline physicians through licensure sanctions, fines, probationary suspensions, or full and permanent licensure revocation. Furthermore, although state boards must adhere to administrative due process, such administrative hearings are typically closed, not bound by legal precedent, limit the introduction of evidence and witnesses, and generally shift the burden of proof to the defendant-physician. In fact, at a DOH tribunal, the provider typically will never know where the inciting complaint or event was initiated; at such hearings, the provider typically does not have the right to face his or her accused. The legal process and legal precedents typically used in courts will not apply in a DOH meeting. Therefore, providers receiving a call from a DOH investigator should immediately retain and engage legal counsel before speaking further with an investigator.

MALPRACTICE LIABILITY INSURANCE

The McCarran-Ferguson Act of 1945 generally delegates the regulation of the business of insurance to the individual states. State legislatures set the policy for the regulation of insurance and appoint a state commissioner of insurance.

In a general sense, insurance is a contract in which one party promises to compensate another for a loss. The purpose of insurance is to distribute risk among a large number of persons. Thus, insurance is made possible not only through a distribution of risk over a large risk pool of insured, but also through a complex system of risk analysis. Premiums, the amount that a policyholder regularly pays in return for coverage, vary on the basis of a large number of factors such as the practitioner's medical specialty/subspecialty, number of years in practice, geographic location, the practitioner's claims history, and the type of policy that is in effect. The malpractice carrier has two principal obligations to the insured: (1) the duty to defend the insured against claims; and (2) the duty to indemnify, which requires the insurer to pay the amount of a settlement or judgment, against a covered claim, within the set policy limits.

There are two basic forms of medical malpractice liability coverage. A claims-made policy covers the insured against loss only as long as both the event and the claim occur during the life of the policy. A claim is said to accrue when the event occurs. Since the average malpractice claim is made 1–2 years following an incident, a provider may no longer be covered under the claims-made policy when a claim is filed. Claims-made policies, therefore, frequently require additional purchases of either "nose" or "tail" coverage in order to maintain coverage during job or insurer-to-insurer transitions. Tails and noses are sold at the then-prevailing rate and will take into account a provider's claim history during the prior policy. Thus, claims-made policies tend to be less expensive since they are closed-ended

TABLE 3.2. Definitions of Professional Misconduct in the State of New York

1. Obtaining the license fraudulently;
2. Practicing the profession fraudulently or beyond its authorized scope;
3. Practicing the profession with negligence on more than one occasion;
4. Practicing the profession with gross negligence on a particular occasion;
5. Practicing the profession with incompetence on more than one occasion;
6. Practicing the profession with gross incompetence;
7. Practicing the profession while impaired by alcohol, drugs, physical disability, or mental disability;
8. Being a habitual abuser of alcohol, or being dependent on or a habitual user of narcotics, barbiturates, amphetamines, hallucinogens, or other drugs having similar effects.
9. (a) Being convicted of committing an act constituting a crime under:
    (i) New York state law or,
    (ii) federal law or,
    (iii) the law of another jurisdiction and which, if committed within this state, would have constituted a crime under New York state law;
   (b) Having been found guilty of improper professional practice or professional misconduct by a duly authorized professional disciplinary agency of another state;
   (c) Having been found guilty in an adjudicatory proceeding of violating a state or federal statute or regulation;
   (d) Having his or her license to practice medicine revoked, suspended or having other disciplinary action taken, or having his or her application for a license refused, revoked or suspended or having voluntarily or otherwise surrendered his or her license after a disciplinary action was instituted by a duly authorized professional disciplinary agency of another state;
   (e) Having been found by the commissioner of health to be in violation of article thirty-three of the public health law;
10. Refusing to provide professional service to a person because of such person's race, creed, color or national origin;
11. Permitting, aiding or abetting an unlicensed person to perform activities requiring a license;
12. Practicing the profession while the license is suspended or inactive;
[...]
[...]
15. Failure to comply with an order;
16. A willful or grossly negligent failure to comply with substantial provisions of federal, state, or local laws, rules, or regulations governing the practice of medicine;
17. Exercising undue influence on the patient, including the promotion of the sale of services, goods, appliances, or drugs;
18. Directly or indirectly offering, giving, soliciting, or receiving or agreeing to receive, any fee or other consideration to or from a third party for the referral of a patient;

(continued)

TABLE 3.2. (continued)

19. Permitting any person to share in the fees for professional services;
20. Conduct in the practice of medicine which evidences moral unfitness to practice medicine;
21. Willfully making or filing a false report;
22. Failing to make available to a patient, upon request, copies of documents;
23. Revealing of personally identifiable facts, data, or information obtained in a professional capacity;
24. Practicing or offering to practice beyond the scope permitted by law, or accepting and performing professional responsibilities which the licensee knows or has reason to know that he or she is not competent to perform;
25. Delegating professional responsibilities to a person when the licensee delegating such responsibilities knows or has reason to know that such person is not qualified, by training, by experience, or by licensure, to perform them;
25-a. With respect to any non-emergency treatment, procedure or surgery which is expected to involve local or general anesthesia, failing to disclose to the patient the identities of all physicians, except medical residents in certified training programs, podiatrists and dentists, reasonably anticipated to be actively involved in such treatment, procedure or surgery and to obtain such patient's informed consent to said practitioners' participation;
26. Performing professional services which have not been duly authorized by the patient or his or her legal representative;
27. Advertising or soliciting for patronage that is not in the public interest. (a) Advertising or soliciting not in the public interest shall include, but not be limited to, advertising or soliciting that:
    (i) is false, fraudulent, deceptive, misleading, sensational, or flamboyant;
    (ii) represents intimidation or undue pressure;
    (iii) uses testimonials;
    (iv) guarantees any service;
    (v) makes any claim relating to professional services or products or the costs or price therefor which cannot be substantiated by the licensee, who shall have the burden of proof;
    (vi) makes claims of professional superiority which cannot be substantiated by the licensee, who shall have the burden of proof; or
    (vii) offers bonuses or inducements in any form other than a discount or reduction in an established fee or price for a professional service or product.
28. Failing to respond within thirty days to written communications from the department of health;
29. Violating any term of probation or condition or limitation imposed on the licensee;
30. Abandoning or neglecting a patient under and in need of immediate professional care;
31. Willfully harassing, abusing, or intimidating a patient either physically or verbally;
32. Failing to maintain a record for each patient which accurately reflects the evaluation and treatment of the patient;

33. Failing to exercise appropriate supervision over persons who are authorized to practice only under the supervision of the licensee;
34. Guaranteeing that satisfaction or a cure will result from the performance of professional services;
35. Ordering of excessive tests, treatment, or use of treatment facilities not warranted by the condition of the patient;
36. Claiming or using any secret or special method of treatment;
37. Failing to wear an identifying badge, which shall be conspicuously displayed and legible;
38. Entering into an arrangement or agreement with a pharmacy for the compounding and/or dispensing of code or specially marked prescriptions;
41. Knowingly or willfully performing a complete or partial autopsy on a deceased person without lawful authority;
42. Failing to comply with a signed agreement to practice medicine in New York state in an area designated by the commissioner of education as having a shortage of physicians;
43. Failing to complete forms or reports required for the reimbursement of a patient by a third party;
47. Failure to use scientifically accepted barrier precautions and infection control practices as established by the department of health pursuant to section two hundred thirty-a of the public health law.

SOURCE: New York State Department of Health, New York State Education § 6530, Definitions of Professional Misconduct (2018), https://www.health.ny.gov/professionals/office-based_surgery/law/6530.htm.

and risk can be better controlled. In order to continue coverage after a claims-made policy has expired, a provider typically must purchase a tail coverage policy. Occurrence policies cover the insured as long as the event occurs during the life of the policy (see Table 3.3).

In order to preserve coverage, and possibly evidence, medical malpractice insurance policies typically require the insured to provide the carrier with prompt notice of any potential claim. The notice requirement is closely tied to the state deadlines for answering a complaint and summons. Failure to provide such prompt notice might contractually negate the carrier's obligations to defend and/or indemnify. The notification regarding potential claims has its basis in risk management, whereby the funds necessary to either settle or pay on a judgment are encumbered through the potential life of the claim.

It is important that providers realize that although the insurance company is providing indemnification, and therefore may have influence on trial strategy, it is in fact the defense attorney who is professionally responsible for the interests of the client or defendant. Therefore, defendants may wish to participate in the

TABLE 3.3. Comparison of Claims-Made versus Occurrence Professional Medical Liability Policies

Specifics	Claims-Made Policy	Occurrence Policy
Covered Acts	The insured is covered for acts upon which claims are made *as long as* both occur during the term of the policy.	The insured is covered for acts that occur during the term of the policy.
Key Distinction	If a medical malpractice claim is brought against the insured after the policy has expired or was terminated, even though provider was insured under the policy at the time of the cause of action, the insurer is not liable for coverage.	The insurer is responsible for coverage for medical malpractice causes of action that arise during the coverage period, regardless of when the claim is brought against the provider.
Extended Reporting / 'Tail' Coverage	Extended reporting coverage, if purchased, will cover those medical malpractice claims arising from actions which occurred during the term of the policy but which were not brought until after the policy expired or was terminated.	Extended reporting coverage is not required because claims arising from actions that occurred during the term of the policy are covered by the insurer regardless of when the action is brought against the insured.
Prior Acts or Retroactive Coverage	Available	Available
Cost of Insurance	Insurance premium costs lower than those for occurrence policies, since the duration of risk exposure to the insurer is defined. Premiums are characterized by an incremental increase over the first 5 years in proportion to the insured's claim history, after which a mature premium level is reached and annual rate adjustments will be the primary drivers of premium increases.	Insurance premium costs are higher than those for claims-made policies; however, the insured's financial exposure for claims brought after the term of the policy is more clearly defined. Uncertainties to the insured provider regarding the potential future costs of tail coverage are eliminated.

choice of their attorney representation, realizing that they may not be bound to the counsel assigned to them by the insurance carrier. It is important that whoever represents the provider/defendant be able to work collaboratively and diligently on the behalf of that provider/defendant. From an ethical point of view, the defense attorney is actually working for both the insurance company/malpractice liability carrier and also the provider/defendant; however, the defense attorney's professional duty of care is to the provider/defendant. Thus, attorneys, as professionals, are also held to high ethical and legal standards and must practice within a standard of care defined by the legal profession.

CONCLUSIONS

A provider/defendant or a health care professional/defendant in litigation that alleges medical malpractice must possess at least a minimal understanding regarding the litigation process and procedure in order to best participate in his or her defense. Clear, open, and honest communication with patients and families is the best way to prevent a lawsuit. However, when a malpractice lawsuit is filed, the best outcomes occur when physicians chose knowledgeable and experienced defense counsel and participate actively in the defense process.

4 · LEGAL REASONING, LEGAL PROCESS, LEGAL PROOF, AND WHY IT IS CONFUSING TO CLINICIAN SCIENTISTS

LAW AND THE AMERICAN LEGAL SYSTEM

"The Law" comprises two separate but complementary parts: (1) substantive law and (2) legal process. Substantive law in turn is derived from either (1) legislation or (2) case law.

The supreme source of legislation in the United States is the U.S. Constitution, from which federal and state powers, and the limitations thereof, are derived, and from which individual and state powers and liberties are defined. Any and all subsequently enacted "lesser" laws must not conflict with the U.S. Constitution. The U.S. Constitution governs not only the federal legislature but also state legislatures. States have their own state constitutions, which must not conflict with the limits and powers delegated to them through the U.S. Constitution. The supremacy clause within the U.S. Constitution expressly empowers it as the pre-eminent source of law in the United States, and therefore state constitutions or laws cannot supersede it. The purpose of federal and state constitutions is to limit and regulate government actions. All laws, in both the federal and state constitutions, are written in language that may be subject to interpretation. The meaning of the U.S. Constitution, as it applies to a litigation, is debated in the U.S. Supreme Court, which, as the highest court of appeal in the United States, is charged with interpretation of the Constitution in that context.

The U.S Constitution empowers Congress, the legislature, with the power to enact statues and also the power to create regulatory bodies that can enact administrative laws to regulate various forms of economic activity. Once a bill is enacted by Congress and signed by the president, it becomes a public law, or federal statute; a similar process applies to the passage and enactment of state statutes. Statutory laws, organized by subject matter, are indexed and published as the United States Code (USC, USCA, or USCS).

A separate but equally important process for enacting laws is represented by the authority of Congress to create and empower federal agencies with rulemaking authority. Federal agencies are empowered through the nondelegation doctrine,[1] which addresses "enabling legislation" designed to develop special and specific, frequently highly specialized, regulations known as rules. The process of rulemaking is governed by the Administrative Procedure Act (APA).[2] Rulemaking by agencies must follow a strict, prescribed process and these rules, which have the force of laws, are published in the Federal Register as the Code of Federal Regulations (CFR), which represents the combined body of U.S. administrative law. Federal agencies in the United States that enact rules pertinent to health care include, but are not limited to, the following: the Agency for Healthcare Research and Quality (AHRQ), Centers for Disease Control and Prevention (CDC), Centers for Medicare and Medicaid Services (CMS), Department of Health and Human Services (DHHS), Drug Enforcement Administration (DEA), and the Food and Drug Administration (FDA).

Case law refers to the library of prior legal cases that litigated the same or similar issues, and is generally referred to as legal precedent. If it is applicable at all, legal precedent is either binding or persuasive. Case law that is binding refers to a case or line of cases that addressed similar legal issues, in the same legal jurisdiction, and that has withstood appeals or reviews by higher courts.

Rules and regulations, and therefore laws, become necessary whenever there is an interaction between persons who may potentially have diverging interests. Persons are legally defined as either individuals or corporations. The law is also important when persons and the state have diverging interests or goals. Optimally, the interests of providers and their patients are aligned in the mutual goal of a successful diagnostic and therapeutic outcome. Disagreements arise when patients' expectations differ from the outcome they perceive has occurred. Such perceptions may be either misperception or reality, and that distinction is not always clear. Peer review, the process by which providers review the quality of the medical care provided by their colleagues, has largely proved ineffectual in regulating quality of care; therefore, the merits of the parties involved in a conflict regarding the quality of medical care provided are generally deliberated in public, in a court of law. English Common Law, state constitutions, and case law generally guide the process and the judicial evaluation of such legal arguments.

The U.S. judicial system is referred to as an adversarial system, because each side is represented by an attorney (legal counsel) who represents his or her client and position through legal argument by using the rules of the legal and judicial process. The adversarial process includes the rights to representation, a fair and impartial hearing, and justice, with the goal of fair conflict resolution. Legal arguments are structured for the presentation of relevant substantive laws, case laws, and legal facts, delivered in a logical way within the boundaries of procedural laws, with the intention of persuading the trier of fact (judge and/or jury) of the merits of their respective case. The aggrieved person (usually the patient or his/her estate) who initiates the lawsuit before a court is called the plaintiff or complainant who is seeking a legal remedy from the court. If the plaintiff is successful, the court will enter a judgment for the plaintiff and issue a court order for damages. The party against whom the complaint is directed is the defendant; in the case of medical malpractice, this party is the provider, hospital, or practice, to which the physician belongs. In litigation, cases are identified by citing the plaintiff first; thus, a lawsuit is cited as *Plaintiff v. Defendant*.

The body of law that addresses the legal process or procedure is referred to as procedural law and is defined strictly within the rules of process and rules of evidence. The law addresses questions or issues, referred to as questions of law or points of law, which are answered through the application of relevant legal principles and their interpretation to reach conclusions based on the facts of the case. There are four basic elements to every legal argument: (1) a statement of the conclusion; (2) the presentation of the statutes, case law, or other rules on which the argument is based; (3) analysis and explanations as well as counter-analysis; and (4) the application of the facts and rules to the particular case, completing the proof of the conclusion. The presentation of legal argument in court must conform to the procedural rules that govern, for example, what evidence is admissible and which is not, who is admissible as a witness, and what questions are reasonable and which are not. Legal argument is not as much about confrontation as it is about logical presentation of the pertinent facts. Legal argument, therefore, includes the pre-argument statements or briefs, the opening arguments, the oral arguments during facts and witness presentation, and the closing argument. Since the introduction of evidence and the development of each counsel's argument must conform to a defined process, sometimes evidence that would otherwise appear naturally important may be excluded on the basis of procedural restrictions.

The goal of the judicial process is justice and not necessarily the truth. Fairness within the judicial context may not be so much about being right as it is about the right to a hearing through due process and a decision rendered upon the merits of the cases as presented. The rules by which the law functions are foreign to providers and therefore there is a great deal of angst within the medical community regarding lawsuits.

LEGAL TERMS OF ART

A term of art is a word or phrase that has a particular meaning within a specific context. Legal terms of art are everyday words and phrases that take on special and specific meanings, meanings that may not be intuitively obvious to even articulate and otherwise well-educated laypersons. Legal terms of art may add complexity, but that may also be difficult to avoid, especially within the context of highly technical transactions. On the one hand, terms of art serve as shorthand for legal concepts; on the other hand, they are also legal traps for the unwary. Legal writing might be simplified if terms of art were abandoned and plain English interpretations were used instead; however, the concepts underlying the terms would then need to be expanded upon and could make the documents unwieldy. Terms of art are often embedded within common documents without a corresponding warning or reference; therefore, these terms are interpreted vastly differently by laypersons than by attorneys. However, legal writing is slowly abandoning Latin legal terms and instead using English terminology.

One area that is replete with legal terms is the area of contracts; contracts may be agreements between parties or policies, such as insurance policies. For example, the use of the term "employment" in an employment contract has implicit references to the myriad of state statues that govern employment laws. The term "consideration" in a contract implies much more than the act of weighing the alternatives. Finally, parties in a contract might state, represent, guarantee, or warrant a particular assumption; these terms have contextual meanings that are not identical.

LEGAL FACTS VERSUS SCIENTIFIC FACTS

Providers are trained in scientific method and the use of factual data to build scientific arguments from which consistent and reproducible conclusions can be derived. Scientific facts are data elements that are characterized by almost absolute certainty, such as the molecular weight of oxygen or pupillary size during physical examination (at least by pupillometric assessment). A scientific observation does not become a scientific fact on its own merit; there must be a demonstration of reproducibility. Clinicians view facts as data points, even though there is an uneasy understanding that data is not always accurate and may be in flux at the time it was obtained. For example, any blood specimen result may vary by as much as 10 percent, even if the same blood is tested repeatedly. Nonetheless, that test result is commonly accepted as a scientific fact. Clinicians are taught to listen to both subjective issues and also pay attention to data; when the story and the data do not match, clinicians will generally side with the data (for example, myocardial infarction in the absence of symptoms but with a positive electrocardiogram [EKG] and troponin level).

Legal facts are the individual elements of evidence introduced in the defense or prosecution of a case and may include scientific facts. However, legal facts will also include written records; photographs; videos; and the testimony of opponents, witnesses, and experts. Facts, in legal terms, are the events that have led to the litigation, points of evidence that are material to the presentation and outcome of the case and potentially require interpretation and deliberation regarding conflicting points of view. Questions of fact during litigation may address veracity, bias, recollection, or relevance, and they are generally within the realm of jury deliberation after each side has presented its case. Things that fall under the realm of legal fact include (1) things which can be understood by a layperson (with knowledge of the subject but not of the law; for example, rules of the road when driving), (2) questions of degree (for example, more or less likely), (3) questions of standard (for example, reasonable versus unreasonable behavior), and (4) the meanings of an ordinary words. For clinicians, the admissibility of recollections, perceptions, or other subjective and not independently verifiable data is confusing: for example, how can the outcome of a trial hinge on what is remembered during the informed consent process that took place 5 years prior? The process and the procedures whereby scientific and legal facts are established are areas in which clinicians frequently become skeptical of the legal process. Scientific facts are measured, replicated, and subject to peer review, whereas legal facts are derived from rulings regarding the admissibility of evidence, testimony under oath, clarification through cross-examination, and assessment by a tribunal of laypersons through burden of persuasion and proof (for example, "more likely than not").

LEGAL PROOF VERSUS SCIENTIFIC PROOF

Legal proof is similar to scientific proof in that it is based in rational logic and analysis. Proof has little to do with right and wrong and everything to do with logic. Clinical proof is a conclusion based on the available facts, occurs in real time, and may be fluid pending further data. Whereas science analyzes quantitative criteria subject to statistical analysis, the law mainly assesses categorical criteria described verbally; in the end, analytically, both processes rest upon subjective judgments or assumptions.[3] Legal proof is based in logic games; occurs in retrospect; and makes conclusions based on narrow interpretations of circumstances, stories, and opinions. Scientists and attorneys both use facts, and they understand these facts in terms of a prevailing theory.[4] The process of drawing inferences from evidence is inductive, although a certain amount of deduction also may be involved. A deductive argument is valid if and only if it is logically impossible that its conclusion is false if the premises are true. In contrast, an inductive argument is strong if and only if it is improbable that its conclusion is false if the underlying premises are true. The measure of the strength of an inductive argument is known as an inductive probability, which is a measure of how probable the conclusion is if the premises are true.[5]

Questions of law are concerned with the applicable legal rules and processes to be decided by the presiding judge, who must deal with applicable legal rules and principles that affect what transpired. The law refers to the actual rules and rulings that determine the parameters within which the facts will be weighed and interpreted through the judicial process. Clinicians frequently draw different conclusions from the facts presented at trial than does the jury; that is because clinicians assign a lesser weight to spoken evidence, which cannot be replicated, and assign a greater weight to documentation or diagnostic studies. Therefore, although the scientific and legal processes whereby a conclusion is reached are not vastly different, legal proof is foreign to clinicians because of the manner in which data and assumptions are deemed factual, and therefore, potentially admissible.

THE COMMENCEMENT OF A LAWSUIT

Commencement of a legal cause of action is the formal procedure by which legal proceedings are initiated. A civil suit is commenced by filing a complaint with the court. Although the procedure varies by state, and whether the proceeding is brought in a federal or state court, a summons (with or without the complaint) must then be served to the defendant. A summons is written notice notifying the defendant and the court that the complaint has been served to all relevant parties and listing the date of the first court appearance for the lawsuit. Due process is a constitutional requirement by which a defendant is entitled to reasonable consideration, notice, and a specified procedure to allow a reasonable response in defense of an allegation or a lawsuit. A motion is a written or oral request is made for a presiding court to make a ruling or to issue an order on a particular legal issue. The purpose of the service of process is to notify the defendant with specificity that he or she has been named in litigation, provide an overview of the circumstances of the complaint, and mandate that that a failure to appear and defend will result in a default judgment.

The filing of a complaint and issuance of a summons trigger specific and strict timelines and deadlines that must be complied with by both parties. The service of process demands must be met and the answer must be provided in a procedurally stipulated time period; if that time elapses without a response, a default judgment may be granted by a court. A default judgment results in an adverse ruling against the defendant, in the plaintiff's favor, and the defendant thus forfeits the opportunity to be heard and yet is subject to any and all sanctions and penalties imposed by the court. A default judgment typically awards the plaintiff reasonable damages as requested in the complaint.

The two most important steps a provider can take when he or she is in receipt of a summons are (1) to notify one's liability carrier and (2) either obtain assigned counsel from the liability carrier or determine if it more advantageous to retain independent counsel, and to do so immediately. Insurance carriers are obligated to defend (and indemnify) the insured and will generally assign legal representation to a defendant from a list of skilled local attorneys with whom the carrier regularly contracts. Nonetheless, there are situations in which that selection may not be optimal in one's particular circumstance. Most insurance contracts allow for an insured to select his or her own counsel, within reason. Situations in which independent counsel may be advantageous include, for example, suits in which a provider is one of many sued, either as a group, or as a team of employees, or as in a suit involving both the hospital and the provider. In such cases, conflicting interests not immediately apparent at the onset but which may become apparent later during the lawsuit may arise, and individual counsel may be better positioned to represent one's own specific interests. An example of such a conflict of interest is one in which a hospital and its employed providers are faced with a difficult-to-defend lawsuit and the hospital wishes to settle to limit legal costs, but in which one or more providers actually have defensible positions and may wish to litigate to avoid an adverse judgement and listing in the National Practitioner Data Bank (NPDB). Communications between a client and an attorney are considered confidential or privileged. The purpose of the attorney-client privilege is to encourage and facilitate the honest and open sharing of information between clients and counsel in order to best allow for effective representation. Legal counsel may not divulge confidential matters without the client's consent; that means that the holder of the privilege is the client. Clients may forfeit privilege by communicating with outside parties. The attorney's work product, such as notes, observations, thoughts, and research prepared in anticipation of litigation are generally protected from discovery processes. The attorney-client privilege extends only to actual communications and materials. It is important to note that the underlying information is not protected if it is available from another source. The notion of client-lawyer confidentiality is broader than the privilege and applies not only to matters communicated in confidence to counsel by the client but also to all information relating to the representation, regardless of its source.

The answer to a complaint is typically filed by legal counsel on behalf of the defendant. The first things that counsel will do before answering the complaint typically are related to potential defenses inherent in the legal process, such as a defective service of process, incorrect jurisdiction, or claims barred by the applicable statute of limitations. The statute of limitations is the time limit imposed by the law for bringing a lawsuit and exists to protect defendants. After the period of the statute has expired, or run, the plaintiff is considered to have been time-barred from bringing the suit. Statutes of limitation vary by jurisdiction, state, and type of action. The purpose of the statute of limitations is to encourage timely litigation while evidence remains accessible. The statute of limitations typically begins to run as of the date of the incident or discovery of a wrong, although it may be tolled, in repose, or extended under specific circumstances, such as in the case of continuing treatment, or, if the injured was a minor at the time at which the alleged malpractice occurred. Statutes of limitations are extremely important to insurers because they represent loss-stop deadlines and thereby limit liability. Counsel may also explore opportunities for counterclaims or the inclusion of other parties; counterclaims generally must be filed with the answer. When the answer is prepared and filed, it will very specifically deny or admit each allegation in the complaint, line by line.

The initiation of a lawsuit is then typically followed by a discovery period, during which interrogatories or depositions are conducted, expert opinions are sought, and evidence is accumulated. When the parties are ready for trial, documents such as a note of issue and motion of trial readiness, or the request for judicial intervention, are filed with the court, and the hearings are scheduled on the court's calendar.

PEER REVIEW AND THE PROCESS OF DISCOVERY IN CIVIL LITIGATION

Although the term "discovery" is also used in the context of the time at which a discovery of injury occurs, we limit this discussion to the process of obtaining evidentiary support in anticipation of litigation. The scope of discovery continues to be contested and litigated.

In 1952, the Joint Commission on Accreditation of Healthcare Organizations (JCAHO) began requiring physician peer review at all U.S. hospitals.[6] Congress subsequently enacted the Health Care Quality Improvement Act (HCQIA)[7] in 1986 with the intent of expanding peer reviewer immunity and improving the quality of patient care.[8] States have also enacted laws that prevent documentation or communications used during the peer review process, such as peer review committee meeting minutes, morbidity and mortality conferences, incident reports, and risk management reports, from being discovered for the purposes of a lawsuit. For example, the New York State Education Law shields from disclosure "the proceedings [and] the records relating to performance of a medical or a quality assurance review function or participation in a medical and dental malpractice prevention program."[9] However, these protections vary and are not absolute.

New York Public Health Law (NY PHL)[10] specifically requires every hospital to maintain a coordinated program for the identification and prevention of medical malpractice; the program must include periodic reviews of physicians' credentials and competence. NY PHL subsequently confers complete confidentiality on information gathered by a hospital in accordance with its mandated functions, expressly exempting it from disclosure and discovery. However, paradoxically, the New York Peer Review Statute goes on to state that:

> [n]either the proceedings nor the records relating to performance of a medical or quality assurance review function or participation in a medical and dental malpractice prevention program nor any report required by the department of health . . . shall be subject to disclosure . . . . No person in attendance at a meeting when a medical or a quality assurance review or a medical and dental malpractice prevention program or an incident reporting function . . . shall be required to testify as

to what transpired thereat. *The prohibition relating to discovery of testimony shall not apply to the statements made by any person in attendance at such a meeting who is a party to an action or proceeding the subject matter of which was reviewed at such meeting.* (Italics added for emphasis.)[11]

Therefore, the protections afforded by peer review may not be absolute and are constantly under scrutiny.[12] In the case of New York, where a person who is a party to an action or proceeding speaks on his or her own behalf at a peer review meeting, that person's testimony may be discoverable; a similar statute is in effect in the state of California, where protection may not apply to the person who is the subject of the peer review discussion. Peer review statutes vary greatly by state and readers are again encouraged to review the applicable statutes in their own states or consult with an attorney.

Documents and reports created in accordance with a hospital's processes for peer review are likely protected. However, if the peer review document was in fact created for another purpose, such as an insurance claim, the privilege may not attach. Therefore, a plaintiff's attorney may be able to find relevant peer review information through alternate original nonconfidential sources. One such source is an attendee at a peer review conference who relates the words of a defendant as he or she spoke at a peer review conference. Other possible sources are the patient and the patient's medical record, perhaps from a disclosure meeting summary. Although members of a peer review committee may not be compelled to testify, any member can do so voluntarily because the privilege against testifying is often held by each individual and not by the committee. Specifically, hallway conversations about peer review or regarding an adverse patient outcome are easily discoverable; protections are lost when a provider-participant in a peer review committee discussion takes it upon himself or herself to reveal peer review discussions outside of the committee meeting. The peer review protection can also be forfeited when committee documents are distributed to persons who are outside the committee; when participants leave the meeting room with documents in hand; or when a protected document is filed in a personnel, administrative, or other nonprivileged location. Increasingly, potential defendants are posting emails or tweets regarding bad outcomes, and these are clearly discoverable under the purview of electronic discovery; untimely deletion of such matters may run counter to a duty to preserve electronic evidence.

The scope of potential discovery is therefore potentially very broad. Rule 26 of the Federal Rules of Civil Procedure (FRCP) provides, in part, that:

[u]nless otherwise limited by court order, the scope of discovery is as follows: Parties may obtain discovery regarding any nonprivileged matter that is relevant to any party's claim or defense and proportional to the needs of the case, considering the importance of the issues at stake in the action, the amount in controversy,

the parties' relative access to relevant information, the parties' resources, the importance of the discovery in resolving the issues, and whether the burden or expense of the proposed discovery outweighs its likely benefit. Information within this scope of discovery need not be admissible in evidence to be discoverable.... Ordinarily, a party may not discover documents and tangible things that are prepared in anticipation of litigation or for trial by or for another party or its representative (including the other party's attorney, consultant, surety, indemnitor, insurer, or agent).[13]

Materials amendable to discovery will include, but are not limited to, hospital and departmental policies and procedures, emails,[14] radiographs, medical records and metadata (see chapter 9), phone logs, pager logs, recordings, correspondence, call schedules, and credentials; however, the requests for production during discovery must not be overreaching and must be justifiable on the basis of the allegations. The courts will impose a proportionality requirement[15] to the discovery demands so that the production burden must be consistent with the needs of the case, the amount in controversy, the importance of the issues at stake, the parties' resources, the importance of the discovery in resolving the issues, and whether the burden or expense of the proposed discovery outweighs its likely benefit.[16]

THE SUBPOENA

A subpoena is a judicial writ or request, a court-ordered demand, for the production of documents or a person to an in-court or other legal proceeding. Subpoenas are common to state and federal as well as criminal, administrative, and civil court proceedings. The term "subpoena" literally means "under penalty of law" and therefore noncompliance with a subpoena can result in court imposed sanctions, civil or criminal penalties (such as fines or incarceration), or both. In addition, a person who has been served with a subpoena and subsequently has failed to appear may be forcibly brought to the proceedings by a law enforcement officer who serves a second subpoena, termed an "instanter." Providers are typically served with subpoenas in cases in which they themselves are sued, in cases in which they are nonparty witnesses to a lawsuit, or in criminal cases in which they have cared for someone subject to an assault or murder.

There are two types of subpoenas. A *subpoena ad testificandum*, which translates as "to testify under penalty," requires the party served to testify before a court or other legal authority. Such a request can be made either to a party to the litigation or proceeding or to a material witness. The *subpoena ad testificandum* will be specific as to the date, time, and location. A *subpoena duces tecum* (deposition subpoena) is a variation of the *subpoena ad testificandum* and requires an individual who is not a party to the legal action to testify or produce documents at a deposition. These types of subpoenas differ in that the timing and location for such hearings may be more negotiable and that the *subpoena ad testificandum* must provide the subpoenaed party with reasonable advance notice. The prosecution in a grand jury is empowered to issue both *subpoenas ad testificandum* and *subpoenas duces tecum* as mechanisms to obtain the evidence and testimony necessary to determine whether to issue an indictment.

A *subpoena duces tecum*, translated as "under penalty you shall bring with you," requires the party served to produce documents, materials, or other real or tangible evidence to a court or law enforcement authority. Subpoena requests for documents are usually highly detailed and specific; however, the subpoena also puts the party on notice that there may be further requests for materials, and that a heightened duty to preserve potentially material evidence is now in place. In some instances, such as medical fraud cases under the Federal False Claims Act, the *subpoena duces tecum* is served with a warrant at the moment the law enforcement officials arrive at a medical practice.

A subpoena may be issued by a court or an attorney on behalf of a court, issued by a court clerk or other trial court administrator's office, and served through a service of process agent. The rules regarding service of process can be state specific. The service of process of a subpoena is the same as it is for a summons and complaint (or its state-specific variations) and can be either (1) hand-delivered, (2) electronically mailed (emailed) to the last known email address of the individual (receipt acknowledgement requested), (3) delivered via certified mail to the last known address (return receipt requested), or (4) read aloud (for example over telephone) to the subpoenaed individual. Similar to a summons and complaint, a subpoena does not need to reach the person named if there is someone in a company who is authorized to receive service of process (such as a receptionist, practice manager, department secretary, or department administrator). Since a subpoena is court ordered, a failure to respond is considered contempt of court. However, legal procedure allows a served party to either formally request the withdrawal of the subpoena, or to file a motion with the issuing court to nullify ("quash") the subpoena for cause. Potentially valid causes to quash a subpoena include errors of person or process or similar reasons. In addition, a party may resist a *subpoena duces tecum* by refusing to comply and requesting a court hearing.[17]

ADMISSIBILITY OF EVIDENCE IN LEGAL PROCEEDINGS

Evidence, or evidentiary facts, are generally categorized as (1) demonstrative evidence; (2) documentary evidence; (3) tangible, or real, evidence; or, (4) testimonial evidence.

The evidence that can be admitted as fact during trial is governed by federal or state rules of evidence; therefore, there are variations on the criteria by which evidence can be admitted. Not all evidence that parties feel is important is admissible. In general, two threshold factors are considered when determining whether evidence is admissible or not: (1) the issue of relevance—the evidence must prove or disprove an important fact required for legal proof; and (2) the issue of reliability, which relates to the authentication of a piece of evidence as credible. Evidence is relevant when it has any tendency to make the fact for which it is offered either more or less probable. The evidence need not make the fact for which it is offered certain, or even more probable than not; there is only a need to establish a tendency to increase the likelihood of the support for the fact for which it is offered. Similarly, the evidence must be material in that it is offered to prove a fact that is at issue in the case. Materiality and relevance are almost synonymous, although materiality relates more to import, whereas relevance relates to a relationship to the issue at trial. Under the Federal Rules of Evidence (FRE), all relevant evidence is admissible unless it is excluded under the United States Constitution, federal statute, the FRE, or other rules prescribed by the Supreme Court.[18] Thus, not all relevant evidence is admissible. The "court may exclude relevant evidence if its probative value is substantially outweighed by a danger of one or more of the following: unfair prejudice, confusing the issues, misleading the jury, undue delay, wasting time, or needlessly presenting cumulative evidence."[19] Prejudice means improper harm but not in the sense that the evidence may be extremely harmful to one party's case. Prejudice requires a showing of improper incitement of emotional bias. Evidence is considered reliable or competent if it meets traditional requirements of reliability and has survived objections as to admissibility.

Real evidence is a thing: it is the contract, the computed tomography (CT) scan images, the medical record documentation, the phone logs. Once it is determined that real evidence is relevant and material, it must be shown to be competent, or authentic. Real evidence may be authenticated in any of three ways: (1) by identification of its uniqueness (for example, a medical record label), (2) by identification of an object that has made it unique (for example, a reference or chronology in the medical record), or (3) by establishing a chain of custody.

Spoliation of evidence is defined as the intentional, reckless, or negligent withholding, hiding, altering, fabricating, or destroying of evidence relevant to a legal proceeding.[20] A party who offers evidence for its proof must establish that the evidence has not been materially altered between the events and the trial—it must be a true and accurate representation. Evidence that is either altered or lost is considered to have been spoliated. Spoliation has three potential consequences: intentional spoliation may be actionable as a criminal act by some state statutes; it may result in fines and incarceration under a charge of contempt; or it may be actionable as a civil tort. More importantly, a demonstration of spoliation of evidence allows opposing counsel to request a jury instruction that the jury may infer that the missing or altered evidence may have been harmful to the non-producing party if it had been available. An inference of evidentiary spoliation can transform a highly defensible case to an indefensible case. The FRCP was amended in 2015; the new rule, 37(e), requires the court to first find an intent to harm the opposing party in order for judges to levy the most severe sanctions.

Failure to Preserve Electronically Stored Information

If electronically stored information that should have been preserved in the anticipation or conduct of litigation is lost because a party failed to take reasonable steps to preserve it, and it cannot be restored or replaced through additional discovery, the court:

(1) upon finding prejudice to another party from loss of the information, may order measures no greater than necessary to cure the prejudice; or
(2) only upon finding that the party acted with the intent to deprive another party of the information's use in the litigation may:
   (A) presume that the lost information was unfavorable to the party;
   (B) instruct the jury that it may or must presume the information was unfavorable to the party; or
   (C) dismiss the action or enter a default judgment.[21]

The preservation of electronically stored evidence has become increasingly significant in the world of electronic medical records not only because the Health Insurance Portability and Accountability Act and the Health Information Technology for Economic and Clinical Health Act require the preservation of electronic health records, but also because in the event of litigation, the inability to respond to a request for electronic evidence can be fatal to a potentially defensible case. Electronically stored health information is now extended to text messages, emails, and similar media through which the patient-provider encounters now occur. In *First Financial Security v. Freedom Equity*, a California federal court imposed adverse inference instructions against the defendant pursuant to Rule 37(e)(2) for failure to preserve text messages.[22]

Demonstrative evidence is adjunct illustrative evidence offered in support of testimony; examples include a skeleton model, an advanced cardiac life support algorithm, an animation, and a model of a brain. Demonstrative evidence is authenticated by the witness whose testimony is being entered into evidence.

Documentary evidence is one specific type of real evidence; in the medical context, documentary evidence is usually related to the patient's medical record, but it may also include correspondence or photographs. Medical records are also business records and require authentication by the custodian of the medical records, usually the health information services supervisor, as to their veracity and completeness. The Best Evidence Rule requires that, when documentary evidence is entered into evidence, a copy or other secondary evidence of its content is not adequate unless there is an adequate explanation as to the absence of the original.

Testimonial evidence is the most well-known form of evidence, and it is unique in that it does not require another form of evidence as a prerequisite for its admissibility. Competency of a witness is established through four elements: (1) the witness must understand and take an oath or substitute (such as an affirmation or pledge, with accommodation to alternative faiths or the irreligious), (2) the witness must have personal knowledge regarding the subject about which he or she will testify, (3) the witness must have the ability to recollect prior perceptions, and (4) the witness must be able to communicate the perceptions offered into evidence.

FORMS OF EXAMINATION UNDER OATH

Out of court examinations usually occur prior to trial (examination before trial [EBT]) and take the form of either a deposition or an interrogatory. During EBTs, witnesses testify under oath. Depositions take the form of oral testimony that takes place before the plaintiff's counsel and the defendant's counsel and that is transcribed by a court reporter. The judge does not preside over a deposition, although a judge is usually available to make rulings regarding the admissibility of certain lines of questioning. Interrogatories are usually in the form of a questionnaire. Depositions are especially useful to opposing counsel because they (1) help clarify the issues, (2) help gauge the witness's later presentation to the jury, and (3) may open new lines of relevant inquiry (or even additional witnesses) prior to trial. Deposition testimony is transcribed and may be read (or, video testimony may be played) at trial; conflicting testimony can be used to impeach or undermine the testifier's credibility. Preparing for a deposition is as important as preparing for trial, and providers must not underestimate the importance of their presentation at an EBT.

Witnesses in court are questioned via direct and cross-examination. Direct examination is questioning by the attorney who calls the witness to testify. Questioning on direct examination must solicit answers in the form of a "yes" or "no" and leading questions are not permitted, albeit with specific exceptions such as age or incapacity. The "yes and no" character of answers can be used by skilled counsel to "box in" a witness through the use of logic game theory to lead to a conclusion that might have been different if the witness could have testified freely. However, the purpose of a subsequent cross examination is to allow further inquiry regarding issues raised during direct examination and potentially clarify the points raised and clarify the conclusions reached.

THE BURDEN OF PROOF

The burden of proof is the affirmative duty imposed upon one litigant party to prove or disprove a disputed fact. The burden of proof is usually associated with the initial burden of production, which refers to the duty of the accuser to provide at least a *de minimis* threshold showing of facts that demonstrate that the case has merit and meets the subsequent requirement to meet the burden of persuasion by a specified weight of evidentiary standard.

In the United States, the accused defendant is considered innocent until proven guilty. Therefore, the plaintiff, or prosecution, has the initial burden to establish the guilt of the defendant. In some instances, there may be a shifting of the burden of proof to the defendant, such as where the defendant raises a legal defense that then requires affirmative proof by the defendant in order to defeat a plaintiff's claim.

Burden of proof subsequently defines the burden of persuasion, or the quantum of proof, by which the party with the burden of proof must establish or refute a disputed factual issue.

In general, the U.S. legal system imposes three standards for burden of persuasion. In civil lawsuits, the lowest legal burden of proof requires a showing by a "preponderance of evidence" or "weight of evidence" that the facts and elements of culpability necessary to win a judgment are have been demonstrated to more likely than not be true. The preponderance of the evidence is also referred to as the balance of probabilities, which is a helpful demonstrative tool to a jury showing that the scale need only be tipped by the least in order to show a preponderance. Thus, a preponderance of the evidence means that one side has more evidence in its favor than the other, even by the smallest degree; this can be 50.1 percent.

In criminal trial proceedings, the burden of persuasion is greatest because criminals found guilty may be deprived of life and liberty in addition to property. If, after the evidence is presented to the judge or jury, there remains a reasonable doubt regarding the accused's guilt, as based in reason and common sense after careful and impartial consideration of all the evidence or lack of evidence, then the required proof of guilt has not been met, and the accused must be acquitted. The "beyond a reasonable doubt" standard of persuasion is the highest standard of proof used in any judicial proceeding.

The clear and convincing evidence standard is an intermediate standard that is a higher level of burden of persuasion than "preponderance of the evidence" but less than the "beyond a reasonable doubt" standard. The clear and convincing standard is most frequently used in administrative court proceedings, although, as we have seen, it is also used to demonstrate the pre-existing wishes in the absence of a living will document in end-of-life care. To meet the clear and convincing proof standard, the evidence presented must be substantially more likely to be true than not, and the trier of fact must have a firm belief or conviction in its factuality.

PROVIDER CONFUSION REGARDING LEGAL PROCESS—THE "SECOND VICTIM"

Providers are, by nature, communicators, and are often taken by surprise by litigation because there is, at least theoretically, a fine line separating a complication from malpractice. Complications can be devastating to patients but may be unavoidable since medicine is not a "zero-defect" science. Providers make diagnosis and treatment decisions in "real time" and without the benefit of all the possible information that could be relevant. Sometimes, not all the data are available; sometimes, there are too much data; and sometimes, even with all the data, the diagnosis is elusive or the procedure is complex. The practice of medicine applies as much art as science to the treatment of diverse and unique individuals. Because of the enormous variation between individuals and the consequent potential for unforeseen anatomic variations, and because of idiosyncratic physiological and psychological reactions, the risk of complications related to anesthesia cannot be completely eliminated at the present time. Arguably the greatest contemporary physician, William Osler, remarked that "errors in judgment must occur in the practice of an art which consists largely of balancing probabilities." The problem with a bad outcome, whether due to negligence or not, is the emotional impact it may have on a jury. Thus, as witnesses to a visible "harm," the impartiality of the jury may be at issue, as biased by the emotional impact on injury.

Providers are traditionally perfectionists who demand a great deal of themselves and who hold themselves to a high standard. Allegations of negligence are powerful in themselves. However, when a bad outcome occurs, and a provider is found guilty of negligence, the emotional impact can be significant, causing powerful feelings of guilt, incompetence, or inadequacy. The emotional impact of a medical error, or a malpractice guilty verdict, upon the provider has come to be known as the "second victim."[23] Second victims are health care providers who are involved in an unanticipated adverse patient event, in a medical error and/or a patient-related injury, and become victimized in the sense that the provider is traumatized by the event. Frequently, these individuals feel personally responsible for the patient outcome. Many feel as though they have failed the patient, second guessing their clinical skills and knowledge base.[24] The provider, as a second victim, frequently experiences anger, hostility, burnout, and a lack of concentration and commitment, and the second victim is even prone to depression[25] or suicidal ideation.[26] Second victims suffer a medical emergency equivalent to post-traumatic stress disorder (PTSD).[27] Research demonstrates that the psychological effects of adverse events on health care professionals can be long-lasting,[28] and in some instances the individual never fully recovers.[29] Emotional reactions were not always linked to the patient outcome, and some providers involved in near-misses are affected by the thought of what might have been.[30]

Providers strive to be, and are expected to be, strong, provide care of the highest quality, and not be a burden to the system.[31] Our culture is one of caring, but also of heroism, which often does not tolerate the idea of victimhood. Institutional responses, such as awareness and proactive planning, are critical steps in supporting and protecting clinicians.[32] In order to support the second victim provider, the institution must have an engaged leadership, a supportive provider staff, and a rapidly deployable procedure.[33] A committed health care system with not only a strong culture of safety but also a commitment to its providers will work simultaneously to support patients and family members as well as support its own clinicians.

Supportive resources have been developed by Medically Induced Trauma Support Services, which has developed the Tools for Building a Clinician and Staff Support Program,[34] and the Institute for Healthcare Improvement has published a white paper entitled "Respectful Management of Serious Clinical Adverse Events."[35] Denham has suggested the five rights of a second victim, described by the acronym TRUST:

1. Treatment that is just and fair with a presumption of good intention.
2. Respect without blame.
3. Understanding and compassion to foster grieving and healing.
4. Supportive care through professional and organized psychological and support services.
5. Transparency and opportunity to contribute through education and prevention.[36]

In summary, the emotional impact of alleged malpractice on providers has yet to be quantified.

MEDICAL ERROR AND DISCLOSURE: LIABILITY RISKS CONFRONT PUBLIC POLICY

An adverse event can be defined as harm to a patient as a result of medical care. The recognition and evaluation of medical errors is fundamental to future error prevention. When providers tell the truth, practitioners and patients share a bond of trust. Numerous ethical precepts are operational when medical errors occur in the health care environment: respect for patient autonomy is paramount, and underscoring the importance of veracity, fiduciary duty, beneficence, and nonmaleficence are also operative in the potential obligation to disclose a medical error. Disclosure of medical errors involves an admission to a patient or family member that a medical error occurred and resulted in harm or an unanticipated outcome. The culture of safety has promulgated a philosophy of transparency with respect to medical errors.[37,38] Many federal and state agencies advocate that hospitals develop and adhere to disclosure policies and protocols. The American College of Physicians and the American Medical Association advocate for the disclosure of errors, and the Joint Commission requires the disclosure to patients of unanticipated outcomes.[39] Disclosure of an error is frequently accompanied by an apology.[40] An apology is a statement that includes recognition of the error, admission of fault with the assumption of responsibility, and a sincere communication of regret or remorse for having caused harm.[41] Many believe that the incorporation of an apology into disclosure conversations between physicians and patients can address the needs of both patients and physicians[42] and is consistent with the ethics of the medical profession, ethics that focus on the necessity for trust between a physician and his or her patient.[43]

Preliminary studies suggest that full disclosure may decrease the risk of litigation.[44,45] However, the optimal policy and procedure for such disclosure remains somewhat controversial.[46] Some, but not all states, and even countries,[47] have developed "safe harbors" to protect the information conveyed during a disclosure meeting from discovery during litigation;[48] furthermore, between states, there is wide variation in the scope of such safe harbor laws.[49,50]

Honesty and empathy are often appreciated and can substantiate the overall atmosphere of professionalism and caring essential to health care. Disclosure of adverse events may even be mandatory under state law, regulatory agency rules, or hospital policy and procedure. However, the process whereby a physician or care team discloses a medical error to a patient or patient's representative should occur only after careful deliberation and consideration.[51] In general, it is a legal tenet that "anything said or done may be used against the defendant," and in some cases, a disclosure may be treated as an "admission against interest" under evidentiary rules. Also, a disclosure that is perceived to be and is thereafter subsequently admitted into evidence as a confession can also eliminate potential defenses to a malpractice claim. In the case of a lawsuit, where an admission or confession eliminates triable issues of fact, the plaintiff may potentially move for summary judgment, leaving only the amount of damages to be determined by the courts or in a settlement. Most insurance policies contain a "cooperation clause," which requires that the insured cooperate fully in the defense of a claim; there is a possibility that engaging in a disclosure meeting might cause the defense of a malpractice claim to be jeopardized, violating the cooperation clause and thereby voiding the policy.

Provider and nursing leadership and hospital administration[52] should be aware of the applicable disclosure policy in effect at their institution and be prepared to develop it, review it, and comply with it.[53] Additionally, although hospital risk-management personnel frequently oversee implementation of the disclosure policy, physicians may need to consider the personal and legal ramifications of a disclosure conference and consider prior consultation with an attorney.

CONCLUSIONS

The practice of medicine is associated with a wide variety of risks, including corporate, contractual, regulatory, criminal, and civil risks. Providers should have a general knowledge of the legal system and the legal process in order to be involved and support their defense. Providers should never make any decision regarding a lawsuit on their own. The most important thing any medical provider can do when involved in a lawsuit is to be proactive and engaged in his or her own defense. However, there is an adage: he who represents himself has a fool for a client. As skilled and intelligent as health care providers are, the importance of obtaining timely assistance of skilled and knowledgeable legal counsel cannot be underscored.

5 · REGULATORY LAW AND THE CLINICAL PRACTICE OF THE NEUROSCIENCES

INTRODUCTION TO THE LAW OF REGULATORY AGENCIES

A regulatory agency is a government body created by and empowered by a federal[1] or state statute to exercise quasi-legislative authority over a specific segment of economic activity, such as health care, technology, communications, or transportation. The federal government empowers more than one hundred administrative agencies. Regulatory agencies exist and function at the local, state, and federal levels of government. An agency has quasi-legislative functions, executive functions, and quasi-judicial functions impacting the areas of administrative law, regulatory law, secondary legislation, and rulemaking. Regulatory agencies oversee activities within their field of jurisdiction, enact laws and regulations, investigate violations, and enforce compliance.

The Administrative Procedure Act[2] (APA) is a federal law that stipulates how agencies propose and enact regulations, and the APA requires that rulemaking be transparent and subject to public input at each stage of enactment. The APA and its state analogs define the roles and powers of all agencies and the procedures by which they must abide by in all their functions. The APA categorizes administrative functions into formal and informal rulemaking and adjudication, which have binding effects; the APA also categorizes the process for issuing guidance documents, which lack the binding effect of a regulation or law. The APA is the main legal interpretative source for federal administrative agencies, whereas states are governed by comparable state acts. The term "rulemaking" refers to the "agency process for formulating, amending, or repealing a rule."[3] The rulemaking process is thus strictly defined and includes advance public notice of a proposed rule, publication of the proposed rule with an inherently defined period of time for notice and public comment, and subsequent finalization as law. The rulemaking process first requires publication of proposed rules in the Federal Register, followed by a prescribed period of public notice and opportunity for comment, and subsequent publication of the final rule. A rule is defined to mean "the whole or a part of an agency statement of general or particular applicability and future effect designed to implement, interpret, or prescribe law or policy or describing the organization, procedure, or practice requirements of an agency."[4]

Regulatory agencies are a part of the executive branch of government and have the statutory authority to function with oversight from the legislative branch, but their actions are also subject to legal review. Administrative law judges adjudicate legal controversies related to agency regulations and provide judicial review of agency decisions. However, courts generally accord deference to government agencies, since they are presumed to have specialized knowledge regarding the technical aspects of the issues that they regulate. The U.S. Supreme Court has established three different levels or standards of judicial deference to agency decisions: (1) under *Chevron v. NRDC*,[5] courts deferred to agency interpretations of enabling statutes unless they are unreasonable on their face; (2) under *Auer v. Robbins*,[6] courts deferred to the agency's interpretations of its own ambiguous regulations; and (3) under *Skidmore v. Swift*,[7] courts did not give a binding deference to the agency's interpretation, but gave a varying amount of deference in accordance with the agency's expertise in a specific matter. The classic legal test for determining whether to grant deference to a government agency's interpretation of a statute that it administers lies with *Chevron*, which gave rise to the two-part framework for a reviewing court's analysis of agency decision-making:

> First, always, is the question whether Congress has directly spoken to the precise question at issue. If the intent of Congress is clear, that is the end of the matter; for the court, as well as the agency, must give effect to the unambiguously expressed intent of Congress. If, however, the court determines Congress has not directly addressed the precise question at issue, the court does not simply impose its own construction on the statute.... Rather, if the statute is silent or ambiguous with respect to the specific issue, the question for the court is whether the agency's answer is based on a permissible construction of the statute.[8]

Finally, agencies are required to publish a "regulatory plan" or "work plan" annually; these are published in the Federal Register in an ongoing fashion[9] and then compiled within the Code of Federal Regulations (CFR) annually.

U.S. DEPARTMENT OF HEALTH AND HUMAN SERVICES

The U.S. Department of Health and Human Services (DHHS) administers overseas health care in the United States through a family of agencies, centers, and quasi-regulatory bodies. The DHHS, previously the Department of Health, Education and Welfare, was established in 1979 and has been in its current role since that time. DHHS is administered by the Secretary of Health and Human Services, who is appointed by the president.

Important administrative bodies within DHHS include the Centers for Medicare & Medicaid Services (CMS, formerly Health Care Financing Administration [HCFA]), the Centers for Disease Control and Prevention (CDC), the National Institutes of Health (NIH), the Food and Drug Administration (FDA), the Health Resources and Services Administration (HRSA), and the Agency for Healthcare Research and Quality (AHRQ). DHHS also administers the Office of the Inspector General (OIG), an investigative arm of DHHS established in 1976 that is primarily charged with investigation of abuse of Medicare and Medicaid and violations of the Stark law and the Anti-Kickback Statute (AKS).

THE FDA AND THE REGULATION OF PHARMACEUTICALS

In the United States, consumers legally obtain access to prescription pharmaceuticals by presenting a valid prescription signed by a licensed health care professional to a pharmacist.[10] A variety of drugs can also be purchased without a prescription through over-the-counter (OTC) purchases. The need for a prescription to obtain certain drugs is determined by the FDA; this determination forms the basis for the legal classification for any specific drug and impacts the drug's marketing and distribution. Prescription and nonprescription drugs may be available as brand-name or generic products; they may also be available as both. There is no federal legislation regarding general prescriptive authority; there is a requirement under the federal Controlled Substances Act[11] that controlled substances be prescribed only by providers registered with the U.S. Drug Enforcement Agency.[12]

The FDA has its origin in the Federal Food and Drugs Act of 1906[13] (also known as the Wiley Act, or the Pure Food and Drugs Act), which was the first federal legislation to address standards for the preparation and the marketing of medicines. Prior to the 1906 act, medicinal products (then consisting largely of proprietary alcoholic tonics, patent medicines, and sometimes even toxic compounds sold as "remedies") remained unregulated in terms of their content, purity, and safety. The 1906 act represented the first statutory prohibition of the marketing of compounds as either medicines or food additives for human consumption when they were known to be poisonous or potentially harmful to human health. The Federal Food, Drug, and Cosmetic Act[14] (FFDCA) took effect on June 25, 1938; it superseded and repealed the Wiley Act, provided the statutory basis for the modern FDA's authority, and is the product of sequential legislative reforms and amendments. In 1951, the Durham-Humphrey Amendment to the FFDCA defined the types of drugs that could not be safely used without medical supervision—effectively creating the defined class of drugs known as "prescription drugs."[15] The FFDCA was further amended in 1962 by the Kefauver-Harris

Amendments. The Kefauver-Harris Amendments represented a landmark change in the regulation of the safety of the U.S. pharmaceutical supply. Kefauver-Harris explicitly required the FDA to review all new drug applications submitted for review specifically to assess pharmaceutical safety in humans; the amendment also stipulated that the FDA ascertain that a drug manufacturer had provided "substantial evidence" through "adequate and well-controlled investigations" to demonstrate that a potential new drug is also effective for its intended use. Thus, it was not until 1962 that U.S. pharmaceuticals required an agency's certification of both safety and efficacy. In 2003, the Medicare Prescription Drug Improvement and Modernization Act (MMA, also known as the Medicare Modernization Act)[16] was enacted. In 2012, the FDA Safety and Innovation Act (FDASIA)[17] and the Medical Device User Fee and Modernization Act were enacted. FDASIA empowered the FDA with a new and powerful expedited drug development tool, known as the "breakthrough therapy" designation, designed to expedite the development and review of new drugs with only preliminary clinical evidence that indicates the drug may offer a substantial improvement over available therapies for patients with serious or life-threatening diseases. After an outbreak in 2012 of an epidemic of fungal meningitis linked to a compounded steroid, Congress enacted the Drug Quality Safety and Security Act.

FDA approval of new drugs implicitly reflects a high degree of administrative tension between two important but competing public health concerns: (1) the risk that a drug will be approved prematurely without an adequate demonstration of safety and efficacy and (2) the risk of unnecessary delay in the availability of medications required for disease treatment. Pharmacologic agents are widely recognized to be inherently toxic; however, they are also potentially therapeutic for prescribed conditions at defined dosages. The process of drug approval by FDA is similar to a risk-benefit analysis, and clinical utility is counterbalanced by a demonstration of relative clinical safety. The FDA cannot approve a new drug until the developer has submitted data from "adequate and well-controlled" studies that provide "substantial evidence" of the safety and effectiveness for the conditions for which it is intended to be prescribed, recommended, or suggested in the product's proposed labeling. The FDA specifies a drug approval process that requires drug manufacturers to follow a defined protocol through which the drugs are tested in animal and human experiments, and to submit data regarding the safety and effectiveness to the FDA before the drugs may be approved for marketing.[18]

During the new drug development process, there are both preclinical and clinical trials designed to demonstrate safety and efficacy. Data from preclinical testing in animal pharmacology and toxicology studies are designed and conducted to permit a preliminary assessment of "reasonable safety." Then, an investigational new drug (IND) application is filed to allow further study and assessment. Phase I clinical trials are designed to gather safety data regarding a new drug, including the safe dosage range, and represent the first administration of a potential drug to a small test population of adults (typically twenty to one hundred normal, healthy volunteers) over a period of several months. Phase I testing involves a determination of basic metabolic, basic pharmacological, and toxicological properties of the IND in humans, with an emphasis on dose ranges, tolerance, and metabolism of the compound (absorption, distribution, elimination, and excretion) as well as preliminary data regarding the effectiveness of the drug in normal humans. Phase II trials test a drug's therapeutic effectiveness in larger populations of patient volunteers; this is the first testing in patients diagnosed with a specific medical condition. The final phase, Phase III, is designed to compare the experimental treatment against other existing standard treatments. To develop valid conclusions regarding a prospective drug, Phase III clinical trials must be large and conducted at multiple centers; the gold standard is the multi-institutional double-blind placebo controlled randomized clinical trial. Once a drug manufacturer has met its evidentiary burdens through clinical studies, it can submit its final application for drug approval, labeling, and marketing to the FDA.

The FDA enforces the sanitary safety of medications through its oversight of adulteration of medications and by its investigational and disciplinary authorities pertaining "Good Manufacturing Procedures" (GMPs). The FDA issues and regularly updates GMP regulations for drugs, and these regulations represent accepted practices and procedures for manufacturing, processing, and packing the products to assure their quality and purity.[19] The FDA polices GMP violations though the use of inspections and the authority to sanction violators and/or suspend productions via injunctive powers. One reason for the drug shortages providers are presently experiencing is that GMPs have become compromised through inadvertent contamination or natural disasters.

Off-label use of a drug occurs when it is used in a manner that is either inconsistent with or not described in the product's FDA-approved labeling.[20] Off-label use of a drug is considered discretionary, and thus involves some additional legal risk in the event of an adverse outcome. However, because the FDA does not regulate the practice of medicine, it cannot regulate the prescribing of drugs for off-label uses.[21] Nonetheless, pharmaceutical manufacturers are explicitly prohibited from promoting non-FDA-approved uses of their drugs or devices. In 2017, the FDA issued a final rule that partially amends the agency's definition of "intended use" for drugs and devices. Previously, "intended use" addressed the questions of whether a manufacturer knows or has "knowledge of facts that would give him notice" that a drug or device would be used for off-label purposes; under the new 2017 rule, the "knowledge" clause in the two regulations is replaced with a "totality of the evidence" standard, providing that "where the totality of evidence is sufficient to establish a new intended use for a medical product."[22]

The learned intermediary doctrine is a rule of law that states that it is the duty of the prescribing provider to be educated and aware regarding (1) the characteristics of the drug he or she is prescribing, (2) the amount of the drug that can be safely administered to a patient, and (3) potential interactions with other medications the patient is taking. Under the learned intermediary doctrine, a pharmaceutical manufacturer/marketer fulfills its duty to warn when it warns providers of the risks associated with the use of the pharmaceutical; the physician then assumes the role of a "learned intermediary" between the manufacturer and the patient.[23] Subsequently, it becomes the duty of the prescribing provider to advise the patient of any dangers or side effects associated with the use of the drug and to supervise its use.[24] The learned intermediary doctrine is a legal risk to providers and serves to insulate pharmaceutical manufacturers from liability; it is also why the package inserts (labeling) for medications are so extensive and complex.

Adverse drug events (ADEs) are integral to the labeling of a medication. A "black box" warning is the highest level of five possible warning categories that may appear in a package insert.[25] The black box warning can have serious ramifications for drug sales, marketing, and even the prescription process; some patient safety advocates argue that the patient should be specifically informed,[26] and that the patient's informed consent should be obtained, prior to initiating treatment with a drug that has an associated black box warning.

Post-marketing surveillance, sometimes referred to as Phase IV trials, reflect data reported to manufacturers and the FDA after a drug is released into commerce. MedWatch is the FDA's voluntary post-marketing reporting system. The Research on Adverse Drug Events and Reports (RADAR) is a project funded independently of the pharmaceutical industry with the goal of detecting previously unrecognized, serious ADEs and to identify new patient populations at high risk. ADE reports are compiled in the Adverse Events Reporting System, then evaluated by clinical reviewers in the Center for Drug Evaluation and Research[27] and the Center for Biologics Evaluation and Research[28] to detect signal events regarding safety and to monitor drug safety.

THE FDA AND THE REGULATION OF MEDICAL DEVICES

Consistent with its mandate over pharmaceutical development and marketing, the FDA has detailed rules and regulations regarding the development, approval, marketing, and post-marketing follow-up for medical devices; these rules and regulations largely parallel those for governing for pharmaceuticals. The Medical Device Amendments Act of 1976 (MDA)[29] expanded the authority of the FFDCA from pharmaceuticals to include medical devices. The MDA expressly pre-empts states from imposing any requirement that is different from, or in addition to, any requirement applicable under the MDA.[30] In *Riegel v. Medtronic*, the U.S. Supreme Court reinforced the regulation by ruling that that a state-law claim for strict product liability; breach of implied warranty; and negligence in the design, testing, inspection, distribution, labeling, marketing, and sale of an FDA-approved medical device was pre-empted by the MDA.[31] The intent of the MDA is to provide consumers of medical devices with a reasonable assurance of both safety and efficacy, which together represent the dual statutorily mandated standards upon which the FDA bases its approval of both pharmaceuticals and devices. However, in the case of devices, FDA approval more heavily favors safety over efficacy. Similar to pharmaceuticals, medical devices must be manufactured under a quality assurance program, be suitable for the intended use, be adequately packaged, be properly labeled, and have establishment registration and device listing forms on file with the FDA.

Within the FFDCA, as amended, a "device" is defined as "any instrument, apparatus, implement, machine, appliance, implant, in vitro reagent or calibrator, software, material, accessory, component part, or related article, intended by the manufacturer to be used, alone or in combination, for humans and for one or more of the specific purposes of (1) diagnosis, prevention, monitoring, treatment or alleviation of disease; (2) diagnosis, monitoring, treatment, alleviation of, or compensation for an injury; (3) investigation, replacement, modification, or support of the anatomy or of a physiological process; (4) supporting or sustaining life; (5) control of conception; (6) disinfection of medical devices; (7) providing information for medical purposes by means of in vitro examination of specimens derived from the human body and which does not achieve its primary intended action in or on the human body by pharmacological, immunological or metabolic means, but which may be assisted in its function by such means." Thus, medical devices can range from simple tongue depressors to complex computerized imaging equipment and biomedical implants.

There are three classification levels for medical devices, largely based on the risks associated with their use. The FDA employs a scale of I to III, in which Class I devices denote the lowest risk and Class III the highest; the classification determines the level of FDA controls associated with the manufacture and marketing of the particular device. Regulatory oversight and control increase from Class I to Class III. A Class III medical device is one that is "purported or represented to be for a use in supporting or sustaining human life or for a use which is of substantial importance in preventing impairment of human health, or presents a potential unreasonable risk of illness or injury."[32] The safety profile of any drug or device is a complex interplay between product design, use, and potential for operator error. Similar to pharmaceuticals, courts have explicitly recognized that no drug or device is completely safe and that such products are "inherently dangerous." The potential for user or operator error is not considered a threshold issue by the FDA, and the FDA recognizes that operator errors can result from a large number of variables over which the manufacturer has no control, such the training and skill of individual operators, ergonomics, patient variability, and the complex clinical environment. However, manufacturers are expected to consider the principles of human factor engineering during product design and encourage appropriate user education and training so that the risk for user errors can be minimized or mitigated.

The formal process whereby the FDA approves a drug or device is highly structured and requires manufacturers to submit data from preclinical trials in order to begin testing in humans; thereafter, data from carefully controlled clinical trials must be submitted to panels of FDA experts. The phases of preclinical and clinical testing parallel those for pharmaceuticals.

The FDA's post-marketing safety-surveillance strategy for medical devices relies on physicians, health care institutions, manufacturers, and patients to report medical device failures and complications through the Medical Device Reporting[33] system. Medical Device Reporting regulations contain mandatory requirements for manufacturers, importers, and device user facilities to report certain device-related adverse events and product problems to the FDA. Medical Device Reporting requirements by manufacturers are mandatory, and failure to report malfunctions can result in punitive damages, rendering a device misbranded, and the rescission of FDA approval. Manufacturers must submit reports to the FDA whenever there are data to suggest that a device (1) may have caused or contributed to a death or serious injury or (2) has malfunctioned, and that the device or a similar device marketed by the manufacturer or importer would be likely to cause or contribute to a death or serious injury if the malfunction were to recur. Adverse event data are logged by both manufacturers and the FDA. The Standards Management Staff of the FDA is charged with the responsibility to ensure that evolving medical device standards are published to provide formal notice to designers and manufacturers and thereby facilitate the incorporation of new regulatory standards into product design and manufacture.[34] In 2009, the FDA launched the Sentinel Initiative, a program that integrates the electronic health records (EHRs) of health care institutions with FDA databases in order to perform continuous and online post-marketing safety analyses. Since medical devices, in contrast to pharmaceuticals, lacked unique device identifiers (UDIs), the FDA was authorized, through the FFDCA Amendments Act of 2007, to develop a comprehensive UDI system for medical devices that is expected to soon be integrated with EHRs as well as administrative and claims databases to identify patients who have been exposed to specific devices and thereby track rare post-exposure risks.

Product liability is the field of legal analysis that refers to liability incurred by one or more parties along the chain of commerce of any product. Once again, as noted above, when a manufacturer discharges the duty to warn through the learned intermediary doctrine, what superficially may appear to be a product liability case may in fact be medical malpractice. A product liability claim might be based on various grounds, such as negligence, strict liability, misrepresentation, or breach of warranty of fitness. Under a product liability claim, a manufacturer or seller is liable if the product contains an inherent defect that is unreasonably dangerous and if that defect causes injury to a foreseeable user of the product.

Product liability is generally considered to be a strict liability offense, meaning that liability is not predicated on the degree of carefulness used in the design, manufacturing, or marketing of a product. Under strict liability, a manufacturer is liable when it is shown that the product is defective. Strict liability does not apply to medical providers.[35] However, product liability claims are increasingly difficult for plaintiffs to bring against manufacturers of medical devices. Since there is no federal product liability law, the laws governing product liability have been codified in state-specific product liability statutes. Product defects may be generally categorized as (1) design defects, (2) manufacturing defects, or (3) marketing defects. In the law of product liability, a design defect is considered to exist when the defect is inherent in the design of the product. In a product liability case, a plaintiff can establish that a design defect exists only if he or she can establish that an alternative design, albeit hypothetical, would be (1) safer, (2) as economically feasible, and (3) as practical as the original design, while retaining the primary purpose. Manufacturing defects, on the other hand, are unintended defects that occur during manufacture or assembly. Marketing defects pertain to inadequate warnings and/or instructions and are typically exemplified by inadequate or faulty instructions and by failures to warn.

Liability claims may also be predicated in a general theory of negligence. Negligence is defined as a failure to exercise proper or ordinary care. A manufacturer might be held liable for negligence if it can be established that a lack of reasonable care in the production, design, or assembly of the manufacturer's product caused harm. One specific type of negligence action pertaining to medical devices is the "failure to warn" case. The duty to warn arises whenever a manufacturer knows or reasonably should have known of latent dangers associated with use of its product under normal circumstances. The manufacturer need not have actual knowledge of the risks; rather, it may be sufficient that the manufacturer had constructive knowledge of latent risks if it reasonably could have or should have known of such risks. Although the plaintiff bears the burden of proof to show that a manufacturer had such actual or constructive knowledge, this evidentiary burden can sometimes be satisfied via documented complaints or prior injuries, reports in relevant scientific or trade literature, recognition of the risks by industry experts, or alerts issued by the FDA or other governmental agencies.

Clinical neurosciences are in the midst of a technological/medical device revolution. Various new technologies include, but are not limited to, neurodiagnostic, neurointerventional, and neurostimulation devices. These devices include functional brain imaging, brain metabolism monitoring, cerebral spinal fluid (CSF) shunts, clot retrievers, snares, embolic coils, flow diversion devices, and neurostimulation devices. The FDA Center for Devices and Radiological Health and the Neurological Devices Panel are especially important resources in this area.

HEALTH INSURANCE PORTABILITY AND ACCOUNTABILITY ACT, HEALTH INFORMATION TECHNOLOGY FOR ECONOMIC AND CLINICAL HEALTH, AND THE OFFICE FOR CIVIL RIGHTS

The privacy and confidentiality of medical records is a well-established principle of both medical ethics and health law. The professional respect for individual dignity and confidentiality is essential to ensure trust and promote the integrity and completeness of health information disclosure within the physician-patient relationship. Without the element of trust, patients will not freely reveal their personal health information, and the scope and quality of the medical encounter is subsequently jeopardized. Therefore, physicians have a fiduciary duty to protect the privacy and confidentiality of their patients and their health information. The ethical principle of confidentiality also has well-established legal ramifications, including, but not limited to, confidentiality, loyalty, contract, and breach of privacy.

In anticipation of later widespread adoption of electronic medical records, the DHHS, upon Congressional mandate, enacted the Health Insurance Portability and Accountability Act (HIPAA), which was passed into legislation by Congress in 1996.[36] The broad goals of HIPAA are to (1) increase the efficiency of electronic health care transactions, (2) ensure the continuity of an employee's health insurance coverage after leaving an employer in the process of changing jobs, and (3) mandate widespread uniform adoption of privacy protection measures for ensuring the security of individually identifiable health information. HIPAA was thus a new but complex regulatory framework designed simply to facilitate portability of health data, reduce administrative costs by increasing efficiency though information technology (IT), and develop a federal mandate for the confidentiality of health information. HIPAA was divided into three inter-related parts: (1) the Administrative Simplification provisions, which mandated the adoption of standard data sets on electronic transaction forms in the use of the Electronic Data Interchange, (2) the Privacy Rule provisions, which set security standards and policies for the way in which providers manage personally identifiable health information, and (3) the Security Rule, which governs relationships between health care business associates who necessarily exchange confidential medical information. Protected health information (PHI) refers to any form of health information that personally identifies a patient. The HIPAA Security Rule requires three levels of safeguards for PHI: (1) administrative, (2) physical, and (3) technical.

The American Recovery and Reinvestment Act of 2009 (ARRA) later established a tiered civil penalty structure for HIPAA violations and also defined the Health Information Technology for Economic and Clinical Health Act (HITECH). The HITECH Act focused primarily on incentivizing the adoption of EHRs but also made the HIPAA Privacy Rule and the HIPAA Security Rule critical issues for health care providers. HITECH specifically mandated that HIPAA-covered entities and their business associates provide notifications after any breach of unsecured protected health information—a provision known as the Breach Notification Rule. HITECH's time frame requires providers notify those affected by a data breach within 60 days of the breach. HITECH also defined financial incentives associated with EHR adoption and use.

The Patient Protection and Affordable Care Act of 2010 (ACA) further broadened liability and increased civil and criminal penalties under HIPAA and HITECH. The civil monetary penalties under HIPAA are based on the level of knowledge that violators are presumed to have had at the time of the breach. Fines for individuals who did not reasonably know that they violated HIPAA begin at $100 per violation with an annual maximum of $25,000; individuals who commit violations with "willful neglect" are fined at $10,000–$50,000 per violation with an annual maximum of $1.5 million. The Department of Justice (DOJ) imposes criminal liability for "knowing" a breach or disclosure of PHI; penalties range from a criminal fine of up to $50,000 with imprisonment up to 1 year through fines of $250,000 and imprisonment for up to 10 years in cases of malicious breach associated with personal gain. The Bipartisan Budget Act of 2015[37] requires all federal agencies to increase the civil monetary penalties within their purview on an annual basis.

"Knowingly" for the purposes of criminal liability requires only a general knowledge that a breach could constitute an offense. Furthermore, civil and criminal penalties can extend to any or all business associates. Physicians must realize that civil prosecutions under HIPAA and HITECH may be associated with exclusion from federally funded payment programs, and such exclusions can rapidly escalate to include state- and private-funded insurers. In addition, criminal prosecutions must be reported to the Department of Health and consequently result in a loss of medical licensure. Finally, depending on the physician's liability insurance policy, it is likely that neither prosecution is covered under traditional malpractice insurance.

The Office for Civil Rights (OCR) within the U.S. DHHS is responsible for enforcing HIPAA privacy and security rules; the OCR investigates privacy violations and enforces penalties for noncompliance. Prior to the HITECH Act, the OCR only audited a HIPAA-covered entity when a patient filed a complaint with the agency. However, the HITECH Act now requires the OCR to conduct periodic audits of providers and HIPAA business associates to ensure they are HIPAA compliant. In addition to federal enforcement of HIPAA by the OCR and the DOJ, individual states are free to enact their own state-specific privacy laws under the jurisdiction of the state attorney general, potentially resulting in both a federal and a separate state level prosecution.

THE FEDERAL FALSE CLAIMS ACT AND THE OIG

The Federal False Claims Act (FFCA)[38] was first enacted during the Civil War in 1863 ("Lincoln's Law") to combat fraud against the federal government by suppliers to the Union Army, but it was largely ineffectual until it was amended in 1986.

The relevant parts of the FFCA state that:

(1) [A]ny person who . . .
   (A) knowingly presents, or causes to be presented, a false or fraudulent claim for payment or approval;
   (B) knowingly makes, uses, or causes to be made or used, a false record or statement material to a false or fraudulent claim; [. . .]
   (D) has possession, custody, or control of property or money used, or to be used, by the Government and knowingly delivers, or causes to be delivered, less than all of that money or property; . . . is liable to the United States Government for a civil penalty of not less than $5,000 and not more than $10,000, as adjusted by the Federal Civil Penalties Inflation Adjustment Act of 1990,[39] plus 3 times the amount of damages which the Government sustains because of the act of that person.

[. . .]

(3) A person violating this subsection shall also be liable to the United States Government for the costs of a civil action brought to recover any such penalty or damages.[40]

The statute goes on to define the terms "knowing" and "knowingly" to "mean that a person, with respect to information (1) has actual knowledge of the information; (2) acts in deliberate ignorance of the truth or falsity of the information; or (3) acts in reckless disregard of the truth or falsity of the information, and no proof of specific intent to defraud is required." Thus, the potential liability to providers, physicians, medical groups, and health care institutions under the FFCA cannot be understated. A claim is a bill submitted for services. The Deficit Reduction Act of 2005 (DRA) became effective in 2017 and granted oversight authority for Medicaid providers and payers to CMS, the DHHS OIG, and individual states. The Fraud Enforcement and Recovery Act (FERA) was enacted in 2009 with the intent of clarifying prior misinterpretations and to otherwise modernize the FFCA and extended FFCA liability to "any person who . . . knowingly makes, uses or causes to be made or used a false record or statement to conceal, avoid or decrease any obligation to pay or transmit property to the government."[41]

Investigations of potential fraud under the FFCA are under the jurisdiction of the OIG and are jointly enforced by the Civil Division of the DOJ. Audits most frequently target outliers, practitioners whose charges vary from the statistical norms for charges by similar practitioners in the same or similar geographic area.

However, random audits are also possible. The Health Care Fraud and Abuse Control Program has invested in enhanced data analysis capabilities, predictive analytics, trend evaluation, and modeling approaches to better analyze and target fraud patterns, identify suspected fraud trends, and calculate ratios of allowed services to national averages.

When a specific instance of alleged miscoding is identified, that claim can be extrapolated statistically to all claims submitted within the statute of limitations. Usually, a single claim in insufficient to justify such an extrapolation; rather, a single claim is used as a basis to define a larger universe of claims. Government auditors will apply sampling methods to allege that the audited sample represents only a fraction of the actual overpayments or actual fraudulent claims and thereby rapidly escalate potential monetary liability. Auditors are required to keep sufficient documentation so that "the sampling frame can be re-created, should the methodology be challenged."[42] CMS Ruling 86-1 states that the use of statistical sampling "creates a presumption of validity as to the amount of an overpayment which may be used as the basis for recoupment."[43] Courts have both excluded and admitted the testimony, methodology, and conclusions of statisticians; however, there is a trend to admit extrapolation as a valid technique. In the case of *United States v. Aseracare, Inc.*, the court held that "[s]tatistical evidence is evidence."[44]

In February 2017, the DOJ announced an increase in the FFCA penalties pursuant to the 2015 budget bill, which requires annual re-indexing of FFCA penalties for inflation. The minimum per-claim penalty increased in 2017 from $10,781 to $10,957 (after increasing from $5,500 to $10,781 in 2016), and the maximum per-claim penalty increase in 2017 to $21,916 (after jumping from $11,000 to $21,563 in 2016). The DOJ reiterated that penalties will continue to be adjusted annually going forward and will be announced in the Federal Register no later than January 15th of each year.

The return on investment under the FFCA and state false claims acts is very significant; therefore, the program and its growth are fiscally viable. Program integrity is a term that is frequently used to underscore the importance of the FFCA with respect to maintaining the integrity of the Medicare and Medicaid health programs. The term is increasingly being applied to false claims not only with respect to flagrant abuse but also with respect to reimbursement for errors and waste within the health care system. There appear to be at least two reasons why the government has been successful in the recuperation of monies from providers and health care organizations: (1) health care fraud, at least in some sectors, appears to be highly pervasive; and, (2) since each instance of an item or a service billed to Medicare or Medicaid counts as a claim, a systematic or recurrent series of false claims will rapidly escalate into a huge payment under the FFCA. It is projected that fraud and abuse account for between 3 and 15 percent of annual expenditures for health care in the United States. The National Healthcare Antifraud Association Report (March 2008) suggests that the cost ranges between 3 and 10 percent; the Government Accounting Office (GAO; in 2008) and the Congressional Budget Office place the estimated cost at 10 percent; and the U.S. Chamber of Commerce Report places it at 15 percent. On the basis of these data, the estimated cost of fraud and abuse ranges from $100 billion to $170 billion annually. For the fiscal year 2016, the U.S. DOJ recovered more than $4.7 billion; since the inception of the program in 1986, the total recovery under the FFCA (as of 2016) exceeds $35 billion. In addition, on the basis of the success of the FFCA, a growing number of states, initially beginning in New York, California, and Virginia, enacted state versions of the FFCA that are administered by the Offices of the Medicaid Inspector General (OMIGs) of the individual states. The DRA obligates CMS to establish and staff a new Medicaid Integrity Program (MIP) similar to the current MIP. The DRA of 2015 incentivized individual states to enact state false claims acts that were equal to or potentially more punitive than the FFCA; financial incentives included an additional 10 percent of the federal Medical Assistance percentage on all recoveries collected by a state pursuant to their own individual false claims programs. Claims data are shared between the OIG and the state OMIGs, and frequently there is overlap in the prosecution.

A claim is considered false or fraudulent if it incorrectly states the charges or mischaracterizes the services rendered. For example, a recent OIG report revealed that 64 percent of claims for surgical debridement cases did not meet Medicare program requirements, resulting in $64 million in overpayments.[45] In plain terms, this means that documentation must support the medical necessity for the services and meet the required elements of both performance/supervision and documentation. For example, the documentation elements and requirements for claims submitted under evaluation and management codes are defined by rules published by the CMS. In general, such elements of documentation must include patient history, examination, and medical decision-making. The intensity of the visit must be reflected in the documentation and the necessary specific elements further defined by CMS. In some cases, the time spent in the encounter must also be documented. A claim for services of higher complexity than those actually provided represents up-coding. Reciprocally, a claim for services of complexity lower than that of services actually performed represents down-coding. Up-coding and down-coding are each considered miscoding, and both are illegal under the FFCA. Unbundling occurs when charges are submitted individually for procedures that are considered to be combined into a single charge; unbundling is illegal under the FFCA. Excessive services and unnecessary services also constitute false claims under the FFCA;[46] although the government has traditionally been reluctant to inquire into the necessity of services deemed by physicians to be necessary, this is changing.

The statute of the limitations period applicable to civil FFCA actions is the later of (1) 6 years after the date on which the violation is committed or (2) 3 years after the date when the material facts giving rise to the cause of action are known or reasonably should have been known by the U.S. official responsible for acting on FFCA violations (i.e., by a DOJ official), but in no event more than 10 years after the date on which the violation is committed. Tolling, or extension of the statute of limitations, is also allowed under the law.

The supervisory and teaching environments require that, in order to submit a claim for services in his or her name, the attending physician must be physically present and immediately available throughout the key portions of the procedure. The reason for the Teaching Rule is based in the way that teaching hospitals are reimbursed. Graduate Medical Education (GME) is funded under Medicare Part A; through GME funding, teaching physicians are paid a stipend for taking responsibility for the hospital's oversight of physicians in training. Medicare also pays teaching hospitals under the prospective payment system for the higher indirect operating costs hospitals incurred by having GME programs, and Medicare supports GME programs in teaching hospitals through claims submitted for the services of attending physicians who involve residents in the care of their patients under Medicare Part B. Thus, a service provided by an unsupervised resident cannot be legitimately billed under Medicare Part B because that service has already been funded under Part A; a separate reimbursement under Part B would constitute a "double reimbursement." The CMS definition of the Teaching Rule might be reasonably distilled as the following:

> [i]f a resident participates in a service furnished in a teaching setting, physician fee schedule payment is made only if a teaching physician is present during the key portion of any service or procedure for which payment is sought. In the case of surgical, high-risk, or other complex procedures, the teaching physician must be present during all critical portions of the procedure and immediately available to furnish services during the entire service or procedure.... In the case of evaluation and management services, the teaching physician must be present during the portion of the service that determines the level of service billed.... [T]he medical records must document that the teaching physician was present at the time the service is furnished. The presence of the teaching physician during procedures may be demonstrated by the notes in the medical records made by a physician, resident, or nurse. In the case of evaluation and management procedures, the teaching physician must personally document his or her participation in the service in the medical records.[47]

DHHS initiated the Physicians at Teaching Hospitals (PATH) program[48] to review Medicare Part B billings by teaching hospitals with the intent of recovering past overpayments for services rendered.[49] The PATH audit of the University of Pennsylvania Health System resulted in a settlement of over $30 million for Medicare claims submitted between 1989 and 1994.[50] The important findings in the University of Pennsylvania PATH audit were (1) a lack of documentation of the physical presence of the teaching physician during services performed by a resident and subsequently billed for payment under Medicare Part B, and (2) upcoding, or billing for a more complex level of care than that which was provided. Compliance with the CMS Teaching Rule requirements may be variably defined by individual institutional compliance policies. The Teaching Rule has been most conservatively interpreted to require that the teaching physician be present for patient examinations and discuss the plan of care with the resident, and, for procedures, to be gowned and gloved at the bedside. Residents who have been credentialed as technically proficient to perform independently may, under some hospital rules, perform procedures in the absence of supervision; however, in these instances, the teaching requirement is not met and claims may not be submitted for procedural reimbursement. Parenthetically, it is important to note that inadequate supervision may also represent a negligence claim under medical malpractice whether or not the encounter is billed, in addition to a potential FFCA action if billed.

The FFCA was amended by FERA, which made retention of overpayments made by the government to a practice illegal.[51] In 2010, Congress enacted significant changes to the FFCA within the ACA. ACA Section 6402 requires that providers and others must report and refund any overpayment made by a federally funded program within 60 days of the date the overpayment is identified, and failure to do so would constitute an FFCA violation with resultant penalties. Before FERA, the reverse false claims provision imposed liability on a person who knowingly made, used, or caused to be made or used "a false record or statement to conceal, avoid, or decrease an obligation to pay or transmit money or property to the [g]overnment." ACA, through FERA, directly placed the affirmative duty on the recipients to identify overpayments, disclose them, and refund them promptly. FERA broadened liability by eliminating the need for a false record or statement and instead imposed a new liability through a new definition of "obligation," which specified that the "retention of any overpayment" can serve as the basis for reverse false claims liability if it is done knowingly and improperly, or if an overpayment is knowingly concealed. In 2016, three hospitals in the Mount Sinai Health System paid a total of $2.95 million to resolve allegations that the hospitals knowingly retained over $844,000 in overpayments made by Medicaid in violation of the Federal and New York False Claims Acts. New York State's share of the settlement is over $1.7 million. Beginning in 2009, because of a software compatibility issue, a coding error caused defendants to submit claims for payment above and beyond what they had received from a managed care organization, and that Medicaid paid these claims as a secondary payor.[52]

Civil penalties include fines, corporate integrity agreements (monitoring programs), and exclusion from CMS and other federally funded payment programs. In addition to civil monetary penalties under the FFCA, liability under the FFCA may also result in either a corporate integrity agreement (monitoring program) and/or exclusion from participating in federally funded payment programs. Criminal penalties for submitting false claims include imprisonment and criminal fines; criminal convictions automatically also implicate provider's exclusion. Provider exclusion is defined by the Exclusion Statute. OIG is legally required to exclude from participation in all federal health care programs individuals and entities convicted of the following types of criminal offenses: (1) Medicare or Medicaid fraud, as well as any other offenses related to the delivery of items or services under Medicare or Medicaid; (2) patient abuse or neglect; (3) felony convictions for other health care-related fraud, theft, or other financial misconduct; and (4) felony convictions for the unlawful manufacture, distribution, prescription, or dispensing of controlled substances. OIG has discretion to exclude individuals and entities on several other grounds, including misdemeanor convictions related to health care fraud other than Medicare or Medicaid fraud. These exclusions can be based on misdemeanor convictions in connection with the unlawful manufacture, distribution, prescription, or dispensing of controlled substances; suspension, revocation, or surrender of a license to provide health care for reasons bearing on professional competence, professional performance, or financial integrity; provision of unnecessary or substandard services; submission of false or fraudulent claims to a federal health care program; engaging in unlawful kickback arrangements; and defaulting on health education loan or scholarship obligations. In the event of an exclusion from participation in the federal health care programs, Medicare, Medicaid, TRICARE, and the Veterans Health Administration will not pay services. Exclusion is a *de facto* loss of livelihood, unless the provider is in a private pay environment. Each practice or hospital is responsible for ensuring that it does not knowingly or inadvertently employ or contract with excluded individuals or entities. This responsibility requires screening all current and prospective employees and contractors against OIG's List of Excluded Individuals and Entities. Furthermore, since both civil and criminal agreements and convictions are reported to both the NPDB and state DOH/boards of medicine, liability under the FFCA will almost certainly result in loss of both hospital privileges and licensure.

The ACA of 2010[53] also added amendments to the 1986 FFCA that simplified and facilitated the whistleblower process. The FFCA empowers private persons and entities who submit evidence of fraud against federal programs or contracts to sue the wrongdoer on behalf of the U.S. government. An action brought by a private party is known as a *qui tam*, or "whistleblower" lawsuit.[54] If the government intervenes in the qui tam action, it has the primary responsibility for prosecution. The whistleblower's reward can amount to 25–30 percent of the judgment or settlement recovered by the government through the qui tam action.[55] Whistleblowers filed 702 qui tam suits in fiscal year 2016, and the DOJ recovered $2.9 billion in these suits.[56] Retaliation against whistleblowers is unlawful, and any employee who is discharged, demoted, harassed, or otherwise discriminated against because of a qui tam claim is entitled to all relief necessary to make the employee whole, potentially including (1) reinstatement; (2) double back pay; and (3) compensation for any special damages, including litigation costs and reasonable attorneys' fees. Nonetheless, the exact protections for whistleblowers continue to be debated in the courts. In 2017, Texas-based MB2 Dental Solutions (MB2) and twenty-one pediatric dental practices affiliated with MB2 agreed to pay $8.45 million to resolve allegations that they knowingly submitted claims for dental services which allegedly were never performed, and that they knowingly received improper kickbacks and misidentified the dentists who actually performed the services. Five owners of the firm and the affiliated practices agreed to each pay $250,000 to resolve claims made against them individually, and the firm's head of marketing agreed to pay $100,000 to resolve alleged individual liability. Notably, the whistleblower, a former employee at the firm, will receive a $1.52 million share of the settlement.[57] On February 1, 2017, a pain management physician, Dr. Robert Windsor, agreed to the entry of a $20 million consent judgment to settle claims brought by three whistleblowers in two lawsuits that involved the physician billing for medically unnecessary diagnostic tests and surgical monitoring services that were never performed. Dr. Windsor owned pain management clinics in Georgia and Kentucky that operated under the umbrella of National Pain Care, Inc., in Kentucky. On October 24, 2016, the physician was also sentenced to more than 3 years in prison and 3 years of supervised release in connection with some of the related conduct. The relators' share of the settlement has not yet been disclosed.[58]

Finally, through the Tax Relief and Health Care Act of 2006, CMS implemented Medicare recovery auditing in 2010 in all states as an additional layer of false claims and overpayment recoveries by using independent Recovery Audit Contractors (RACs). The goal of the recovery audit program is to identify improper payments made on claims. RACs were selected in an open bidding process. RACs function as independent contractors under the authority of CMS; they employ trained coders and perform focused chart reviews to identify both overpayments and underpayments in return for a contingency fee of up to 12.5 percent. For the purposes of delineating RAC jurisdiction, the United States was divided into four regions. As of October 2016, Region A (CT, DE, DC, ME, MD, MA, NH, NJ, NY, PA, RI, and VT) is administered through Performant Recovery, Inc., managed by Diversified Collection Services; Region B (IN, MI, MN, IL, KY, OH, and WI) is administered through Cotiviti, LLC, Inc.; Region C (AL, CO, FL, GA, LA, MI, NC, NM, OK, SC, TN, TX, VA, WV, PR, USVI) is administered through Cotiviti, LLC; and, Region D (AK, AZ, CA, HI, IA, ID, KS, MS, MO, ND, NV, OR, SD, UT, WA, WY, Guam, American Samoa, and Northern Marianas) is administered through HMS Federal Solutions.[59] Each RAC is allowed to use its own proprietary software and develop an independent interpretation of Medicare rules and regulations.

EMERGENCY MEDICAL TREATMENT AND ACTIVE LABOR ACT: THE DUTY TO SCREEN AND STABILIZE

The Consolidated Omnibus Reconciliation Act,[60] which includes the Emergency Medical Treatment and Active Labor Act (EMTALA) as one of many provisions, imposes several requirements on acute care hospitals that accept Medicare funding (participating hospitals). Generally referred to as the "anti-dumping" law, the law's initial intent was to ensure patient access to emergency medical care and to prevent the practice of patient dumping, in which uninsured patients were transferred, solely for financial reasons, from private to public hospitals without consideration of their medical condition or stability for the transfer.[61]

EMTALA requires Medicare-participating hospitals with emergency departments to screen and treat the emergency medical conditions of all patients in a nondiscriminatory manner, regardless of their ability to pay, insurance status, national origin, race, creed, or color. EMTALA defines an emergency medical condition as "[a] medical condition manifesting itself by acute symptoms of sufficient severity such that the absence of immediate medical attention could reasonably be expected to result in—(1) [p]lacing the health of the individual... in serious jeopardy; (2) [s]erious impairment to bodily functions; or (3) [s]erious dysfunction of any bodily organ part."[62]

The EMTALA statute imposes specific obligations upon treating hospitals. First, any individual who comes to the emergency department must be provided "an appropriate medical screening examination within the capability of the hospital's emergency department, including ancillary services routinely available to the emergency department, to determine whether or not an emergency medical condition exists."[63] EMTALA obligations are triggered when an individual first presents to the emergency department; specifically, when an individual arrives on hospital property. In fact, EMTALA might actually be triggered before the patient's actual arrival as long as the patient is en route and the emergency department has been notified of the patient's pending arrival.[64] The appropriate medical screening examination must be conducted by individuals who have been determined to be qualified in hospital bylaws to perform such an examination.[65] Second, if it is determined that an emergency medical condition does exist, the hospital must provide the necessary treatment to stabilize the patient's medical condition or appropriately transfer the patient to another hospital. Appropriate transfer of unstable patients requires that the referring hospital (1) provide ongoing care within its capability until transfer to minimize transfer risks, (2) provide copies of medical records, (3) confirm that the receiving facility has space and qualified personnel to treat the condition and has agreed to accept the transfer, and (4) ensure that the transfer be made with qualified personnel and appropriate medical equipment. However, if that hospital chooses to accept the patient as an inpatient for further treatment, the EMTALA obligation ends. Specialized hospitals, such as tertiary care facilities, cannot refuse to accept a transfer if they have the capacity to treat the patient. However, if that patient had previously been admitted as an inpatient to the referring hospital, there is no EMTALA obligation.[66] Third, patients may be transferred under EMTALA only on the basis of medical necessity; such transfers must be appropriate and include a consideration of the medical benefits of transfer against the medical risks of transfer, and such a determination must be certified in writing by a physician.

Accepting hospitals have a duty to report potential EMTALA violations to the CMS. Thus, EMTALA violations are primarily complaint driven after complaints are filed by accepting hospitals. Such complaints are investigated by the OIG, and penalties may include termination of the hospital's or physician's Medicare provider agreement and civil monetary fines imposed on hospitals and/or physicians. Under EMTALA, a hospital may be fined up to $50,000 per violation ($25,000 for a hospital with fewer than one hundred beds); physicians may be fined up to $50,000 per violation, and the fines may extend to on-call physicians. A receiving facility that has suffered a financial loss as a result of another hospital's violation of EMTALA can also bring a lawsuit to recover damages. The statute of limitations under EMTALA is 2 years. Whistleblowers under EMTALA are protected by law.

EMTALA also governs on-call obligations. Facilities must maintain a list of physicians who are on call, as either treating or consulting physicians. Treating and consulting physicians may provide consultation by telephone, video conferencing, or any other reasonable means of communication, and there is no specific requirement that the on-call physician evaluate the patient in person. However, the on-call physician must evaluate a patient in person if specifically requested to do so; failure to comply is a violation under EMTALA.[67]

STARK

The Physician Self-Referral Law,[68] commonly referred to as the Stark law, prohibits physicians from referring patients to receive "designated health services" payable by Medicare or Medicaid from entities with which the physician or an immediate family member has a financial relationship, unless an exception applies. The federal government interprets the term "financial relationship" broadly to include any direct or indirect ownership or investment interest by the referring physician, as well as any financial interests held by any of the physician's immediate family members.

> The referral prohibition contained in the Stark law applies only to the referral of patients for statutorily defined "Designated Health Services." Currently, Designated Health Services are defined as: clinical laboratory services; physical therapy services; occupational therapy services; radiology services, including ultrasound, MRI

and CT scans; radiation therapy services; durable medical equipment; parenteral and enteral nutrients, equipment and supplies; prosthetics, orthotics and prosthetic devices and supplies; home health services; outpatient prescription drugs; and inpatient and outpatient hospital services.[69]

Although the Stark law was initially enacted in two separate parts, references to the Stark law as either "Stark I" or "Stark II" are purely preferential, since the two statutes have been fully integrated.[70] Unlike the federal AKS, the Stark law is not a criminal statute. However, the OIG for DHHS can pursue a civil action against Stark Law violators under the civil monetary penalties law. The Stark law is a strict liability statute, which means proof of specific intent to violate the law is not required. Referrals and claims that violate the Stark statute are each punishable by a $15,000 civil money penalty; any claim paid as the result of an improper referral is an overpayment, and circumvention schemes are punishable by a $100,000 civil money penalty.

ANTI-KICKBACK

The Stark and AKS laws are similar, but there are certain differences. Thus, there is a lot of confusion about the exact nature of the laws. Where there is a legal question, an attorney should be consulted. In short, the Physician Self-Referral Statute ("Stark") prohibits a physician from making referrals for certain designated health services payable by Medicare to an entity with which he or she, or an immediate family member, has a financial ownership interest, unless an exception applies. On the other hand, the AKS provides criminal penalties for individuals or entities that knowingly and willfully offer, pay, solicit, or receive remuneration in order to induce or reward the referral of business reimbursable under any of the federal health care programs.

AKS[71] is a criminal law that prohibits the knowing and willful payment, or receipt, of remuneration to induce or reward patient referrals or the generation of business involving any item or service payable by a federal health care program (e.g., drugs, supplies, or health care services for Medicare or Medicaid patients). The Social Security Amendments of 1972 included the original AKS. Remuneration includes anything of value. The AKS is designed to protect patients and federal health care programs from fraud and abuse by inhibiting the use of money to influence health care decisions.

In 1977, the Medicare-Medicaid Anti-Fraud and Abuse Amendments increased the penalty for violating the statute from a misdemeanor to a felony. DHHS and the DOJ jointly created the Health Care Fraud Prevention and Enforcement Action Team in 2009. Thus, since the AKS is a criminal statute, it is different from the civil violations under the other statutes discussed in this chapter. A criminal conviction has substantially greater repercussions on credentialing and licensure than does a civil conviction. Criminal penalties and administrative sanctions for violating the AKS include fines, jail terms, and exclusion from participation in the federal health care programs. Conviction for a single violation under the AKS may also result in a fine of up to $25,000 as well as imprisonment for up to 5 years.[72] In addition, conviction results in mandatory exclusion from participation in federal health care programs.[73] Absent a conviction, individuals who violate the AKS may still face exclusion from federal health care programs at the discretion of the DHHS.[74] Finally, under the AKS, the government may also assess civil money penalties, which could result in treble damages plus $50,000 for each violation of the AKS.[75] The OIG was given the authority to issue civil penalties in addition to the already authorized criminal penalties set forth in the Medicare and Medicaid Patient and Program Protection Act of 1987.[76] The AKS is broadly drafted and establishes penalties for individuals and entities on both sides of the prohibited transaction. It is noteworthy that, similar to rise of state-level false claims acts that parallel the FFCA, at this time, approximately thirty-six states and the District of Columbia have enacted state laws that prohibit remunerations for health care program business referrals. Therefore, similar to the FFCA, there can be simultaneous liability under both federal and state statutes for kickback law violations.

The AKS is an intent-based statute requiring "knowing and willful" engagement in prohibited conduct. In *United States v. Greber*, a landmark case regarding the scope of the AKS, the scienter requirement was defined under the "one purpose" test: "if one purpose of the payment was to induce future referrals, the Medicare statute has been violated."[77] In 2010, the ACA amended the intent requirement of the AKS so that government agencies are no longer required to prove that the defendant intended to violate the AKS. The importance of substantiating the fair market value of payments so as to insulate against future allegations of AKS violations has led the growth of valuation services.

Safe harbors protect certain payment and business practices that could otherwise implicate the AKS from criminal and civil prosecution. The purpose of safe harbor provisions is to insulate certain behavior that would otherwise be a felony under the AKS. To be protected by a safe harbor, an arrangement must squarely fit within the safe harbor and it must satisfy all of the safe harbor provision elements. Details regarding safe harbors are found at 42 CFR §1001.952.

Physicians frequently contract with organizations to perform administrative services; these frequently take the form of medical director and other advisory agreements.[78] Although it is reasonable to reimburse a medical director who is providing genuinely necessary services and many compensation arrangements are legitimate, a compensation arrangement may violate the AKS if even one purpose of the arrangement is to compensate a physician for his or her past or future referrals.[79] Physicians working as independent contractors can potentially violate the AKS it there is an imbalance between the compensation and the services performed. In *United States v. McClatchey*, a hospital paid physicians a stipend of $75,000 per year for positions as medical directors; there was a lack of services provided, and the government alleged violations of the AKS on the basis that the payments for medical director services greatly exceeded the value of services rendered, and that the payments were instead intended to induce the physicians to refer patients.

The reach of the AKS affects not only medical practices but also corporations. For example, in 2012, GlaxoSmithKline paid a $3 billion settlement to resolve allegations that it, *inter alia*, (1) promoted the drugs Paxil, Wellbutrin, Advair, Lamictal, and Zofran for uses not approved by the FDA; (2) made false and misleading statements concerning the safety of Avandia; and (3) reported false best prices and underpaid rebates owed under the Medicaid Drug Rebate Program. It is noteworthy that the settlement involved multiple qui tam actions in which the relators received $131 million as their share of the settlement.[80] In *United States v. Campbell*,[81] the University of Medicine and Dentistry of New Jersey entered into clinical assistant professor (CAP) agreements with a number of private practice cardiologists to perform a variety of teaching-related services, for which they were paid between $50,000 and $180,000 per year under contracts. The government contended that the primary service performed under the CAP agreements was the referral of patients for private cardiology services to the hospital. The court found that the AKS was violated because the physicians were not compensated at fair market value, and the arrangements were not commercially reasonable. In 2016, Tenet Healthcare Corp. paid $244.2 million to resolve allegations that its hospitals paid kickbacks in return for patient referrals. Tenet paid an additional $123.7 million to state Medicaid programs; subsidiaries pleaded guilty to related charges and were assessed $145 million, and the total settlement amounted to $513 million.[82]

On May 18, 2017, two Missouri-based hospitals, Mercy Hospital Springfield (formerly known as St. John's Regional Health Center) and its affiliate, Mercy Clinic Springfield Communities (formerly known as St. John's Clinic), agreed to pay $34 million to settle allegations that they engaged in a kickback scheme with referring physicians for chemotherapy services. The compensation of the oncologists was based in part on a formula that improperly took into account the value of their referrals of patients to the infusion center operated by the hospitals. The whistleblower, a physician formerly employed by one of the hospitals, received $5.4 million.

6 · DIGITAL MEDICINE AND THE DATA REVOLUTION

Managing Digital Distraction and Electronic Medical Record Liability While Leveraging Opportunities in Teleneurology and Telecritical Care

Without a reasonable financial margin, even the most dedicated health system cannot accomplish its mission. Financial stewardship is essential in a time when health systems are fiercely competitive in terms of quality metrics and outcomes, market share, and consumer satisfaction. Patients are seeking value from health care delivery. The system-wide shift to value-based care requires that organizations and providers make clinical, workflow, and operational changes that will increase the perceived value of the health maintenance and therapeutic services provided. It is axiomatic that health care is not a priority—until it is needed. The healthy will see no value in critical care—until they need it.

TRENDS THAT WILL SHAPE HEALTH CARE OF THE FUTURE

Technology and health system delivery will likely be the driving forces that will probably have the greatest impact on the health care landscape of the future. After all, despite the attention to fitness and healthy lifestyle management in certain market segments, social inequities will continue, emerging diseases will alter the current epidemiologic landscape, and unhealthy lifestyles will continue.

The first driver of change is likely to be the advent of personalized telehealth. Telehealth is a mix of both remote monitoring and telemedicine. Devices similar to the Apple Fitbit will allow continuous tracking and trending of vital signs. Paroxysmal atrial fibrillation, blood pressure monitoring, and even almost continuous glucose and electrolyte monitoring will create a new paradigm for preventative health. For many, the first presentation of paroxysmal atrial fibrillation is a debilitating stroke, the first manifestation of hypertension is intraparenchymal hemorrhage, and the first manifestation of occult diabetes is either diabetic ketoacidosis or acute renal disease. Telemedicine will change the point of contact for the majority of patients from the emergency department or primary care office, with their associated inconveniences, to virtually anywhere that a digital signal can be accessed. Almost everyone in America has a smartphone and is almost always connected; the capacity for wearable technologies continues to evolve. Perhaps the days of a person suffering with acute chest pain who is trying to find a phone booth are finally over. The importance of personalized health care lies not only in the individual uniqueness of each person's anatomy and physiology, but also in the uniqueness of their psychology and their individual capabilities and needs. The "one-size-fits-all" approach to health care—the model upon which current health care delivery has been predicated—respects neither individual lifestyle preferences nor schedules. In order to provide a health care model that most respects patient autonomy and individual needs, the delivery of that health care service must be available when it is needed. The inability to coordinate lifestyle and health care interactions is frequently at the root of failure to comply with preventative health as well as routine health care visits and follow-up care. Empowering patients to help manage their own health supports both autonomy and engagement.

The second driver of enormous change in the health care environment will likely be artificial intelligence (AI). The processing speed, digital memory, and the capacity for self-evolving analytical capacity will change the nature of the provider interaction from its current state, with its associated cognitive biases, distractions, and knowledge limitations, to a Siri or Alexa type of encyclopedic diagnostic and treatment capability. Although IBM's Watson remains prototypic and immature, the potential for technology evolution along the line of Watson is almost endless given the history of technology growth, especially over the past 10 years. Diagnostic and treatment algorithms most often fail because of outlier, erroneous, overwhelming, or incomplete data. AI goes beyond computerized processing and algorithms; AI connotes learning and meaningful integration of both available medical knowledge and patient data. Especially in the areas of highly complex images with subtle changes such as mammography, chest and brain computerized tomography, magnetic resonance imaging, and ultrasonography, medical imaging has already been impacted by computer assisted reconstruction and may be amenable to automated reading. AI could drastically change the manpower landscape of health care and both dramatically decrease costs and dramatically increase access to health care. The issue of liability with respect to decisions made by or with the aid of AI is, at present, probably well beyond the scope of the law. Malpractice claims involving AI have not been addressed; given the complexity of AI, expert medical opinions challenging the best practice algorithms incorporated into AI may be difficult to posit. However, processing errors leading to erroneous input or application of output will undoubtedly continue to be relevant in situations in which a bad outcome or adverse event occurs.

The third important driver of health care change will be in the landscape of the delivery of therapy. Drones are already delivering defibrillation units to cardiac arrests in larger cities much more quickly and efficiently than ambulances can travel. Mergers between payers and pharmacies and the advent of rapid package deployment systems such as Amazon may eliminate the trip to the pharmacy.

Thus, the pace of change and the limits of technology continue to evolve and have great potential. However, at present, despite the opportunities, technology continues to introduce risks into the patient care encounter.

LEGAL RISK AND LIABILITY ASSOCIATED WITH THE ELECTRONIC MEDICAL RECORD

The electronic medical record (EMR) is the new medical record. Documentation in a patient's medical record has always served a number of equally important purposes: (1) creation of a record memorializing the patient-physician/provider encounter; (2) creation and perpetuation of a patient's medical history; (3) facilitation of formal communication among various members of the health care team; (4) contemporaneous memorialization and explanation of medical decision-making that occurs during a specific encounter; (5) creation of a foundation for peer-review and quality-assurance activities; (6) justification of the level of professional and/or hospital charges submitted to third-party payers; (7) to provide data for medical research; and, (8) compliance with administrative and regulatory requirements. The EMR allows providers to accomplish each of these goals, but also leverages technology to allow for (1) simultaneous use by multiple providers who are geographically separate; (2) auto-population of fields with laboratory, radiology, and telemetry data; (3) remote accessibility; (4) Boolean search capability to scan medical records for key words of phrases; (5) rapid digital input via voice recognition or keyboard, vastly increasing both the ability to enter data and to read the data legibly; and (6) rapid transmission via the electronic data interchange to support billing claims and facilitate both preservation and portability.

The legal risks associated with EMRs can be divided into the following categories: (1) civil litigation and errors in data entry, pull down menus, and metadata; (2) regulatory risks associated with false claims compliance; (3) privacy risks associated with the Health Insurance Portability and Accountability Act (HIPAA); and (4) patient satisfaction risks associated with contemporaneous documentation.

The concept of metadata is fundamental to a discussion of legal risks associated with digitally created and stored information. The *Business Dictionary* defines metadata as

> [d]ata that serves to provide context or additional information about other data. For example, information about the title, subject, author, typeface, enhancements, and size of the data file of a document constitute metadata about that document. It may also describe the conditions under which the data stored in a database was acquired, its accuracy, date, time, method of compilation and processing, etc.[1]

Metadata is generally not visible and can only be accessed in specific document view modes. Metadata is embedded within and follows the digital file and is therefore evidence.

The key areas of risk associated with data entry into an EMR focus around the probability for erroneous data entry and perpetuation of erroneous information carried forward through the "copy and paste" function. Data entry errors can occur through auto-population, a mouse click error, an error associated with pull down menus, or erroneous voice recognition. Although auto-population can automate data entry into a chart entry, it can introduce errors and must be verified. Although the risk of error introduced through field auto-population may be statistically lower than by the paper-based transcription of the past, it is also less likely to be scanned and edited during the field population process. Mouse clicks and pull down menus can introduce errors based on the rapidity with which such clicks and decisions are made; these errors involve not only data entry but also diagnoses and prescriptions. Metadata also tracks the time that a provider spent accessing and reviewing EMR pull down menus and alerts. Digital voice recognition software has vastly increased the potential for more complete documentation. However, voice recognition is not perfect: the microphone may not be on during the dictation; there may be erroneous recognition and transcription; or there may simply be too much information, creating a record that is to verbose for other providers to read. The autocorrect function in digital document creation and in texting software has similar, and sometimes as frustrating or embarrassing, results as the word recognition software. Since the standard of care with respect to the review of the patient's medical record is a complete review, over-documentation carries risks associated with information overload. Large volumes of data can be especially difficult to access in cases in which referring providers send data in the form of written or printed paper records, which are subsequently scanned in as PDF files and annexed to an EMR, but are extremely difficult to search. The time spent editing a specific encounter note and the subsequent addenda and alterations are also accessible through a review of the metadata. Where EMRs are linked to clinical decision-support systems, the use of such reference information can also be accessed at a later date to support or rebut due diligence; such information can involve diagnostic or treatment algorithms, drug interactions and doses, or where available, integrated external databases such as Up to Date. Subsequent review of electronic documentation, through the process of electronic discovery and computer forensics, can disclose exactly how, where, and when the document was created and the intricacies of the creation process. Increasingly, photographs and videos are being used as adjunct documentation of either the physical examination or the informed consent/treatment plan process. Such adjunct documentation will represent an increasingly important area of risk mitigation in the future, but it can also open the visual assessment to alternate subsequent interpretations in the event of litigation. The growing importance of EMRs also imposes liability on the health care system because, in the event of an EMR failure, access to critical patient data and the documentation of other treating providers can be hampered and interfere with patient care.

The term "false claims" refers to the submission of claims for services that were either not provided or that purported to provide a level of service different from that which was billed. Auto-population and copy-and-paste functions can make notes appear more complex and robust than they truly are, and these functions introduce a risk of systematic up-coding for intensity of service. Lengthy notes with carryover and auto-population but that reflect only a minimal professional analysis or professional judgment are red flags to investigators regarding the potential for false claims violations.

The EMR has great potential for privacy breaches under HIPAA. Electronic data transmission not only facilitates the transmission of large volumes of data to multiple parties almost instantaneously, it is also vulnerable to cybersecurity breach. A click of a mouse can transmit data instantaneously and irretrievably. Simultaneously, while HIPAA continues to legislate safeguards with respect to the privacy of health information and penalize providers and institutions for security breaches, cybersecurity breaches are increasingly commonplace within the financial and industrial sectors, and almost every government agency has been the victim of a cybersecurity breech. Thus, it can be reasonably argued that privacy laws such as HIPAA and HITECH disproportionately impact the health care sector, and that the health care sector is being not only victimized by cyberhackers, but also is unreasonably penalized given the prevailing cybersecurity environment. Finally, there may be evolving generational differences regarding expectations of privacy; the more connected younger generations may have come to expect less personal privacy given the digital environment to which they have become accustomed. Expectations of privacy may be changing over time despite a historical ethical and professional tradition of privacy between the provider and patient.

THE PROVIDER AND SOCIAL MEDIA

Social media includes a variety of social networking and electronic community websites that allow users to share information, communicate online, and network within electronic communities. Examples of social media include, but are not limited to, Facebook, Google+, MySpace, Instagram, LinkedIn, Pinterest, Reddit, Tumblr, Twitter, Snapchat, and YouTube. Social media promotes connectedness and communication. Providers can access social media in a professional capacity, participate in online communities, access continuing education, and network and communicate with colleagues. Patients as well as health care providers may access social media, individually or via a shared network, but the information communicated is not private. Breaches of patient confidentiality can result in legal liability for a provider under civil privacy laws or under HIPAA or HITECH.

Risks associated with postings can involve either the provider or online reviews of the provider. Social media can convey subjective impressions about personality, values, and priorities, and these may reflect on the provider in an unprofessional manner.[2] Unprofessional behavior might involve the use of profanity or discriminatory language; images of sexual suggestiveness or intoxication; and negative comments about patients, the profession, or an employer. Employers, patients, colleagues, and even state licensing agencies may monitor social media content. In the event of litigation, social media content may be introduced into evidence. State medical boards have the authority to discipline providers for unprofessional behavior, and such disciplinary action can include sanctions, license suspension, or even revocation.[3] In addition, providers who interact with patients via social media may be in violation of provider-patient boundaries.[4] In the event of litigation, social media is discoverable; Facebook policy regarding the use of data states that "we may access, preserve, and share your information in response to a legal request" both within and outside of U.S. jurisdiction.[5] Health care systems are increasingly aware of the risks associated with social media and have developed policies and procedures both to insulate themselves from liability and also to help providers understand the legal implications of social media postings. Providers in violation of hospital or organization policies may be subject to disciplinary action.

Social networks may also post information about providers and the perceived quality of care rendered. Patients who chose to post personal health information on social media are not in violation of HIPAA or HITECH since they themselves are the holders of the privacy privilege. Reciprocation on social media may, however, put the provider at liability if additional information is disclosed without the patient's permission. Professional health care-focused online reputation-management services can be used to monitor a provider's online reputation. In such cases, communication, rather than online or legal retaliation, may be the best option because of the risk of escalation and further dissemination of opinions.

ELECTRONIC DISTRACTION

The importance of focus and mindfulness to situational awareness and patient safety cannot be underscored. Mobile personal digital devices represent the opportunity for instantaneous connectedness that embodies tremendous potential for health care providers: not only do these devices allow immediate access to huge databases of information previously available only in libraries, these devices also provide the opportunity to connect with other experts for help and advice with complex clinical management. Nonetheless, technology also represents a risk of distraction, with a subsequent loss of focus, a loss of situational awareness, and the potential for patient harm. The commonly touted skill of multitasking is actually a fallacy since the human mind is unable to truly fully focus simultaneously on multiple competing sensory data points; instead, multitasking is actually a process of task-switching with attention rapidly alternating between data points. Therefore, more engaging data points will detract from other potentially equally or even more important information. Additionally, mobile technology can create highly entertaining and highly engaging digital sensory worlds, wherein the stimulation provided can actually be highly addictive. Such a loss of focus is now commonly understood to represent digital distraction both in private life and in the work environment.[6]

Providers have a moral, legal, and ethical duty of care; good care demands focus. Although competing data points, information overload, and competing priorities are not new to clinicians, electronic technology brings an additional layer of sensory complexity to the patient care environment. Digital distraction sits squarely into the paradigm of lost situational awareness and a latent condition that can exacerbate errors such as slips, lapses, mistakes due to inattention, and other mistakes that fall under theories of human error. Where previously providers were able to shift their attention between tasks and conversations, the opportunity to "lose oneself" completely in a digital environment represents a new threat. Increasingly, in medical negligence lawsuits, evidence regarding electronic and digital activities of providers at or around the time of an adverse patient care event is being introduced. Just as the EMR is embedded with metadata that provides information about the circumstances under which a digital file was created, electronic communications can be traced. For example, in motor vehicle accidents, cell phone logs are now being routinely subpoenaed to provide information about whether or not a driver involved in a motor vehicle accident was on the phone or texting at the time of the accident. Similarly, cases involving medical providers have determined that a provider was potentially distracted on the internet, social media, or in a digital conversation and therefore may have lost focus and breached a duty of care to patient. Medical and nursing negligence can occur as a failure of monitoring, failure to timely diagnose, failure to supervise, and failure to rescue. Such failures, if they can be attributed to provider distraction, can provide a causal link between breach of duty and subsequent injury/damages.[7]

Increasingly, health care organizations and health care systems are becoming aware that digital media and its potential for distraction can implicate not only the provider but also the group, team, and institution in legal liability. Just as states are increasingly outlawing texting and driving, cell phone use and driving, and cell phone use and crossing intersections, some health care organizations have developed policies regarding boundaries for the use of electronic technology and personal digital devices within the patient care environment to minimize the risk of institutional liability. The airline industry, which is credited for developing the Crew Resource Management model of team safety, has also developed the Sterile Cockpit Rule whereby, during episodes of higher workload, at times where flight crews are especially vulnerable to error and where situational awareness is critical, distractions to the flight crew must be minimized. The Joint Commission has embraced the Sterile Cockpit Rule and recommends that distractions to the health care team be minimized during critical operations such as drug dispensation and administration, critical assessments, and critical procedures.

Therefore, distraction due to electronic technology is being increasingly recognized as a contributing factor to cognitive dissonance and distraction in the health care workplace. Attorneys and patients are becoming increasingly sensitized to the importance of focus in accident prevention and the ability to mine digital data during electronic discovery for subsequent litigation. Health care providers would be well advised to use extreme caution when accessing non-work-related digital communications while being charged with patient care.

TELENEUROLOGY AND TELEMEDICINE OPPORTUNITIES AND LIABILITY

Telemedicine has the potential of providing a critical platform for the extension of better-integrated, population-based models of medical care. Specifically, telemedicine can link tertiary care hubs with more rurally-based points of health care encounters where subspecialists may not be readily available. In addition, telemedicine can be structured so that specialists and subspecialists can be available to multiple centers throughout the course the day. Thus, telemedicine promises improved access to more complex care. Telemedicine has become possible and increasingly refined through advances in visual communication technologies, enabling legislation, and marketing that has facilitated provider acceptance of remote medical care. Not long ago, a telemedicine encounter was no more than a video conference between providers; today, telemedicine can continuously and remotely monitor a multitude of patients scattered through various communities with software designed to detect physiological aberration, remote video conferencing and monitoring, computerized physician order entry to intervene with therapies as needed, and the opportunity to documented directly into the respective EMRs of the health care organizations where the patients are located. The key limitation with the current state of telemedicine remains the inability to intervene procedurally.

Telecritical care represented the first widespread application of telemedicine technology, because critical care physicians and their expertise in managing complex acute disease were, and to a large extent continue to remain, inaccessible to smaller community hospitals. Telemedicine represented an opportunity to fill the manpower void and to broaden patient access to critical care specialists. Two models of telecritical care evolved simultaneously: (1) the corporate model, wherein a team of the intensivists are hired specifically to provide telecritical care from corporate headquarters, linking expertise with multiple hospitals simultaneously online, and (2) the health system model, wherein a large tertiary care center provides consultative services to either smaller hospitals within the system or local referral bases. Early warning technology and software algorithms are increasingly making it easier to identify at-risk patients.[8] Teleneurology, teleneurosurgery, telecritical care, and/or teleneurocritical care consultation can help facilitate the management of the neurologically impaired patient with respect to immediate interventions, such as the administration of thrombolytic therapy with tissue plasminogen activator (tPA) for stroke,[9,10] anticoagulation reversal in the setting of intraparenchymal or intracranial hemorrhage, blood pressure goals and management, seizure management or prophylaxis, and recommendations for airway management or vasoactive therapy. In many cases, patients might even be spared transfers from small communities to larger cities for diagnoses such as small traumatic subarachnoid hemorrhages, which may not require special intervention or management; not only may such conditions be as easily managed in the community setting as in a tertiary care center, but making the necessary care available immediately and locally would also potentially improve the patient's and family's satisfaction. Telemedicine consultation can easily be multidisciplinary and, as long as the ability to provide procedures and any necessary basic interventions, such as electroencephalography, arterial cannulation, airway support, or central venous cannulation are available, patients can frequently be well managed in community hospital intensive care units (ICUs) with telemedicine support.[11]

Therefore, data demonstrates that telemedicine can not only increase patient access to critical care and subspecialist critical care services, but also improve nursing[12] and patient satisfaction. Typically, in rural and community hospitals, patients in the respective ICUs are managed by internists, family practitioners, surgeons, or hospitalists, although generalists may provide excellent ICU patient care. However, such ICUs are typically lacking in the kind of specialist-driven value that an experienced and highly trained intensivist might add to patient care. The process of introducing a tele-ICU program will require cultural acceptance by the medical staff, which, in turn, will require an understanding that the issue is individual patient care. Tele-ICU physicians can frequently facilitate working relationships by visiting the ICUs with which they are connected, working with the medical staff in medical staff leadership and educational programs, and meeting with the ICU staff to enact standardized protocols and best practices at the bedside.

Financial outcomes with respect to contribution margins have been repeatedly demonstrated to be favorable,[13] especially when the umbrella effect of regional collaboration has been accounted for. Hospitals may strategically leverage telecritical care to increase the volume and intensity of their diagnosis-related group (DRG) payments; they can do this by either increasing services and/or by increasing severity-of-illness or case-mix indices. Hospitals that can broaden their "DRG-reach" are most likely to derive immediate financial benefit from tele-ICU programs. Also, experienced critical care providers can improve hospital reimbursement through more accurate documentation and thereby drive more accurate coding and subsequent reimbursement. On the other hand, even if the hospital's DRG mix does not change, hospitals can still derive an improved bottom line profit margin by decreased ICU and hospital resource utilization, decreased complication rates, and decreased readmission rates. Hospitals may also be able to better negotiate with payers for preferred reimbursement rates based upon the availability of the subspecialist, improved outcomes, and decreased cost of care. Moreover, optimally functioning tele-ICUs allow hospitals to retain the care for their sickest patient population and decrease transfers of patients out of their systems for higher level of critical care. In addition, hospitals may be able to launch a public relations or advertising campaign highlighting the availability of enhanced tele-ICU and/or telemedicine services to the community in an effort to capture market share. Finally, hospitals that have been unsuccessful in recruiting intensivist coverage and to choose to use a tele-ICU program will frequently realize an "opportunity cost" savings by using a standard contract for services rather than using a salaried full time equivalent (FTE) model, hourly reimbursement model, or locum tenens model, thereby decreasing expenses associated with recruitment, salary, and benefits. Reimbursement by government and private payors for telemedicine services continues to evolve. The 2017 American Medical Association Current Procedural Terminology (AMA CPT) Manual introduced modifier 95 to indicate that one of a series of predefined telemedicine services has been provided. Modifier 95 designates synchronous telemedicine services that are rendered via real-time interactive audio and video telecommunication systems and provided by a physician or other health care professional to a patient who is located at the distant site from the provider. DHHS and CMS included critical care consultation codes, Healthcare Common Procedure Coding System (HCPCS) codes G0508 and G0509, to facilitate reimbursement for telehealth services.[14] Telemedicine parity laws mandate that for telemedicine services, commercial payers provide coverage and reimbursement comparable to what they pay for in-person services; at the present time, forty states have either approved or proposed legislation that would allow for full or partial telemedicine parity. A detailed state-by-state analysis of telehealth laws and reimbursement policies has been delineated by the National Telehealth Policy Resource Center.[15] Nonetheless, payor compliance with parity laws is not universal.

Legal risk and liability associated with telemedicine remains an evolving area of tort law. The foundation for liability in medical malpractice will always begin with an analysis of whether a provider-patient relationship had indeed been established. The importance of diligently structuring contracts within the realm of telemedicine relationships cannot be overemphasized. Liability can be influenced greatly by the shifting of risk via contract formation. Contracts should clearly delineate, for example, duties to monitor, duties to inform, duties to supervise, teaching obligations, prescriptive obligations, hours of coverage, malpractice coverage, and responsibility for procedural interventions. Contracts should also address responsibility for ensuring the reliability of the technology and back-up systems as well as third-party and vendor obligations. The liability for ensuring adequate training should also be contractually defined, since it has implications with respect to credentialing, standard of care, and contractual liability. Institutions and providers may share liability for lack of training or improper use of telemedicine technology. Nonetheless, because telemedicine usually involves care by multiple providers, the question of which provider or provider team did in fact have constructive control over the patient at the time of a mishap will generally determine the amount of negligence assigned to each provider. Joint and several liability is a legal principle by which multiple parties can share liability for an adverse event, and that liability may be apportioned to each party based upon a contribution analysis with respect to malfeasance. Therefore, state medical malpractice case law, tort laws, laws regarding telecommunications and electronic technology, and federal laws will all potentially govern potential liability related to allegations of telemedicine-related medical malpractice. Since telemedicine providers are largely consultants, consent-to-treat issues are usually addressed by intermitting telemedicine into the provider care team. Paradoxically, as the adoption of telemedicine becomes increasingly accepted, rural treating physicians or rural hospitals may actually be penalized for not reaching out to potentially available expertise and therefore not utilizing available telemedicine technologies; these inactions would be deemed a failure to appropriately consult in the care of complex patients.

Each hospital has a legal duty to responsibly select its medical staff, and that process of selection is known as credentialing. Providers of medical care within an institution must be appropriately credentialed within that institution; specifically, credentialing not only delineates general privileges such as admitting privileges, but also delineates procedure-specific privileges such as those for critical care. Providers must practice within the scope of their privileges. In addition, licensed providers must also hold a valid license to practice within the state in which they provide services to patients—the place where the patient is located. The unlicensed practice of medicine constitutes a felony. With respect to individual providers, liability for credentialing is minimal as long as the credentials are accurately reported without misrepresentation. Non-physicians participating in telemedicine services must practice within the scope of their certification or licensure. Lawsuits against hospitals related to credentialing via the legal doctrine of negligent credentialing could, in the case of telemedicine, spread liability across institutions. There is an implied specificity with respect to the provider pool such that the hospital receiving telemedicine services be on notice regarding each provider providing telemedicine services.

Compliance with legal and regulatory mandates pertaining to the practice of medicine is complex and extensive. Telemedicine is particularly affected by the HIPAA and HITECH rules governing the protection of personally-identifiable health information as it is stored and transmitted in electronic format. The Federal False Claims Act prohibits knowingly submitting or causing to be submitted false or fraudulent claims for payment to the government. In telemedicine, the threshold for meeting each element of care required to justify reimbursement at a particular level of the Evaluation and Management code is the same as that for an in-person clinical visit; however, the limitations of telemedicine may not allow for each element to be met. The most common telemedicine restriction with respect to federal, state, and private-payor reimbursement contracts is that medical encounters are not considered "medically necessary and appropriate" if the physician was not in face-to-face contact with the patient.

CONCLUSIONS

In conclusion, the future of specialty care in relatively low-volume rural hospitals is likely to be shaped by telemedicine services in at least one way or another. Given the current limited available pool of critical care providers, the even more limited pool of neurocritical-care certified providers, and the continuing incidence of acute critical illnesses including sepsis and stroke, a plan for telemedicine services should be considered as mission critical to both referring community hospitals as well as regional medical centers.

7 · DEVELOPING AND LEADING A SUSTAINABLE HIGH-RELIABILITY, HIGH-PERFORMING UNIT

Theories of Quality, Teamwork, Medical Error, and Patient Safety

THE IMPACT OF CULTURE AND TEAMWORK ON PATIENT OUTCOMES AND EXPERIENCE

In health care, great leadership is absolutely critical to the organization's success. It is axiomatic that an organizational culture that supports cohesive and dedicated teamwork is essential to excellence in patient care. Where leaders participate in team problem solving, there is a positive impact on morale, and the team feels empowered and supported. The practical importance of Tom Peters' principle of "management by walking around" (MBWA) cannot be overstated.[1] When organizational leadership not only encourages but supports disciplined yet compassionate behaviors that focus on a common goal of optimal outcomes, then the patient, family, care team, and institution all succeed together. Health care organizations that do not achieve optimal outcomes frequently lack the leadership culture that is necessary to inspire and support the provider team. The transformational theory of leadership emphasizes a shared sense of mission and requires leaders to communicate a vision that is engaging to team members and creates a sense of unity, collective purpose, and shared goals.[2] Therefore, transformational leaders, through an ability to influence attitude, can motivate a level of performance that exceeds expectations.[3] The collaborative theory of leadership emphasizes collaborative communication strategies through which a collaborative work environment can produce synergy through teamwork.[4] Great leaders, however, not only catalyze commitment to a vigorous pursuit of a clear and compelling vision to stimulate higher performance standards, but also build enduring greatness through a paradoxical blend of personal humility and professional will.[5] Good to great organizations focus first on assembling the right team, rather than defining a vison, and then driving people towards it; greatness is then bred through a team with passion and a focus on being the best, within the context of the overall mission of the organization. Through a process of bringing together disciplined people and using disciplined thought and disciplined action, health care systems can build up and break through the barriers that hold them back from greatness.

Physicians are not typically selected on the basis of a personality of team orientation. The selection process, course of study, and the traditional mindset of personal ownership for each and every therapeutic success and failure is vastly different from managerial cultures that foster and develop teamwork as a core competency. Indeed, "extreme ownership" remains a tenet of military leadership training and is somewhat analogous to traditional medical training with respect to ingrained dedication and responsibility.[6] Nonetheless, the tradition of individualism is being replaced in medical school curricula with increased focus on shared decision-making and shared responsibility.

Characteristics of high-performing teams can be poorly defined but tend to include the following: (1) a solid sense of trust in both each other and in the team's purpose and goals; (2) a clear understanding of goals and expectations; (3) respectful but open communication with an encouragement of contribution; (4) a shared sense of leadership with empowerment; (5) flexibility and adaptability; and (6) an atmosphere that fosters continuous learning.[7,8] The importance of a continuous learning environment, through mutual support and leadership with a focus on group problem-solving, is the foundation of learning organizations. Learning organizations focus on developing three core learning capabilities: (1) fostering aspiration; (2) developing reflective conversation; and (3) understanding complexity.[9] According to Senge, a learning organization employs five disciplines to create a culture of excellence: (1) a shared vision; (2) mental models that describe the presumptions and generalizations by people that define their owns actions and overcome the shortcomings of traditional hierarchical power; (3) personal mastery by which members of the organization develop the strength to be proactive and foster learning to continuously achieve results that are important; (4) team learning whereby team members develop a willingness to shift their mental models and be open to learn from their colleagues; and (5) systems thinking, which creates the synergy of effort and vison to effect great outcomes.

Through cooperative problem-solving, collaboration, and communication, a high-functioning health care team can not only learn and grow, it can foster learning and growth, promote brainstorming and the sharing of viewpoints, and define shared goals and values. High-functioning teams are defined by collaboration, which involves analyzing situations in a culture of shared goals and commitment.

Health care organizations are complex systems. Systems thinking is more than just management-speak, it is a concept that defines how the pieces of the whole work together. The Joint Commission has defined leadership standards essential to the provision of high-quality health care. Inclusive leadership is in health care is essential to the goal of high-quality patient care.

> An organized body of physicians and other licensed independent practitioners has not only the technical knowledge, but also the standing to provide clinical supervision and oversight of its members' clinical care and performance. Therefore, to fail to adequately incorporate into the organization's leadership the licensed independent practitioner leaders who can evaluate and establish direction for the clinical care and decision making of licensed independent practitioners throughout the organization, is to create a fundamental gap in the leadership's capability to achieve the organization's goals with respect to the safety and quality of care, financial sustainability, community service, and ethical behavior.[10]

Tribal leadership is a philosophy by which leadership not only identifies subcultures within the organization but effectively uses principle-based specific leverage points to motivate and energize, through inclusiveness, to foster a remarkably efficient and motivated culture that embraces excellence.[11] Therefore, the challenge of leadership is not only to inspire a shared vision but to enable others, especially professionals within the health care system, to pursue their passion while feeling as though they are capable and powerful leaders within their own rights, to the good of the system.[12] Teamwork and communication are the keys that enable health care professionals to safely and consistently deliver high-quality patient care, and a culture of teamwork is fostered through effective senior leadership in health care institutions.

OVERVIEW OF THE DEVELOPMENT OF CRITICAL CARE AND NEUROCRITICAL CARE IN THE UNITED STATES

Intensive care units (ICUs) represent microsystems within a larger health care system that are defined by their specific leadership culture. Clinical microsystems represent the functional, front-line care units that provide the majority of health care; they are the essential building blocks of larger organizations and of the health care system, and they represent the point of interface between patients and providers. The quality and value of care produced by a large health care system can be no better than the services generated by the small systems of which it is composed. A seamless, patient-centered, high-quality, safe, and efficient health care system cannot be realized without transformational leadership at the level of these essential microsystem building blocks that combine to form the entire care continuum.[13]

Since ICUs represent the safety net by which a health care system cares for its sickest and most vulnerable patients, the culture of the ICU takes on a pivotal importance to the success of the whole hospital. The ICU safety net allows a hospital to admit and care for acutely-ill patients who present to the emergency department, to perform technical, highly complex surgeries and other procedures, and to rescue patients who develop unexpected complications while hospitalized. Without a capable critical care unit, a hospital is limited in the scope and intensity of the services it can provide to its patient community and must refer more complex patients elsewhere, thereby jeopardizing its ability to serve the community in which it operates. In addition, a higher complexity of illness and a greater complexity of care allow a hospital to seek and achieve higher levels of reimbursement and thereby generate the margin that furthers the hospital's mission. In addition to complex patient care, ICUs have also traditionally been home to innovation, research, and teaching. Specialized ICUs have long led innovation in medical technology, treatment, and the setting of standards in patient care.[14] Finally, ICUs also represent a special environment where, when the most complex and intensive care fails to offer benefit, the focus shifts to the compassionate limitation of life support and the delivery of patient- and family-focused end-of-life care.

Johns Hopkins Hospital is credited with the establishment of the first neurosurgical ICU in the United States in 1932; neurosurgeon Walter Dandy envisioned a ward dedicated to the specialized care needs of sick postoperative neurosurgical patients. Later, multidisciplinary specialists with training and experience in the care of patients with critical neurologic illnesses concentrated their expertise in neurocritical care units, both to support neurosurgeons and to more effectively and safely manage patients with non-surgical acute neurologic illnesses, such as ischemic strokes, neuromuscular weakness, and cerebrovascular catastrophes. Specialists who founded and led the first neurocritical care ICUs included neurosurgeons, neurologists, and anesthesiologists.[15] In parallel, nurses with a passion for critical care also developed the subspecialty of critical care nursing. Critical care nurses established the American Association of Cardiovascular Nurses in 1969, which subsequently evolved into the American Association of Critical Care Nurses; later, subspecialty training and certification in critical care nursing followed. The Society of Critical Care Medicine[16] was established in 1970 as a multidisciplinary international organization dedicated to promoting excellence and consistency in the practice of critical care;[17] soon afterwards, critical care became recognized as a separate medical specialty with fellowship training programs and national examination and certification requirements through the American College of Critical Care, created in 1988.[18] Adjunct clinical specialists such as pharmacists, nutritionists, respiratory therapists, and social workers with interests in critical care gravitated to the ICU, where they enhanced the scope of patient care and began to enhance the team model of critical care. The further development of neurocritical care as a subspecialty of critical care brought neurologists into neurocritical care units (at that time led primarily by neurosurgeons and anesthesiologists) and into the care of neurologic patients with life-threatening critical illnesses. Neurocritical care fellowship training programs were established, and the Neurocritical Care Society was founded in 1999 as an international, multidisciplinary medical society, although the organization was not formally established until 2002. Subspecialty certification in neurocritical care was established as a formal demonstration of training and competency. Neurocritical care as a subspecialty was accepted in the United States by the United Council of Neurological Subspecialties in 2006, and the first neurocritical care board examination was held in 2007.[19] In 2004, the journal *Neurocritical Care* was launched to promulgate research and standardization in neurocritical care.[20] Neurocritical care intersects with many of the neuroscience and critical care specialties, and it continues to evolve in its scope of practice and practitioners.[21]

THE IMPORTANCE OF TEAMWORK IN NEUROCRITICAL CARE

High-intensity neurosciences clinician staffing lowers mortality and improves quality of care in ICUs.[22] The Leapfrog Group has published hospital safety standards based on the premise that the quality of care in hospital ICUs is strongly influenced by whether intensivists are providing care and how the staff is organized in the ICU.[23] Mortality rates have been demonstrated to be significantly lower in those hospitals with closed ICUs managed exclusively by board certified intensivists.[24,25,26] Leapfrog contends that more than 54,855 deaths that occur in U.S. ICUs could be avoided if the Leapfrog Group's ICU Physician Staffing Safety Standard were implemented in all urban hospitals with ICUs across the United States.[27] Mortality from critical illnesses, such as acute lung injury and sepsis, ranges from 25 percent to 50 percent, and 20 percent of Americans die in ICUs.[28] With improvements in medical care, especially with respect to the management of complex comorbid conditions, there has been an increase in the rate of sepsis. Sepsis, acute respiratory failure, and renal failure have correspondingly led to a higher utilization of procedures such as mechanical ventilation, bronchoscopy, or renal replacement therapy in ICUs,[29] and these require specialized medical and procedural expertise within a closed, high-intensity model ICU in which ICU-qualified physicians manage patients.[30]

More recently, multidisciplinary team-based critical care has emerged as a model of patient safety[31] in critical care and neurocritical care. It is well established that leadership cultures that emphasize teamwork increase corporate effectiveness. Historically, the health care industry underutilized the fundamentals of corporate teamwork and fostered ineffective team leadership at the physician level.[32] A multidisciplinary care team may be defined as a collaboration of health care workers from different areas of expertise with the goal of providing high-quality, continuous, comprehensive, and efficient health services to patients. Specifically, physician-led multidisciplinary teams that focus on collaboration and continuous learning have demonstrated value,[33] although others have argued that simply employing a team-based structure in a critical care unit does not ensure improved patient outcomes.[34]

A multidisciplinary care model in which physicians, nurses, respiratory therapists, clinical pharmacists, and other staff members provide critical care as a team can complement physician intensivist staffing. Such a multidisciplinary approach takes into consideration the complexities of contemporary critical care and acknowledges the importance of communication within the team to better provide comprehensive care. Care teams blend multidisciplinary skills and focus individuals' unique professional insights and training on each patient's problems; these teams efficiently delegate responsibilities in a way that is commensurate with each member's training and skill set. The multidisciplinary team model of critical care of is endorsed by the Society of Critical Care Medicine and the American Association of Critical Care Nurses.[35] Daily rounds by a multidisciplinary care team were independently associated with lower mortality in ICU patients.[36] For example, the ABCDEF bundle is an evidence-based guide for clinicians to coordinate multidisciplinary ICU patient care. The ABCDEF bundle includes the following: (1) Assess, prevent, and manage pain; (2) Both spontaneous awakening trials and spontaneous breathing trials; (3) Choice of analgesia and sedation; (4) Delirium: assess, prevent, and manage; (5) Early mobility and exercise; and (6) Family engagement and empowerment.[37]

It is indisputable that where professionals are respected for the intellectual capital, they contribute to problem-solving, their level of engagement and dedication rises, and the environment of safety as well as the outcomes is positively impacted. Not only must each member of the team be respected professionally, but each member must also be respected personally as long as he or she remains engaged and dedicated. Creating and nurturing an environment of teamwork may be the single most important role of leadership; in the event of suboptimal outcomes, the effectiveness of leadership must be questioned.

HIGH-RELIABILITY ORGANIZATIONS

The Joint Commission incorporated an accreditation requirement discharging hospital leadership to create and maintain a "culture of safety."[38] In general, high-reliability organizations (HROs) exemplify, in practice, the traits of learning organizations, teamwork, and multidisciplinary collaboration already outlined. HROs have been defined in terms of their results—namely, highly predictable and effective operations in the face of hazards that can harm hundreds or thousands of people at a time.[39] Nonetheless, the concept of HROs has been imported into health care from the industrial sectors, where a preoccupation with safety is critical not only to corporate mission but also to public health. Thus, HROs are those organizations that have demonstrated a record of successful operation within complex, high-hazard domains for extended periods without serious accidents or catastrophic failures. The principles of high reliability extend well beyond the standardization of operating procedures. In fact, the notion of high reliability is considered to be an extension of mindset: persistent collective mindfulness and focus.[40] HROs consciously, through leadership, strive to create an environment in which potential problems are anticipated, detected early, and virtually always responded to early enough to prevent catastrophic consequences. These principles are inherent in error management and are referred to as error anticipation, error detection, and mitigation of effect. Furthermore, the mindset is characterized by five specific cognitive focuses: (1) preoccupation with failure; (2) reluctance to simplify explanations for operations, successes, and failures; (3) sensitivity to operations (situational awareness); (4) deference to frontline expertise; and (5) commitment to resilience. HROs cultivate resilience by relentlessly prioritizing safety over other performance pressures.[41] In order to maintain a high-reliability mindset, everyone must maintain a full sense of ownership in every element of structure, process, and outcome. Freedom to speak up, without criticism or judgment, regarding a potentially dangerous situation must be encouraged. Therefore, the hierarchy of leadership must empower process-level workers with sufficient decision-making authority and deference to expertise so that ownership is preserved and respected. The hallmark characteristic of an HRO is not so much that there are no problems or errors, but that the errors do not impact operations. The High Reliability Health Care Maturity (HRHCM) model is designed specifically to help health care organizations achieve and organizational culture of high reliability with zero patient harm. HRHCM incorporates three major domains critical for promoting HROs: Leadership, Safety Culture, and Robust Process Improvement; the model has consistently achieved good validity.[42]

More than four million admissions occur annually in the United States[43] in the ICU, which is typically is an extremely complex clinical environment. The critical care unit environment represents a high-risk, high-hazard setting that can benefit from high-reliability organizing: the opportunity for error in the ICU is ubiquitous, and critically ill patients are especially vulnerable to harm. Furthermore, flexibility in mindset and response to unexpected events are hallmarks of ICU-based patient care. Since no hospital or health care system has achieved consistent high-reliability excellence, high reliability is considered more of an ongoing process, not a state of achievement.[44] The important corollary is that hospitals are currently characterized by low reliability, which implies strongly that hospitals cannot solve these problems by simply and directly adopting high-reliability principles and practices all at once. On the journey to high reliability, health care organizations and systems would need to operationalize three strategic initiatives: (1) the leadership's commitment to the ultimate goal of zero patient harm, (2) the incorporation of all the principles and practices of a safety culture throughout the organization, and (3) the widespread adoption and deployment of the most effective process improvement tools and methods.[45] Moreover, the inevitable investment required to incorporate these three strategic initiatives into a successful program is that of leadership commitment from the level of the board of trustees and the board of directors through senior leadership and to the level of clinical leaders, because every incremental change depends on visible and genuine leadership commitment.

QUALITY IMPROVEMENT IN HEALTH CARE

It can be reasonably argued that if a critical care unit is well led, embraces the multidisciplinary care team model, and embraces a culture of learning, quality will follow.

The Institute of Medicine (IOM) defined quality as the degree to which health services for individuals and populations increase the likelihood of desired health outcomes and are consistent with current professional knowledge. Despite the intent of the IOM when it defined quality as a health care system concept, the six key dimensions of quality articulated by the IOM remain relevant at the point of care to each individual patient. Health care should be (1) safe, (2) effective, (3) patient centered, (4) timely, (5) efficient, and (6) equitable.[46] True to a long history of health care quality improvement efforts, the precise practical definition of quality in health care remains elusive.

Quality review evolved from utilization review, initially a program intended to review the appropriateness of care, as mandated by the Condition of Participation of the Medicare and Medicaid Programs as Titles XVIII and XIX of the Social Security Act of 1965. The broad reach of utilization review programs soon gave rise to professional standards review organizations (PSROs) established under Medicare to more specifically focus on quality. In 1966, Avedis Donabedian developed a framework within which to assess the quality of care in his orthopedic practice, linking structure and process to outcomes.[47] In 1983, PSROs were replaced by peer review organizations (PROs), which were initially intended to focus on the reduction of unnecessary admissions, unnecessary readmissions, complications, and mortality rates.[48] Congress created the Agency for Health Care Policy and Research (now the Agency for Healthcare Research and Quality [AHRQ]) in 1989 to study geographic variation in health care utilization, cost, and outcomes. The National Committee for Quality Assurance (NCQA) was established as a not-for-profit quality monitoring organization in 1990. The NCQA is credited with the establishment of the Healthcare Effectiveness Data and Information Set and the Consumer Assessment of Healthcare Providers and Systems programs. In 1992, the Health Care Financing Administration established the Quality Improvement Initiative in an effort to achieve evidence-based continuous quality improvement.[49] The National Surgery Quality Improvement Project was established by the Veterans Administration (VA) in 1994 to study surgical mortality in VA hospitals;[50] the program collected risk adjustment and outcome data and was subsequently expanded by the American College of Surgeons as a voluntary quality monitoring and benchmarking database for participating hospitals. The IOM published a transformational treatise in 1999 to underscore the state of health care quality in the United States,[51] and subsequently followed with a blueprint for systemic quality improvement in 2001.[52] In 2010, the Patient Protection and Accountable Care Act (PPACA, more commonly known as the ACA)[53] became law and mandated the creation of a non-profit Patient-Centered Outcomes Research Institute to conduct comparative effectiveness research; the National Quality Strategy, which prohibited the payment of federal funds to states in the event of certain hospital-acquired conditions;[54] and Accountable Care Organizations designed to guide health care systems and providers toward value-based reimbursement through initiatives such as the Quality Reporting and Hospital Value-Based Purchasing Program and the Physician Value-Based Modifier Program.[55] Value-based purchasing (VBP) is a program intended to replace fee-for-service reimbursement; the program bases reimbursement on quality metrics established by payers. Pay for performance is one such VBP initiative whereby health care institutions are evaluated on the basis of their performance on pre-established quality metrics and are then either rewarded or penalized financially on the basis of the quality of care that they provide. For example, in October 2008, the Centers for Medicare and Medicaid Services (CMS) stopped reimbursing hospitals for conditions that patients acquired during their hospital stay. Although VBP remains an attractive theory, especially to both government and private payers, it is unclear whether the complexity of health care will allow for reimbursement constraints without imposing significant access (cost) controls similar to those already in place in countries with single-payer/government-sponsored health care. Public reporting is also becoming mandatory for both institutions and providers under the CMS "Hospital Compare" and "Physician Compare" websites designed to promote transparency in quality and enable consumers to compare results across institutions and providers over time.[56]

Despite legislative mandates and significant government funding, quality improvement remains a cottage industry. Quality assurance and quality improvement models vary greatly between institutions and even between ICUs within single institutions. The reason for variation in quality improvement approaches is largely based on the needs, opportunities, and resources available. Not every quality improvement metric is universally applicable.

The Plan-Do-Study-Act Cycle, also known as the Deming Wheel or Deming Cycle, represents one systematic process for continual improvement of a product, process, or service. Deming emphasized that the process of knowledge growth occurs through learning and is always guided by a theory. Thus, Deming's first step is planning, which involves identifying a goal or purpose, formulating a theory, defining success metrics, and putting a plan into action; the next steps are effecting a change, measuring the effect, and implementing a new process.[57] Deming advocated three core principles that he believed were at the heart of every quality improvement program: (1) that quality improvement is the science of process management; (2) that if an outcome cannot be measured, then it cannot be improved; and (3) in order to manage quality, the key data need to be presented in the optimum format, at the right time, to the right people.

Almost contemporaneously, the Toyota Corporation in Japan implemented Kaizen, a quality program in manufacturing production processes.[58] The Kaizen method strives to advance a process toward perfection by eliminating waste (*muda*) in the workplace (*gemba*).

Subsequently, programs such as Lean, Total Quality Management (TQM), Agile, Waterfall, and Six Sigma were developed by consultants as marketing brands to underscore the quality focus of a product. More recently, Rapid Cycle Performance Improvement (RCPI) has been advocated as an easily flexible intervention typically used to effect short-term, high-intensity performance improvement, especially within health care systems. The attractiveness of RCPI as a concept, especially to quality leaders, underscores the slow response and typically shallow leadership interest and commitment to quality improvement. What is remarkable is that all the methodologies share the core characteristics of (1) leadership, creativity, and innovation; (2) team engagement; and, (3) closed loop performance.[59] Although the each of the various different methodologies may have specific situational applicability, the most important priorities in any quality improvement program remain unchanged and involve continuous surveillance for improvement opportunities, team empowerment and engagement, flexible adaptation, and data collection.

Risk management in health care is not synonymous with quality assurance, although there is substantial overlap and one goal of both disciplines is patient safety. The purpose of risk management is to assess, develop, implement, and monitor risk management plans with the goal of minimizing exposure to legal, administrative, and regulatory risk. Quality assurance programs help avoid and detect risk.

MEDICAL ERRORS

The goals of patient safety and high-quality care and the quest to avoid medical errors stem from the ethical principle of "primum no nocere," or "first, do no harm." In *To Err is Human: Building a Safer Health System*, the IOM reported that medical errors account for at least 98,000 inpatient deaths annually, or at least 270 inpatient deaths daily, making medical error the third leading cause of death in the United States.[60] It is noteworthy that the IOM only looked at errors of omission in its calculation of the incidence of medical error in the United States. The definition of medical error is strongly contextual; error may be defined differently depending on whether the issue is being addressed by clinicians, researchers, quality control specialists, ethicists, insurers, legislators, lawyers, or legislators.[61] The U.S National Patient Safety Foundation defines patient safety as the avoidance, prevention, and amelioration of adverse outcomes or injuries stemming from the process of health care.[62] Medical error has been variably defined as an unintended act (either of omission or commission) or one that does not achieve its intended outcome,[63] the failure of a planned action to be completed as intended (an error of execution), the use of a faulty plan to achieve an aim (an error of planning),[64] or a deviation from the process of care that may or may not cause harm to the patient.[65] James Reason's definition of error distinguishes between errors of execution and errors in planning, acknowledging that both mental/judgmental and physical/technical failures contribute to errors, but fails to recognize errors of omission. In contrast, Lucian Leape's definition recognizes that both actions (acts of commission) and inactions (acts of omission) contribute to medical errors, but fails to recognize intended acts that are based on a faulty plan.

Similarly, an adverse event can be defined as an unintended injury to patients caused by medical management (rather than the underlying condition of the patient) that results in measurable disability, prolonged hospitalization, or both.[66,67] An adverse event is considered to be preventable when there is a failure to follow accepted practice at an individual or system level.[68] Errors are also classified as to whether they are latent or unrecognized errors, which have a high potential for future repetition, or active errors, which generally are violations of rules. Well-designed systems are exemplified by Reason's Swiss Cheese Model of error as those that have several layers of defense that protect against adverse consequences of error "passing through." On the other hand, error-prone systems are characterized by the holes in the Swiss cheese that allow errors to pass or penetrate through and reach the patient.[69] A near miss is such an error, an event that could have had an adverse patient consequence but did not because of safety protocols or processes.[70] Near misses are important because they have potential to recur.

CREW RESOURCE MANAGEMENT

The medical model for team collaboration for patient safety has its origin in the Crew Resource Management or Cockpit Resource Management (CRM) paradigm developed by the airline industry. Studies of aviation mishaps in the 1970s determined that the majority of airline accidents were attributable to pilot or crew errors, frequently because of a breakdown in communication, rather than a mechanical failure.[71] CRM promoted wide recognition of the fact that the majority of crew errors were failures in leadership, team coordination, and decision-making and that human interactions are an integral part of team performance and outcome.[72] Federal Aviation Administration (FAA) and National Aeronautics and Space Administration (NASA) studies repeatedly demonstrated that CRM-trained crews operated more effectively as teams and were able to cope more effectively with non-routine situations than aircrews without CRM training. The essential components of CRM are (1) situational awareness, (2) effective communication, (3) team management or management of group dynamics and conflict resolution, (4) workload management through planning and workload distribution, (5) stress awareness and management, and (6) effective leadership.

Situational awareness can be defined as a continuous perception of self and the relevant environment as they apply to the mission and the ability to execute tasks based on that perception; situational awareness is also referred to as the "big picture." Situational awareness also requires the appropriate interpretation of situational cues so as to recognize that a potential or real problem exists and may require a decision or action. When one's perception matches reality, one is situationally aware. Situational awareness involves integrating all of the information received. One's ability to make a correct decision under any given circumstance depends upon the timely acquisition of appropriate data, accurate assessment of the data and their priority, accurate assessment regarding the probability of outcomes, and assessment of risk. Loss of situational awareness is considered to represent the most important cause of all human performance-related mishaps. Loss of situational awareness occurs in circumstances of attention threats, task saturation, distraction, overly fixated or channelized attention, inattention, habituation, or misdirected peer pressure.[73] Moreover, loss of situational awareness is an important consideration in the risks of digital distraction due to electronic devices (discussed in chapter 6). CRM stresses that teams must become adept at expressing appropriate disagreement and giving and taking feedback; communication requires that the critical information be conveyed clearly, attended to, understood, and acknowledged. Group dynamics in CRM promotes the notion that leadership is a complex process and that a leader's ideas and actions influence the thoughts and behavior of others. The group dynamic paradox inherent in CRM lies in the reconciliation that, in a hierarchical institution, there will exist individual leaders with shared technical responsibilities who are operationally interdependent on each other. Thus, conflict resolution, which is fundamental to problem solving, must be recognized as an opportunity to seek better solutions.[74]

Clearly, the ideas exemplified in the CRM model compose a template for developing and leading a sustainable high-reliability and high-performing (critical care) units. Thus, the U.S. Department of Health and Human Services, the DoD, and the AHRQ jointly developed a program designated as TeamSTEPPS as a model to improve communication and teamwork skills among health care professionals;[75] conceptually, TeamSTEPPS parallels CRM.

MEASURES OF QUALITY IN NEUROCRITICAL CARE

The pursuit of excellence in health care is a fundamental priority; therefore, continuous quality improvement is essential. However, the definition and the measurement of quality in health care remains elusive.[76] Metrics, as quality indicators, may be classified on the basis of whether they are measures of structure, process, or outcome. Some have proposed that metrics include the following: (1) structure indicators, such as the availability of intensivists (hours per day), patient-to-nurse ratio, strategy to prevent medication errors, and measurement of patient/family satisfaction; (2) process indicators, such as length of ICU stay, duration of mechanical ventilation, proportion of days with all ICU beds occupied, and proportion of glucose measurements exceeding 8.0 mmol/L or lower than 2.2 mmol/L; and (3) outcome indicators, such as standardized mortality (Acute Physiology And Chronic Health Evaluation [APACHE] II), incidence of decubitus, and number of unplanned extubations.[77] It is also widely known, but not widely discussed, that quality has become politicized because hospitals and health care systems compete on the basis of quality measures; therefore, reporting bad outcomes or data that may negatively impact a hospital's competitive edge is often tacitly discouraged unless that reporting is legislatively mandated. Metrics should be important, feasible, valid, and actionable.[78]

Standardized mortality ratios, risk adjusted mortality, and risk adjusted outcome data could potentially represent a starting point for optimal data analysis; however, these data are widely impacted by documentation, the acceptance and transfer of patients between hospitals and services within hospitals, and large variations in samples sizes. Admission, length of stay, and readmission data are similarly impacted by unit size and staffing, ward capabilities, and the influences exerted by primary team attendings. Whereas catheter-related urinary tract infections (CAUTIs) may be a good measure of compliance with current recommendations for early urinary catheter discontinuation, there are data to suggest that early catheter discontinuation can be associated with higher rates of delayed acute kidney injury detection. In addition, neurologically ill patients frequently represent the patient population most in need of long-term urinary catheters for management of diabetes insipidus, salt wasting, and subarachnoid hemorrhage fluid balance. Nonetheless, best practices regarding the minimization or elimination of ventilator associated pneumonia,[79] catheter-related bloodstream infections,[80] and CAUTIs should be implemented wherever possible. Thus, there is confusion and uncertainty about the extrapolation of quality of care metrics between types of ICUs.

The environment of care and the team in collaboration achieve the synergy necessary for excellence in patient care. However, intensivist staffing alone may not be sufficient to improve outcome;[81] similarly, the introduction of a neurocritical service without a neurocritical care unit may be insufficient to achieve quality outcomes.[82] Suarez et al. have repeatedly demonstrated that the introduction of a neurocritical care team care model, led by full-time neurosciences clinicians who coordinate care, is associated with significantly reduced in-hospital mortality and length of stay without changes in readmission rates or long-term mortality;[83] in similar studies by other researchers, the outcomes have included lower intensive care unit mortality, higher rates of discharge to a skilled nursing facility, and higher rates of discharge to home.[84] Patients with acute intracerebral hemorrhage may have a more favorable outcome if they are admitted to a neurocritical care unit as opposed to a general ICU.[85] Dedicated neurosciences clinicians and the creation of a neurocritical care team have been shown to positively impact quality outcome metrics such as rates of mortality, CAUTI, central line-associated bloodstream infection, and ventilator-associated pneumonia and, ultimately, to decrease the length of stay. Importantly, the appointment of neurosciences clinicians positively impacted patient satisfaction.[86]

CONCLUSIONS

With the primary goals of patient safety and optimal outcomes, well-led and optimally functioning units are best positioned to provide high-quality care and patient and family satisfaction, and to minimize legal and regulatory risks. Since attitudes reflect culture and influence the processes of care, leadership culture defines the team and its work product.

8 · NEUROLAW AND THE INTEGRATION OF NEUROSCIENCE, ETHICS, AND THE LAW
The New Frontiers

In this chapter we come full circle, but we emerge with greater uncertainty. Whereas we started by finding common themes among ethics, morality and the law, we now find that when we introduce the rapid technological advances in the field of neurosciences into the analysis, the relationship between commonly held beliefs, a specific state of mind, and a state of brain impact not only individual behavioral norms, but also the legal analysis of behaviors. How can we explore the thoughts of our patients? Is it even ethical to do so? If so, who decides, and under what circumstances? What do we do with what we find?

Within the clinical neurosciences, there is often great uncertainty regarding the cognitive capacity of our patients and their prognosis. These are some of the many questions that arise:

- How can we communicate with a patient who has "locked-in" syndrome? How can we potentially explore a patient's wishes for heroic support in a credible way?
- Can we use current or future technology to assess cognitive function in patients in a vegetative state? Is communication possible with such patients?
- If communication were possible with patients in comas or vegetative states, how could that communication change the prognosis and level of care?

Technology-forcing regulations or policies are regulatory strategies that establish unachievable and perhaps economically unfeasible performance standards;

these standards then set incentives for technology development in order to keep up with the regulations or laws. Technology forcing is common in regulatory policy. Less well defined is the converse of technology forcing: law forcing by technology. The legal system can be slow to respond to scientific information and new scientific development in its early stages; sometimes, these developments may not be accepted or even recognized as science. Nonetheless, as new technology emerges, scientific, ethical, and legal questions will inevitably emerge, and these will need our guidance and input as neuroscientists.

NEUROLAW

The term "neurolaw" is attributed to Sherrod J. Taylor, who, in 1991, began to categorize the impact of developments in neuroscience on the law and legal processes.[1] Thus, in general terms, neurolaw refers to an emerging field of interdisciplinary study at the intersection of neurosciences, ethics, law, and social policy development. More specifically, neurolaw explores the relationship between the potential structural, physiological, biochemical, and pharmaceutical bases of cognition and behavior and the consequent legal analyses of cognition and behavior such as propensity, capacity, and state of mind. The implications of neurolaw range from expectations regarding expert witness neuroclinician testimony, to the evolution of legal standards regarding prosecutorial and defensive boundaries, to predictions of a person's potential future behaviors. Neurolaw is therefore an organized attempt to understand the relationship between the law and the brain by applying neuroscientific data within the context of ethical boundaries and legal contentions.[2,3] Neurolaw addresses the interface between neuroscience and legal rules.[4]

LEGAL IMPLICATIONS OF BRAIN INJURY

Neurolaw applies to legal testimony only to the extent that the foundations of behavior can be validated.[5] *Mens rea* is Latin for "guilty mind." Determination of *mens rea* is a legal construct that allows the criminal justice system to implicate intent. The Model Penal Code recognizes four escalating levels of *mens rea*: (1) purpose/intent, (2) knowledge, (3) recklessness, and (4) negligence. In order to be found guilty under a criminal statute, unless the statute specifically states otherwise, the defendant must commit all elements of the crime with a mental state of recklessness or greater. A person is said to act "purposefully" (or intentionally) if he or she acts with the intention that the action causes a certain result. A person is said to act "knowingly" if he or she is aware that the conduct will cause a specific result. A person is said to act "recklessly" if he or she is aware of a substantial risk that a certain result will occur because of his or her actions. Finally, a person is said to act "negligently" if he or she should have been aware of a substantial and unjustifiable risk of a specific consequence that would result from his or her actions.[6]

Expert testimony regarding state of mind, or *mens rea*, has significant implications within the criminal context and forms the basis for legal terms of art such as "malice," "intent," "knowingly," "recklessly," and "willfully." Expert opinion, although well respected, can differ, and such variability in expert opinion has important ramifications for an accused's personal freedoms and for the justice system. If neuroscience could correlate neurophysiology with a state of mind, expert testimony could be validated, replicated, and fair.

Neuroscience considerations are increasingly being applied to the legal areas of intellectual property law, tort law, consumer law, health law, employment law, and criminal law.[7] Moreover, Constitutional law becomes implicated not only at a legal level but at an ethical level, since a question of whether or not an individual's neural makeup or functioning could constitute legally discoverable evidence, and whether or not such an intrusion into one's personal thoughts or motivations, potentially arising from neurochemical and neuroanatomical processes, would challenge individual rights and freedoms.[8]

The legal system necessarily assumes that humans are "practical reasoners" and that a conscious deliberation underlies actions, free will, and free decisions in the absence of duress or deceit. Nonetheless, there are many examples of neurological disorders in which either there is a will to act and action is not possible, or there is action without will. Tourette's syndrome is one example of a condition where actions occur in the absence of free will, and there is no conscious override ability to repress actions. Conventionally, behavior has been in the realm of psychiatry or psychology, whereas neurologic disorders have been addressed by neurology or neurosurgery. Biology and decision-making are now increasingly seen as intertwined. Neuroimaging advances may now be at the threshold of elucidating the functional microcircuitry and functional biochemistry that link brain to behavior, and, as this happens, the law will need to reconcile with neuroscience to both help those in need but also to potentially protect the vulnerable.[9]

Critical neuroscience, like neurolaw, endeavors to study links between psychological theories of violence, criminality, deception, and general antisocial behavior through a mapping of these behaviors to cognitive constructs and neurobiological evidence to test the assumption that social and psychological approaches to explanations of crime can be superseded by neuroscience.[10]

Neurolaw necessarily addresses highly controversial situations. Concrete legal examples might include any of the following:

- At what point will a person with latent dementia no longer be liable for contract obligations? Or, at what point can a person with latent dementia no longer contract?

- Can the person whose status is immediately post closed head injury and concussion be administered the Miranda warning?
- What are the limits of neuromonitoring regarding tests for falsity or recall?
- Is it ethical to use neuroscientific techniques to predict human behavior, establish a possible propensity for criminal behavior, or evaluate incarcerated persons for potential future offenses?
- Is there a reliable tangible neuroscientific measure to support or contend an insanity defense?
- As a parallel to plastic surgery, should cognitive enhancers become widely available to allow for a competitive edge in school or the workplace? Or, should cognitive enhancers be required in certain fields of work to minimize the risk of error?

As neurosciences continue to evolve and there is an increasing body of data to support scientifically valid conclusions, neurolaw will bridge the various disciplines of neuroscience, law, social sciences, and ethics.

FUNCTIONAL BRAIN IMAGING, CONSCIOUSNESS, AND BEHAVIOR

The advent of computed tomography (CT) imaging made it possible to use rapid noninvasive brain imaging to evaluate structural anomalies and lesions. CT also catalyzed the development of positron emission tomography (PET) and magnetic resonance imaging (MRI), which not only made possible functional imaging but also created an opportunity to examine neurobiological correlates of behavior.[11] Advances in cognitive neuroscience also increasingly make it possible to use neurophysiological techniques to measure and assess mental states within diverse cognitive states.[12] Event-related potentials (ERPs) as measured by electroencephalography (EEG) have long been used in neurophysiological research.[13] Polygraph machines have long been used to measure physiological reactions associated with anxiety, such as diaphoresis, respiratory rate, blood pressure, and galvanic potentials in the skin, which are presumed to correlate with sympathetic nervous system changes; these reactions have then been used to infer the state of mind of the testifier in question. More recent advances in functional brain imaging include magnetoencephalography (MEG), magnetic resonance spectroscopy (MRS), and functional magnetic resonance imaging (fMRI). Blood flow and metabolism in the brain are measured by fMRI. MEG can be used to measure fields of electric currents in the brain to identify aberrant brain activity; it can also be used to localize seizure focuses and perform cortical localization in preparation for brain surgery (e.g., epileptogenic focus excision and/or tumor excision).

The use of functional brain imaging techniques, such as PET, single-photon emission computed tomography (SPECT), and fMRI allows the monitoring of neuronal and neurochemical patterns in the living human brain during various states of functioning.[14] fMRI especially is increasingly being used to develop three-dimensional mapping of cortical and subcortical brain activities. In 2010, a grouping in Europe studied patients with severe brain injuries, including vegetative state and minimally conscious state, by using fMRI to detect imaging correlates of functional communication and to otherwise measure and detect awareness; the researchers found that among the 23 patients who received a diagnosis of being a vegetative state, four demonstrated the ability to willfully modulate the brain activity to mental imagery consistent with behavioral evidence of awareness.[15] Further studies continued to reveal that spatial navigation and motor imagery correlated with volitional brain activity, suggesting that fMRI could potentially establish consciousness in noncommunicative brain-injured patients.[16] Subsequently, researchers hypothesize the concept of a "default mode network" (DMN) of brain function,[17] through observations that a number of areas, including the precuneus,[18] bilateral temporo-parietal junctions, and medial prefrontal cortex, were more active at rest than when the subjects were involved in an attention-demanding cognitive task. The fMRI provided data to suggest that signal strength within the DMN could possibly be a reliable indicator of a patient's level of consciousness, differentiating unconscious patients such as those in a coma or vegetative state from patients who are minimally conscious or have locked-in syndrome.[19]

The theoretical ramifications of fMRI with respect to awareness and potential communication in patients with severe brain injury or locked-in states with motor paralysis could have profound ethical and legal significance, as this technology could, at some point, be used to establish the presence of pain or anxiety or communicate regarding wishes for continued life support or heroic interventions. Pain and suffering are important determinants of damages in personal injury litigation, but they are not easily verifiable. A reliable objective measure of pain would revolutionize tort litigation and pain management. Moreover, at present, the severity of vegetative states is assumed to be homogeneous; potentially, fMRI may present opportunities for identification of subclasses of brain injury severity and also prognostic determinations in such patients.

Resting-state fMRI has also been used to image functional brain connectivity and is thus increasingly under consideration as a potential marker for Alzheimer's disease (AD), because in such degenerative disease states, functional brain changes are widely believed to precede structural brain changes. Structural and functional neuroimaging studies may help visualize dysfunctional nodes and networks underlying neurologic and psychiatric disease and thereby develop potential future targets for neuromodulation.[20] Noninvasive functional imaging, together with functional manipulation of the human brain, is creating new opportunities and treatment modalities, such as psychosurgery, for disorders of the human mind, mood, and behavior.[21] The ethical implications of such imaging and interventions are enormous both with respect to the potential for abuse and with respect to the forced normalization of social behavior.

Brain fingerprinting detects concealed information stored in the brain by measuring a specific EEG ERP, the P300 Memory and Encoding Related Multifaceted Electroencephalographic Response (P300-MEMER), which is elicited by stimuli that are significant in a specific context such as EEG responses to words or pictures relevant to a crime scene or terrorism event. Brain fingerprinting detects information by measuring cognitive information processing and to date, unlike the classic lie detector, no one has beaten a brain fingerprinting test with countermeasures.[22]

Research linking the brain to antisocial and criminal behavior also raises neurophilosophical questions concerning our liberty.[23] Some neuroscientists believe that "minds are simply what brains do."[24] Some researchers have hypothesized that brain activity associated with deliberate decisions may actually be detected before the brain itself becomes conscious of making the decision.[25] Brain lesions are known to affect behavior as well as mood. Such behaviors and cognitive states are pathological, caused by the disease or lesion. Cognitive neuroscience may speak to at least two familiar conditions of criminal responsibility: intention and sanity. If in fact some behaviors can be initiated by the brain at a subconscious level, the question of free will and therefore liability will require ethical and legal reconsiderations. Liability for criminal behavior requires a specific state of mind, a *mens rea*, which, if it is in fact subconscious and proven to be so, could theoretically require a reconsideration of how we define intent.

Aggressive behaviors associated with seizure disorders have been previously well described, and, for the most part, such patients are thought to share common characteristics. These patients are generally younger males with a long history of drug-resistant epilepsy and lower than average intelligence; the onset of aggression usually occurs in the postictal state and is generally follows a cluster of seizures, is of sudden onset, is related to stressful situations, and is exacerbated by alcohol abuse.[26] Therefore, prediction of such behavior might be possible. It has been hypothesized that homicidal and violent behaviors associated with postictal psychosis may be avoided with early recognition and treatment.[27]

The legal implication of reliable prediction of a predilection for bilateral behavior is exemplified by the Tarasoff doctrine.[28] Under *Tarasoff v. Regents of University of California*, a therapist who determines, or reasonably should have determined, that patient may pose a serious danger to others, has a duty to exercise reasonable care and to protect the foreseeable victim. In *Ewing v. Goldstein*, the decision in *Tarasoff* is extended to include reasonable bases for protection, which may be decided by a jury on the basis of prior knowledge.[29] Furthermore, in addition to epilepsy and seizure disorders, structural lesions of the brain are also associated with violence and aggressive behavior. For example, ventromedial frontal lobe lesions may increase the risk of violent behavior,[30] and the dorsolateral prefrontal cortex is associated with an implicit attitude toward violence that under most normal situations would be considered inappropriate.[31] Evidence appears to be strongest for the association between focal prefrontal damage and impulsive subtype aggressive behavior.[32]

Although there is currently no cure for AD or dementia, neuroimaging techniques and biomarkers may identify neural tissue changes in people with AD before they manifest observable behavioral changes.[33] At the present time, there is evidence to suggest that PET can accurately diagnose AD; however, at this time, there is no evidence to suggest that a diagnosis of AD through PET can alter the clinical course of the disease or patient outcome.[34]

The Alzheimer's Disease Neuroimaging Initiative is an ongoing, longitudinal, multicenter study designed to develop clinical, imaging, genetic, and biochemical biomarkers for the early detection and tracking of AD.[35] The legal and ethical considerations regarding the manner of legal treatment of a person who does not yet exhibit behavioral symptoms but whose brain is documented to have already been altered by the disease process are unclear. Core legal domains such as contract formation, liability in torts, and *mens rea* in criminal law all impact issues of "capacity," "competency," and "liability," and legal proof may be affected by AD biomarkers.[36]

It is increasingly well accepted that neurodegenerative diseases may cause neural dysfunction in brain areas that are involved in the modulation of judgment, executive function, emotional processing, sexual behavior, violence, and self-awareness and that such neurobiological dysfunction might in turn lead to antisocial and criminal behavior.[37] Examples of such neurodegenerative diseases include AD, behavioral variant of frontotemporal dementia, semantic variant of primary progressive aphasia, Huntington's disease, human immunodeficiency virus–related dementia, and alcohol-induced dementia.[38]

Although the link between neuroimaging and behavior is a highly controversial and evolving area of neuroscience research as well as of ethical and legal debate, the important conclusion is that the subconscious neurophysiology may influence actions, potentially causing actors to act in ways they would not have, and thus it is reasonable to ask: can a tumor or brain injury mitigate or nullify responsibility for illegal conduct?

TRAUMATIC BRAIN INJURY

Traumatic brain injury (TBI) is a nondegenerative, noncongenital insult to the brain from an external mechanical force, possibly leading to permanent or temporary impairment of cognitive, physical, and psychosocial functions, with an associated diminished or altered state of consciousness. TBI comprises a spectrum of injuries to the brain encompassing (1) open head injuries that include penetrating or blast/avulsive cranial trauma and (2) closed head injuries, which are the result of blunt impact injuries to the head.

With respect to closed TBIs, the mechanism of injury generally involves a force transmitted to the head or body that results in damage to the brain matter and causes a subsequent functional impairment. Depending on the severity, TBI may not be amenable to neuroimaging. TBI severity can be quantified by using various measures such as the Glasgow Coma Scale score, the presence or duration of loss of consciousness, post-traumatic amnesia, or the degree of functional impairment. Loss of consciousness occurs in less than 10 percent of patients who suffer a concussion; however, when it does occur, it provides incontrovertible evidence of significant acute TBI.[39]

Closed TBI is also divided into acute and repetitive, and it is also classified as mild, moderate, or severe. Closed head injuries cause the brain to undergo shear and rotational stresses that may tear axons, disrupt neural pathways, or contuse the brain by direct (coup) or indirect (contra coup) movements within the cerebrospinal fluid against the inner table of the skull. Shear stresses are most frequently due to deceleration-acceleration forces and rotation forces. In some cases, the injuries can cause petechial hemorrhages or local or generalized cerebral edema. Symptoms will depend on the severity of the injury.[40]

The term "concussion" is derived from the Latin *concussus*, which means "to shake violently."[41] In its mildest form, a patient with a mild concussion will be dazed or momentarily confused. In the case of more severe injury, loss of consciousness may occur and be followed by a brief period of amnesia. Thus, a concussion is a mild TBI, which is most often sustained during sports injuries, falls, motor vehicle accidents, and blunt weapon assault. Concussion is difficult to diagnose and treat. An appropriate index of suspicion is vital to the diagnosis; that index of suspicion is based on both the mechanism of injury as well as the history. Symptoms frequently include disorientation and temporal amnesia. The American Medical Society for Sports Medicine, The American Academy of Neurology, and the International Conference on Concussion in Sport have developed and published evidence and consensus-based guidance for the diagnosis and management of sports-related concussions. The diagnosis of concussion can be largely clinical without specific diagnostic signs, imaging abnormalities, or laboratory abnormalities. Concussions generally cannot be seen on CT or MRI scans, but they represent real brain injuries and are thus a type of functional brain injury rather than a pathological diagnosis.

Animal models of concussion demonstrate that neurochemical changes in the post-traumatic brain develop over hours and may last up to 10 weeks. After injury, there is a release of excitatory neurotransmitters, particularly glutamate, which bind to N-methyl-d-aspartate (NMDA) receptors; this event causes a transmembrane flux of potassium into the extracellular space and is followed by an influx of calcium into the cell, causing a transient hypermetabolic glycolytic state with associated lactate production.[42] The loss of consciousness is thought to be precipitated by the rotational forces at the junction of the midbrain and thalamus, resulting in a transient disruption of the reticular activating system.[43] The search for human biomarkers to help diagnose and classify the severity of traumatic brain injury continues.[44] For example, a single serum concentration elevation of glial fibrillary acidic protein (GFAP), ubiquitin carboxy-terminal hydrolase L1 (UCH-L1), or S100 calcium-binding protein B (S-100beta), any of which can occur within 6 hours of head injury, may be useful in the identification and stratification of the severity of brain injury in patients with head trauma. A positive GFAP is associated with the presence of concussion but the absence of biomarkers and cannot reliably exclude a diagnosis of concussion.[45] GFAP proteins are present in the blood of concussion patients, and they are detectable for up to a week after the injury. There may be less invasive measures of brain injury; a buccal salivary swab is being developed to diagnose concussion without the need for a blood test.[46] In addition, matrix metallopeptidase 2 (MMP-2), C-reactive protein (CRP), and brain type creatine isoenzyme (CKBB) biomarkers can successfully predict postconcussion injury visualized on CT, and a serum-based biomarker panel can accurately differentiate patients with complicated mild TBI from those with uncomplicated mild TBI.[47]

Postconcussion Syndrome (PCS) is a complex set of acute cognitive impairments that result from concussion. Headache is the most common symptom of PCS; other symptoms include vertigo, disequilibrium, and cognitive difficulty affecting memory and concentration. The recognition of chronic traumatic encephalopathy (CTE) as a clinical syndrome evolved from the terms encephalitis pugilistica or dementia pugilistica, which referred to progressive dementia. CTE has now been recognized as an occupational hazard, especially in athletes, who are frequently subjected to concussions or subconcussive repetitive closed head injury. Early descriptions of traumatic encephalopathy,[48] dementia pugilistica,[49] and CTE[50] subsequently gave way to clinical-pathologic findings characterized by cerebellar or extrapyramidal disorders with dysarthria and motor deficits associated with cognitive and behavioral disturbances. In 2002, however, the possibility that repetitive concussions could result in chronic brain damage and a progressive neurologic disorder was raised by a postmortem evaluation of a retired National Football League player.[51] Subsequently, the term *traumatic encephalopathy syndrome* was introduced.[52]

Concussion scores have been used to help practitioners determine the risk of concussion after injury. For example, the Standardized Concussion Assessment Tool, the Symptom Checklist, the Standardized Assessment of Concussions, and the Balance Error Scoring System are validated for assessment of concussion.[53] Concussion symptoms include photosensitivity, headaches, fatigue, and poor concentration and may include loss of consciousness.[54] The evidence underlying the mechanisms of the neuropathology and clinical features of CTE is still limited.[55] Severe concussion, on the other hand, may have neuroanatomical correlates. Histopathologic changes can occur at microscopic levels in patients after a single episode of TBI.[56] Similar to the legal and ethical considerations involved in AD patients who may have subclinical disease and thus have an impairment in neurocognitive functioning that in turn may impair their judgment, patients with a TBI, such as a concussion, may have a similar subclinical impairment.

The legal effect of acute TBI and mild concussion is important, for example, in the case of a person who is involved in a violent altercation or accident and is subsequently questioned by the police. The Miranda warning protects the Fifth Amendment constitutional rights of custodial suspects against self-incrimination. The U.S. Supreme Court decided *Miranda v. Arizona* in 1966, and the holding applies to all jurisdictions. Under *Miranda*, a person must be informed of four rights prior to interrogation: (1) the right to remain silent, (2) that anything said can and will be used in an adverse way in a court of law, (3) the right to an attorney, and (4) that if the person cannot afford an attorney, one will be appointed on that person's behalf.[57] Several U.S. jurisdictions have added additional rights. In addition, the wording and sentence complexity of Miranda warnings and waivers can vary significantly from jurisdiction to jurisdiction. For individuals to knowingly, intelligently, and voluntarily waive their rights, they must both understand and appreciate those rights. Court decisions have established a totality of circumstances test for evaluating the validity of a rights waiver decision; these require the court to consider the suspect's capacities as well as the procedures and circumstances surrounding the waiver. The knowing requirement component presupposes more than a simple understanding and instead requires an appreciation of the significance of the right as it applies to the situation. The waiver must be made voluntarily, which requires that a suspect waive his or her rights independently, free from coercion or duress. Similar to the doctrine of informed consent, without an understanding of the implications, consent or waiver is meaningless: "a person makes a knowing and intelligent waiver of Miranda rights when he has full awareness of the nature of the right being abandoned and the consequences of its abandonment."[58] A variety of cognitive testing instruments have been developed in the context of Miranda waivers, and there is general agreement that among certain demographic groups, such as adolescents, the implications of Miranda may not be well understood.[59,60]

In *Colorado v. Jewell*, a case involving an intoxicated suspect arrested after his car rolled over during a police chase, the Colorado court considered the potential impact of intoxication on the defendant's Miranda waiver; the court relied on a prior decision in *People v. Platt*, which held that self-induced intoxication diminishes a defendant's mental faculties but does not necessarily invalidate a Miranda waiver.[61] In *Jewell*, the court reaffirmed that "intoxication only invalidates an otherwise valid Miranda waiver if the court finds through a preponderance of the evidence that the defendant was incapable of understanding the nature of his rights and the ramifications of waiving them."[62] Thus, the rebuttal of voluntariness with respect to waiver of a Miranda warning is a high legal standard. Still, if advances in neurosciences and an understanding of mild TBI and concussion can demonstrate that organic brain injury, as an acute and not self-induced confusional state, can in fact demonstrably interfere with cognition to the extent of not understanding the implications of a Miranda waiver, the law may need modification. In fact, under the doctrine of informed consent in the medical setting, medications and acute delirium are widely held to invalidate informed consent.

COGNITIVE ENHANCEMENT

Human behavior comprises molecular, cellular, structural, and neural circuit determinants. Just as psychopharmacology has been applied to psychiatric disorders, neuropharmacology is the use of drugs to manage neurologic disorders; however, the distinction may be increasingly blurring. Initially, molecular biology defined receptors and their ligands; subsequently, neuropharmacology introduced chemical compounds that modulated neurotransmission and altered behavior. The modern era has ushered in molecular neuropharmacology, which includes advances in pharmacogenetics and pharmacogenomics using genomic and proteomic technologies along with genome mapping to a potentially begin an era of gene therapy for neurologic disorders. For the treatment of conditions such as attention-deficit/hyperactivity disorder (ADHD), drugs acting on the noradrenergic and dopaminergic systems, such as methylphenidate[63] and atomoxetine, are commonly used;[64] in the treatment of neurodegenerative disorders such as AD and Parkinson's disease, acetylcholinesterase inhibitors (AChEIs) and memantine [an NMDA receptor antagonist] represent commonly used standard treatment approaches.[65] Within the realm of clinical neurosciences, performance-enhancing medications have been used with various success in the care of patients with severe neurologic impairment, such as stroke patients, TBI patients, and patients with severe cognitive decline.

The term "brain enhancement" refers to pharmacologic (and non-pharmacologic) interventions that improve cognitive function and performance. Nootropics (Greek *noos* for "mind" and *tropos* for "turn") refer to smart drugs and cognitive enhancers, which are substances that improve cognitive functions, particularly executive functions, such as memory, creativity, or motivation, in otherwise healthy individuals.[66]

Cognitive enhancement typically impacts the realms of (1) learning and memory, (2) concentration and attention, (3) cognitive processing speed, (4) visual-spatial relationship intubation, and (5) enhanced executive functions including planning ability and the ability to carry out abstract reasoning. With cognitive enhancement, pharmacologic interventions to enhance performance begin to pose questions similar to surgical interventions designed to enhance appearance.

Interventions with risk are justified based on a risk/benefit ratio; all interventions and all treatments have some level of risk. In the event in which interventions and treatments have risks and the benefits are personally desired but not necessarily medically indicated, interventions such as cognitive enhancement begin to have ethical ramifications.[67]

Although current nootropic compounds can offer, at best, modest improvements in cognitive performance, it is certain that more effective compounds will be developed in the future and that their off-label use will increase. One sphere in which the use of these drugs may be commonplace is by healthy students within academia.[68] Students have long used methylphenidate and dextroamphetamine to enhance cognitive functioning as well as intellectual stamina during studying and test taking. Armed Forces have long used dextroamphetamine to enhance performance and reaction time. More recently, modafinil has been introduced into the Armed Forces to maintain acceptable levels of mood and performance during periods of sleep deprivation.[69] Although the physiologic long-term ramifications of such nootropic compounds have not been well-defined, these compounds do confer a competitive edge. At an ethical level, the question of whether such a competitive edge is justifiable, especially in civilian populations in which certain segments of the population may have access to these compounds and others may not, raises issues regarding equality. At a different level, the question of whether civilians (such as surgeons) charged with tasks that require high levels of concentration and vigilance as well as sustained performance should be encouraged to use performance-enhancing agents is also a subjective ethical debate. Finally, whether the prohibition of nootropics can be effectively enforced is doubtful. As nootropic use becomes widespread among students in the future, the discussion of this issue will become more pressing in the years to come.[70] Therefore, key ethical issues regarding pharmacologic performance enhancement include the following: (1) medical safety, (2) authenticity of thought versus performance under the influence, (3) coercion of use, (4) unequal access, (5) and whether or not cognitive enhancement constitutes an unfair advantage.[71] Many argue that the use of cognition-enhancing drugs does not unnaturally cheapen accomplishments achieved under their influence[72] Thus, the legal system will need to potentially re-evaluate present restrictions on such compounds and potentially face public policy arguments that could claim that widespread cognitive enhancement provides a social benefit. At the same time, the legal system will need to monitor abuse and addiction as well as setting a standard for assessing whether or not errors or accidents rising from cognitive enhancement are related to medication failure, personal idiosyncrasies, or exhaustion.

CONCLUSIONS

Neuroscientists are in a position to serve society by contributing special knowledge and expertise to legal proceedings.[73] *Black's Law Dictionary* defines an expert witness as one "qualified by knowledge, skill, experience, training, or education to provide a scientific, technical, or other specialized opinion about the evidence or a fact issue."[74]

In federal and state courts, the admissibility of scientific expert testimony in the last century has been governed by one of three legal standards. From *Frye v. United States*,[75] the "general acceptance" test requires that any technique or method introduced in court be generally accepted by the relevant community of scientists. Some states, such as New York, still adhere to the *Frye* standard. In federal courts, the Daubert standard (from *Daubert v. Merrell Dow Pharmaceuticals*) defines the admissibility of expert evidence on the basis of the following criteria:

1. Whether the theory or technique in question can be (and has been) tested;
2. Whether it has been subject to peer review and publication;
3. Its known or potential error rate and the existence and maintenance of standards controlling its operation; and
4. Whether it has attracted widespread acceptance within a relevant scientific community.[76]

In *Daubert*, the Supreme Court decided that, while admissible scientific evidence need not be known with certainty, it must rest on a valid foundation of scientific knowledge. Although *Daubert* is widely accepted as the standard, some states continue to use the admissibility test articulated in *Frye*, which requires that expert evidence "have gained general acceptance in the particular field in which it belongs."[77] *Daubert* has been recently modified through the standard set in *Kumho Tire Company v. Carmichael*,[78] although this is not in itself a new standard. It has been argued that although the federal rules of evidence govern admissibility of scientific evidence, it might be reasonable to expect that objective and nonobjective opinion might together be admitted as expert opinion;[79] however, this is not presently a legal standard. In *United States v. Semrau*, the courts disallowed a motion to introduce fMRI-based deception detection as evidence, ruling that fMRI failed to meet the standards of general acceptance and known error rates outlined by *Daubert*.[80]

The science continues to evolve and is forcing the law to adapt. The evolving science will drive controversy in the fields of law and ethics. Neuroscientists must be at the front line of these developments.

9 · AFTERWORD

The practice of medicine is highly regulated, involving multiple layers of hospital-based, state, and federal regulations. Practitioners need to be aware of all the regulations and rules that impact their specific practices in order to minimize the risk of disciplinary proceedings, which can adversely affect both their reputations and their livelihoods. In addition, practitioners who assume leadership roles must be prepared to work diligently to create and cultivate a culture of identification and teamwork to optimize unit functioning, patient safety, and outcomes. There are a myriad of criteria that leaders must take into consideration throughout daily operations as well as in strategic planning for the future. Although the risk of medical malpractice is potentially present in every patient encounter, a multidisciplinary focus with medication and patient safety is a key line of defense. The future of neurocritical care, like the future medicine, is both exciting and uncertain. New technologies, medications, and procedures will undoubtedly bring both rewards and challenges as well as legal and regulatory risks.

Legal risk mapping is best accomplished with partners who understand the administrative and legal/regulatory environment so as to prepare adequately for changes and opportunities.

ACKNOWLEDGMENTS

When I think of where my learning began, I remember my mother taking me on my first visit to the public library; thereafter, never a day went by without my mom and dad asking what books I had read that day and what lessons I had learned. Gene Roddenberry and *Star Trek* not only inspired a voyage of lifelong discovery but also taught me my first lessons on cultures, ethics, and the hope for the future: IDIC—infinite diversity in infinite combinations. Roddenberry also taught me that as important as logic is, there is no substitute for humanism. Throughout my formative years I was fortunate to have the company of friends whose competitive spirit and innate curiosity rivaled my own. I must thank a long line of teachers and professors who not only pushed me harder but also opened my mind to infinite possibilities. From there, I realized that I and I alone would define the limits of learning, but I also realized that knowing for knowing's sake was not enough and it was all about what could be accomplished through knowledge. So, it was obvious, first medical school, then graduate business school, and finally law school . . . all with the aim of seamlessly navigating the various disciplines but with the end goal of constant contribution—to patients, clients, families, health systems, professional societies, and of course, society.

First, I especially thank my lifetime mentor, Professor Peter J. Papadakos, who has not only been an inspirational role model but also a source of constant support. Dr. Papadakos, in whom the "teaching lamp is always lit" taught me not only critical care but the skill to care for the critically ill patient. In addition to a great deal of advice and support on so many other projects, Dr. Papadakos first presented me with the opportunity to embark on this project. I thank Professor Ronald A. Gabel for believing in me and giving me an opportunity to purse my dreams in the field of anesthesiology. I thank Professor Phillip Boysen for seeing the potential in me and supporting my professional career when I was fresh out of fellowship and still finding my way. More recently, I thank Dr. Ralph P. Pennino, without whose mentorship, support, and friendship this project could not be possible; Dr. Pennino continues to inspire me to make a difference—every day.

Lastly and most importantly, I thank my parents for instilling in me a lasting and deeply ingrained work ethic and both a love for and a respect for learning, life, and the world around us; my baby sister, without whose admiration all of this would mean less; and my loving wife, Doris, who is my life companion and best friend, and without whom none of this could be possible.

NOTES

CHAPTER 1 MORALITY, ETHICS, AND THE LAW

1. Patrick Devlin, *The Enforcement of Morals* (Oxford: Oxford University Press, 1959).
2. Dorothy Lee, *Freedom and Culture* (Saddle River, NJ: Prentice Hall, 1959).
3. John Stuart Mill, *On Liberty* (Mineola, NY: Dover Press, 2002).
4. Morris Ginsberg, *On Justice in Society* (Baltimore: Penguin Books, 1965), 50–73.
5. *The Constitution of the United States of America* (New York: Barnes and Noble Books, 1995).
6. H. Widdows, "Western and Eastern Principles and Globalised Bioethics," *Asian Bioethics Review* 3, no. 1 (2011): 14–22.
7. D. P. Sulmasy, "What Is an Oath and Why Should a Physician Swear One?" *Theoretical Medicine and Bioethics* 20, no. 4 (August 1999): 329–346.
8. Hippocrates, "Hippocratic Oath," trans. Ludwig Edelstein in *The Hippocratic Oath: Text, Translation, and Interpretation* (Baltimore: Johns Hopkins Press, 1943).
9. R. D. Orr et al., "Use of the Hippocratic Oath: A Review of Twentieth Century Practice and a Content Analysis of Oaths Administered in Medical Schools in the U.S. and Canada in 1993," *Journal of Clinical Ethics* 8, no. 4 (1997): 377–388.
10. A. C. Kao and K. P. Parsi, "Content Analyses of Oaths Administered at U.S. Medical Schools in 2000," *Academic Medicine* 79, no. 9 (September 2004): 882–887.
11. "A Modern Hippocratic Oath by Dr. Louis Lasagna," Physician Oaths, AAPS, accessed November 11, 2017, http://www.aapsonline.org/ethics/oaths.htm.
12. "Declaration of Geneva of the World Medical Association," Physician Oaths, AAPS, accessed November 11, 2017, http://www.aapsonline.org/ethics/oaths.htm.
13. "Model Rules of Professional Conduct," American Bar Association, accessed November 11, 2017, https://www.americanbar.org/groups/professional_responsibility/publications/model_rules_of_professional_conduct/model_rules_of_professional_conduct_table_of_contents.html.
14. E. D. Pellegrino, "Thomas Percival's Ethics: The Ethics beneath the Etiquette," *Thomas Percival, Medical Ethics* (Birmingham, AL: Classics of Medicine Library, 1985), 1–52.
15. "AMA Code of Medical Ethics," American Medical Association, accessed November 11, 2017, https://www.ama-assn.org/delivering-care/ama-code-medical-ethics.
16. D. S. Agliano, "Study Aid-in-Dying as End-of-Life Option," *CEJA Report 5-A-13* (Chicago: Council on Ethical and Judicial Affairs, American Medical Association, 2013).
17. M. Rubin et al., "The Code of Professional Conduct for the Neurocritical Care Society," *Neurocritical Care* 23, no. 2 (October 2015): 145–148.
18. "About NCS," Neurocritical Care Society, accessed November 11, 2017, http://www.neurocriticalcare.org/About-Us/Bylaws-Procedures-Codes-of-Professional-Conduct.
19. "American Academy of Neurology Code of Professional Conduct, December 2009," American Academy of Neurology, accessed November 11, 2017, https://www.aan.com/siteassets/home-page/footer/membership-and-support/member-resources/professionalism—disciplinary-program/09codeofprofssionalconduct_ft.pdf.
20. "AANS Code of Ethics," American Association of Neurologic Surgeons, last modified April 13, 2007, https://zneurosurgery.com/wp-content/uploads/2014/05/AANS-Code-of-Ethics-2007-version.pdf.

21. D. O. Quest, "Professional Conduct-Witness Testimony," *American Academy of Neurological Surgery Bulletin* 15 (2006): 3–4.
22. F. L. Cohen, "The Expert Medical Witness in Legal Perspective," *Journal of Legal Medicine* 25 (2004): 185–209.
23. A. Gallegos, "Expert Witnesses on Trial," *American Medical News*, August 1, 2011.
24. "Model Rules of Professional Conduct," American Bar Association, accessed November 11, 2017, https://www.americanbar.org/groups/professional_responsibility/publications/model_rules_of_professional_conduct/model_rules_of_professional_conduct_table_of_contents.html.
25. Tom L. Beauchamp and James F. Childress, *Principles of Biomedical Ethics*, 3rd ed. (Oxford: Oxford University Press, 1989).
26. S. J. Youngner et al., "A National Survey of Hospital Ethics Committees," *Critical Care Medicine* 11, no. 11 (1983): 902–905.
27. In re Quinlan 70 NJ 10, 355 A2d 647 (NJ 1976).
28. S. A. Hurst et al., "How Physicians Face Ethical Difficulties: A Qualitative Analysis," *Journal of Medical Ethics* 31, no. 1 (2005): 317–314.
29. Schloendorff v. Society of New York Hospital, 105 N.E. 92 (1914).
30. Union Pacific Railway Co. v. Botsford, 141 U.S. 250, 251 (1891).
31. Cruzan v. Director, Missouri Department of Health, 497 U.S. 261 (1990).
32. *The Constitution of the United States of America* (New York: Barnes and Noble Books, 1995).
33. The Patient Self-Determination Act, 42 U.S.C. 1395cc(f)(1), 1396a(w)(1) (1990).
34. Agreements with Providers of Services: Enrollments Processes, 42 U.S.C. § 1395cc(f)(3), 2018.
35. Health Care Agents and Proxies, New York Consolidated Laws, Ch. 45, Article 29C (2017).
36. CMS Manual System, State Operations Provider Certification: Survey Procedure. CMS Tag A-0131, §482.13(b)(2) (November 9, 2017).
37. "Health Care Financing Administration Final Rule," *Federal Registry*, 60, no. 123 (June 27, 1995): 33262–33294.
38. The Joint Commission 2009 Requirements Related to the Provision of Culturally Competent Patient-Centered Care, Hospital Accreditation Program (HAP), TJC. RI.01.03.01, EP 1, EP 2, EP 3, EP 4, EP 5, EP 6, EP 7, EP 9, EP 11, and EP 13.
39. The Joint Commission 2009 Requirements Related to the Provision of Culturally Competent Patient-Centered Care, Hospital Accreditation Program (HAP), TJC RI.01.05.01, EP 1, EP 5, PE 6, and EP 13.
40. *Trials of War Criminals before the Nuremberg Military Tribunals under Control Council Law No. 10*, vol. 2, pp. 181–182, Washington, DC: U.S. Government Printing Office, 1949, last accessed November 11, 2017, https://history.nih.gov/research/downloads/nuremberg.pdf.
41. E. Shuster, "Fifty Years Later: The Significance of the Nuremberg Code," *New England Journal of Medicine* 337 (1997): 1436–1440.
42. M. A. Grodin, G. J. Annas, "Legacies of Nuremberg: Medical Ethics and Human Rights," *Journal of American Medical Association* 276 (1996): 1682–1683.
43. "WMA Declaration of Helsinki—Ethical Principles for Medical Research Involving Human Subjects, 64th WMA General Assembly, Fortaleza, Brazil, October 2013 ed.," World Medical Association, accessed November 11, 2017, https://www.wma.net/policies-post/wma-declaration-of-helsinki-ethical-principles-for-medical-research-involving-human-subjects/.
44. P. Riis, "Perspectives on the Fifth Revision of the Declaration of Helsinki," *Journal of the American Medical Association* 284 (2000): 3045–3046.
45. Robert V. Carlson et al., "The Revision of the Declaration of Helsinki: Past, Present, and Future," *British Journal of Clinical Pharmacology* 57, no. 6 (June 2004): 695–713.

46. Department of Health and Human Services, "Common Rule," Code of Federal Regulations, Part 46 (1981).
47. United States Food and Drug Administration, Code of Federal Regulations, Parts 50 (Protection of Human Subjects), 56 (Institutional Review Boards), 312 (Investigational New Drug Application), and 812 (Investigational Device Exemptions), 2018.
48. G. J. Annas, "Medical Privacy and Medical Research—Judging the New Federal Regulations," *New England Journal of Medicine* 346, no. 3 (2002): 216–220.
49. Code of Federal Regulations Part 160 (General Administrative Requirements) and Part 164, subparts A and E (Security and Privacy), 2018.
50. Rebecca Skloot, *The Immortal Life of Henrietta Lacks* (New York: Crown Publishers, 2010).
51. M. B. Kapp, "Ethical and Legal Issues in Research Involving Human Subjects: Do You Want a Piece of Me?," *Journal of Clinical Pathology* 59, no. 4 (2006): 335–339.
52. "National Bioethics Advisory Commission Research Involving Human Biological Materials: Issues and Policy Guidance (1999)," National Bioethics Advisory Commission, accessed August 1, 2018. https://bioethicsarchive.georgetown.edu/nbac/hbm.pdf.
53. B. J. Evans and E. M. Meslin, "Encouraging Translational Research through Harmonization of FDA and Common Rule Informed Consent Requirements for Research with Banked Specimens," *Journal of Legal Medicine* 27, no. 2 (2006): 119–166.
54. Office of Human Research Protection, United States Department of Health and Human Services Guidance on Research Involving Coded Private Information or Biological Specimens, Office of Human Research Protection (August 10, 2004).
55. S. F. Kurtz and C. W. G. D. Strong, "The 2006 Revised Uniform Anatomical Gift Act—A Law to Save Lives," *Health Lawyers News* (February 2007): 44–49.
56. T. G. Beach et al., "The Sun Health Research Institute Brain Donation Program: Description and Experience, 1987–2007," *Cell Tissue Bank* 9, no. 3 (2008): 229–245.
57. T. G. Beach et al., "Arizona Study of Aging and Neurodegenerative Disorders and Brain and Body Donation Program," *Neuropathology*, 35, no. 4 (2015): 354–389.
58. P. Riis, "The Danish Brain Collection and Its Important Potentials for Future Research," *IRB* 15, no. 6 (November–December 1993): 5–6.
59. O. C. Glenn et al., "Interpreting Gene Expression Effects of Disease-Associated Variants: A Lesson from SNCA rs356168," *Frontiers in Genetics* 8 (2017): 133.
60. A. Deep-Soboslay et al., "Psychiatric Brain Banking: Three Perspectives on Current Trends and Future Directions," *Biological Psychiatry* 69, no. 2 (2011): 104–112.
61. J. Morales Pedraza, "A Model of a Code of Ethics for Tissue Banks Operating in Developing Countries," *Cell Tissue Bank* 13, no. 4 (December 2012): 607–622.
62. R. Ravid, "Standard Operating Procedures, Ethical and Legal Regulations in BTB (Brain/Tissue/Bio) Banking: What Is Still Missing?," *Cell Tissue Bank* 9, no. 2 (June 2008): 121–137.
63. J. N. Gibbs, "State Regulation of Pharmaceutical Clinical Trials," *Food and Drug Law Journal* 59 (2004): 265–285.
64. E. H. Morreim, "Litigation in Clinical Research: Malpractice Doctrines versus Research Realities," *Journal of Law, Medicine & Ethics* 32, no. 3 (2004): 474–484.
65. P. M. Tereskerz, "Data Safety Monitoring Boards: Legal and Ethical Considerations for Research Accountability," *Accounting Research* 17, no. 1 (January 2010): 30–50.
66. A. M. Grant et al., "Issues in Data Monitoring and Interim Analysis of Trials," *Health Technology Assessment* 9, no. 7 (2005): iii–iv, 1–238.
67. J. Illes et al., "Ethics. Incidental Findings in Brain Imaging Research," *Science* 311, no. 5762 (2006): 783–784.
68. A. C. Milstein, "Research Malpractice and the Issue of Incidental Findings," *Journal of Law, Medicine & Ethics* 36, no. 2 (2008): 356–360.

69. The Free Dictionary, s.v. "fiduciary duty," accessed November 11, 2017, https://legal-dictionary.thefreedictionary.com/fiduciary+duty.
70. Beauchamp and Childress, *Principles of Biomedical Ethics*, 194–195.
71. M. Sutrop, "Viewpoint: How to Avoid a Dichotomy Between Autonomy and Beneficence: From Liberalism to Communitarianism and Beyond," *Journal of Internal Medicine* 269, no. 4 (April 2011): 375–379.
72. Bouvia v. Superior Court, 179 Cal. App. 3d 1127, 1135–36, 225 Cal. Rptr. 297. (Ct. App. 1986), review denied (Cal. June 5, 1986).
73. Bouvia, 170 Cal. App. at 1142–1143.
74. Barber v. Superior Court, 195 Cal. Rptr. 484 (Cal. App. 2 Dist.1983).
75. Washington v. Glucksberg, 521 U.S. 702 (1997).
76. Vacco v. Quill, 521 U.S. 793 (1997).
77. Dispensing of Controlled Substances to Assist Suicide, 66 Fed. Reg. 56607 (November 9, 2001).
78. Gonzales v. Oregon, 546 U.S. 243 (2006).
79. Gonzales v. Oregon, 546 U.S. 243 (2006) (Scalia, J., dissenting).
80. H. T. Greely, "What If? The Farther Shores of Neuroethics: Commentary on 'Neuroscience May Supersede Ethics And Law,'" *Science and Engineering Ethics* 18, no. 3 (September 2012): 439–446.
81. C. J. Frost and A. R. Lumia, "The Ethics of Neuroscience and the Neuroscience of Ethics: A Phenomenological-Existential Approach," *Science and Engineering Ethics* 18, no. 3 (September 2012): 457–474.
82. T. R. Scott, "Neuroscience May Supersede Ethics and Law," *Science and Engineering Ethics* 18, no. 3 (September 2012): 433–437.
83. D. Schmitz and P. C. Reinacher, "Informed Consent in Neurosurgery—Translating Ethical Theory into Action," *Journal of Medical Ethics* 32, no. 9 (2006): 497–498.
84. M. Munyaradzi, "Critical Reflections on the Principle of Beneficence in Biomedicine," *Pan African Medical Journal* 11 (2012): 29.
85. Heller v. Doe, 509 U.S. 312.
86. J. K. Hall, "Legal Consequences of the Moral Duty to Report Errors," *JONA's Healthcare Law, Ethics and Regulation* 5, no. 3 (September 2003): 60–64.
87. D. Finkelstein et al., "When a Physician Harms a Patient by a Medical Error: Ethical, Legal, and Risk-Management Considerations," *Journal of Clinical Ethics* 8, no. 4 (Winter 1997): 330–335.
88. T. H. Gallagher, D. Studdert, and W. Levinson, "Disclosing Harmful Medical Errors to Patients," *New England Journal of Medicine* 356, no. 26 (June 28, 2007): 2713–2719.
89. M. P. Sweet and J. L. Bernat, "A Study of the Ethical Duty of Physicians to Disclose Errors," *Journal of Clinical Ethics* 8, no. 4 (Winter 1997): 341–348.
90. The Joint Commission 2009 Requirements Related to the Provision of Culturally Competent Patient-Centered Care, Hospital Accreditation Program (HAP), Joint Commission on the Accreditation of Healthcare Organizations, "Standard RI.2.90," in *Hospital Accreditation Standards* (Oak Brook, IL: Joint Commission Resources, 2005).
91. M. Wei, "Doctors, Apologies, and the Law: An Analysis and Critique of Apology Laws," *Journal of Health Law* 40, no. 1 (Winter 2007): 107–159.
92. Stamos v. Davies, 21 DLR (4th) 507 (Ont HC, 1985).
93. L. T. Kohn, J. M. Corrigan, and M. S. Donaldson, eds. *To Err is Human: Building a Safer Health System* (Washington, DC: National Academy Press, 2000).
94. Charles S. Bryan, *Osler: Inspirations from a Great Physician* (New York: Oxford University Press, 1997), 119.

95. M. L. Olsen, K. M. Swetz, and P. S. Mueller, "Ethical Decision Making with End-of-Life Care: Palliative Sedation and Withholding or Withdrawing Life-Sustaining Treatments," *Mayo Clinic Proceedings* 85, no. 10 (October 2010): 949–954.
96. J. E. Szalados, "Discontinuation of Mechanical Ventilation at End-of-Life: The Ethical and Legal Boundaries of Physician Conduct in Termination of Life Support," *Critical Care Clinics* 23, no. 2 (April 2007): 317–337, xi.
97. "The Principle of Nonmaleficence: Illustrative Cases," Ethics in Medicine, last modified April 8, 2008, https://depts.washington.edu/bioethx/tools/prin2cs.html.
98. L. Y. Cabrera, E. L. Evans, and R. H. Hamilton, "Ethics of the Electrified Mind: Defining Issues and Perspectives on the Principled Use of Brain Stimulation in Medical Research and Clinical Care," *Brain Topography*, 27, no. 1 (January 2014): 10.
99. D. Larriviere et al., "Responding to Requests from Adult Patients for Neuroenhancements: Guidance of the Ethics, Law and Humanities Committee," *Neurology* 73, no. 17 (October 27, 2009): 1406–1412.
100. V. Cakic, "Smart Drugs for Cognitive Enhancement: Ethical and Pragmatic Considerations in the Era of Cosmetic Neurology," *Journal of Medical Ethics* 35, no. 10 (October 2009): 611–615.
101. S. M. Outram, "The Use of Methylphenidate among Students: The Future of Enhancement?," *Journal of Medical Ethics* 36, no. 4 (April 2010): 198–202.
102. G. R. Winslow, *Triage and Justice* (Berkeley: University of California Press, 1982): 169.
103. "Laws of War: Amelioration of the Condition of the Wounded on the Field of Battle (Red Cross Convention), August 22, 1864," The Avalon Project, Yale Law School, accessed November 17, 2017, http://avalon.law.yale.edu/19th_century/geneva04.asp.
104. "Universal Declaration of Human Rights," United Nations, accessed November 17, 2017, http://www.un.org/en/universal-declaration-human-rights/.
105. K. V. Iserson and J. C. Moskop, "Triage in Medicine, Part I: Concept, History and Types," *Annals of Emergency Medicine* 49, no. 3, (2007): 275–281.
106. J. Szalados, "Triaging the Fittest: Practical Wisdom Versus Logical Calculus?," *Critical Care Medicine* 40, no. 2 (2012): 697–698.
107. J. L. Nates et al., "ICU Admission, Discharge, and Triage Guidelines: A Framework to Enhance Clinical Operations, Development of Institutional Policies, and Further Research," *Critical Care Medicine* 44, no. 8 (2016):1553–1602.
108. Barry Schwartz and Kenneth Sharpe, *Practical Wisdom: The Right Way to Do the Right Thing* (New York: Riverhead Books, 2010).

CHAPTER 2 CASE STUDIES

1. H. Brodaty et al., "The GPCOG: A New Screening Test for Dementia Designed for General Practice," *Journal of American Geriatric Society* 50, no. 3 (2002):530–534.
2. W. G. Rosen et al., "A New Rating Scale for Alzheimer's Disease," *American Journal of Psychiatry* 141, no. 11 (1984): 1356–1364.
3. F. I. Mahoney and D. W. Barthel, "Functional Evaluation: The Barthel Index," *Maryland State Medical Journal* 14 (1965): 61–65.
4. EuroQol Group, "EuroQol: A New Facility for the Measurement of Health-Related Quality of Life," *Health Policy* 16, no. 3 (December 1990): 199–208.
5. R. Logsdon et al., "Assessing Quality of Life in Alzheimer's Disease: Patient and Caregiver Reports," *Journal of Mental Health and Aging* 5 (1999): 21–32.
6. M. Arcand, "End-of-Life Issues in Advanced Dementia. Part 1," *Canadian Family Physician* 61, no. 4 (April 2015): 330–334.

7. M. A. Pisani et al., "Short-Term Outcomes in Older Intensive Care Unit Patients with Dementia," *Critical Care Medicine* 33 (2005): 1371–1376.
8. M. J. Souter et al., "Recommendations for the Critical Care Management of Devastating Brain Injury: Prognostication, Psychosocial, and Ethical Management: A Position Statement for Healthcare Professionals from the Neurocritical Care Society," *Neurocritical Care* 23, no. 1 (2015): 4–13.
9. J. A. Frontera et al., "Integrating Palliative Care into the Care of Neurocritically Ill Patients: A Report from the Improving Palliative Care in the ICU Project Advisory Board and the Center to Advance Palliative Care," *Critical Care Medicine* 43, no. 9 (2015): 1964–1977.
10. S. D. Yeatts et al., "Challenges of Decision Making Regarding Futility in a Randomized Trial: The Interventional Management of Stroke III Experience," *Stroke* 45 (2014): 1408–1414.
11. Bernard S. Cayne, ed., *The New Lexicon Webster's Dictionary of the English Language* (New York: Lexicon Publications, 1989).
12. S. J. Reiser, A. J. Dyck, and W. J. Curran, eds, *Ethics in Medicine: Historical Perspectives and Contemporary Concerns* (Cambridge, MA: MIT Press, 1977): 6–7.
13. "Medical Futility in End-of-Life Care: Report of the Council on Ethical and Judicial Affairs," *Journal of the American Medical Association* 281, no 10 (1999): 937–941.
14. N. S. Jecker, "Medical Futility," Ethics in Medicine, University of Washington School of Medicine, last modified March 14, 2014, https://depts.washington.edu/bioethx/topics/futil.html.
15. D. L. Kasman, "When Is Medical Treatment Futile? A Guide for Students, Residents, and Physicians," *Journal of General Internal Medicine* 19, no. 10 (October 2004): 1053–1056.
16. Maryland Code, Health—General, § 5-601(o).
17. Delaware Code Annotated Title 16 §2501(m).
18. Alaska Statutes § 13.52.060(f).
19. New Mexico Statute Annotated §24-7A-7(F).
20. In re Helen Wanglie, PX-91-238 Minnesota District Court, Probate Division, 1991.
21. In re Baby K, 16 F3d 590, Petition for Rehearing en banc Denied, no. 93-1899 (L), CA-93-68-A, March 28, 1994.
22. Texas Health and Safety Code §166.046 (a).
23. R. L. Fine, T. W. Mayo, "Resolution of Futility by Due Process: Early Experience with the Texas Advance Directive Act," *Annals of Internal Medicine* 138 (2003): 744.
24. R. L. Fine, T. W. Mayo, "Resolution of Futility by Due Process: Early Experience with the Texas Advance Directive Act," *Annals of Internal Medicine* 138 (2003): 744.
25. Texas Health and Safety Code § 166.046(E).
26. Texas Health and Safety Code § 166.046(g).
27. Idaho Code 39-4514(5).
28. New Jersey Statutes Annotated §26:2H-67.
29. J. E. Szalados, "Discontinuation off Mechanical Ventilation at End-of-Life: The Ethical and Legal Boundaries of Physician Conduct in Termination of Life Support," *Critical Care Clinicians* 23, no. 2 (April 2007): 317–337.
30. *Merriam-Webster*, s.v. "prognosis," accessed November 17, 2017, https://www.merriam-webster.com/dictionary/prognosis.
31. J. M. Luce, "Physicians Do Not Have a Responsibility to Provide Futile or Unreasonable Care If a Patient or Family Insists," *Critical Care Medicine* 23, no. 4 (1995): 760–766.
32. J. C. Hemphill III, B. Douglas, D. B. White, "Clinical Nihilism in Neuro-Emergencies," *Emergency Medical Clinics of North America* 27, no. 1 (February 2009): 27–37.
33. J. C. Hemphill et al., "The ICH Score: A Simple, Reliable Grading Scale for Intracerebral Hemorrhage," *Stroke* 32, no. 4 (2001):891–897.

34. T. J. Fendler et al., "American Heart Association's Get with the Guidelines-Resuscitation Investigators: Association between Hospital Rates of Early Do-Not-Resuscitate Orders and Favorable Neurological Survival among Survivors of In-Hospital Cardiac Arrest," *American Heart Journal* 193 (2017): 108–116.
35. N. N. Sarkari, S. M. Perman, and A. A. Ginde, "Impact of Early Do-Not-Attempt-Resuscitation Orders on Procedures and Outcomes of Severe Sepsis," *Journal of Critical Care* 36 (December 2016): 134–139.
36. J. J. Siracuse et al., "Impact of 'Do Not Resuscitate' Status on the Outcome of Major Vascular Surgical Procedures," *Annals of Vascular Surgery* 29, no. 7 (October 2015): 1339–1345.
37. D. B. Zahuranec et al., "Early Care Limitations Independently Predict Mortality after Intracerebral Hemorrhage," *Neurology* 68, no. 20 (2007): 1651–1657.
38. K. J. Becker et al., "Withdrawal of Support in Intracerebral Hemorrhage May Lead to Self-Fulfilling Prophecies," *Neurology* 56, no. 6 (2001): 766–772.
39. J. C. Hemphill III, D. B. White, "Clinical Nihilism in Neuro-Emergencies," *Emergency Medical Clinics of North America* 27, no. 1 (February 2009): 27–37.
40. P. Mollaret, M. Goulon, "The Depassed Coma (Preliminary Memoir)," *Revue Neurologique (Paris)* 101 (1959): 3–15.
41. National Conference of Commissioners on Uniform State Laws, "Uniform Determination of Death Act," National Conference of Commissioners on Uniform State Laws Annual Conference Meeting in Its Eighty-Ninth Year, Kauai, Hawaii, July 26–August 1, 1980, accessed August 17, 2018, http://www.uniformlaws.org/shared/docs/determination%20of%20death/udda80.pdf.
42. Florida Statute § 382.009.
43. 10 New York Codes, Rules and Regulations §400.16(e)(3) (2017).
44. The Quality Standards Subcommittee of the American Academy of Neurology, "Practice Parameters for Determining Brain Death in Adults (Summary Statement)," *Neurology* 45, no. 5 (1995): 1012–1014.
45. "Criteria for the Diagnosis of Brain Stem Death: Review by a Working Group Convened by the Royal College of Physicians and Endorsed by the Conference of Medical Royal Colleges and Their Faculties in the United Kingdom," *Journal of the Royal College of Physicians (London)* 29, no. 5 (1995): 381–382.
46. E. F. Wijdicks, P. N. Varelas, G. S. Gronseth, D. M. Greer, American Academy of Neurology, "Evidence-Based Guideline Update: Determining Brain Death in Adults: Report of the Quality Standards Subcommittee of the American Academy of Neurology," *Neurology* 74, no. 23 (2010): 1911–1918.
47. D. M. Greer, P. N. Varelas, S. Haque, E. F. Wijdicks, "Variability of Brain Death Determination Guidelines in Leading US Neurologic Institutions," *Neurology* 70, no. 4 (2008): 284–289.
48. E. F. Wijdicks, "Brain Death Worldwide: Accepted Fact but No Global Consensus in Diagnostic Criteria," *Neurology* 58, no. 1 (2002): 20–25.
49. S. Wahlster, E. F. Wijdicks, P. V. Patel, et al., "Brain Death Declaration: Practices and Perceptions Worldwide," *Neurology* 84, no. 18 (2015): 1870–1879.
50. C. N. Shappell et al., "Practice Variability in Brain Death Determination: A Call to Action," *Neurology* 81, no. 23 (2013): 2009–2014.
51. D. M. Greer et al., "Variability of Brain Death Policies in the United States," *JAMA Neurology* 73, no. 2 (2016): 213–218.
52. An Act Relating to the Determination of Death, Nevada Acts, Chapter 315 (A.B. 424) (effective October 1, 2017).
53. Small v. Howard, 128 Mass 131 (1880).

54. Pederson v. Dumouchel, 431 P.2d 973 (Wash 1967).
55. A. Joffe, "Confusion about Brain Death," *Nature Reviews Neuroscience* 7 (2006).
56. B. Copnell, "Brain Death: Lessons from the McMath Case," *American Journal of Critical Care* 23, no. 3 (2014): 259–262.
57. R. S. Olick, E. A. Braun, and J. Potash, "Accommodating Religious and Moral Objections to Neurological Death," *Journal of Clinical Ethics* 20, no. 2 (2009): 183–191.
58. Q. Yang, G. Miller. "East-West Differences in Perception of Brain Death. Review of History, Current Understandings, and Directions for Future Research," *Journal of Bioethical Inquiries* 12, no. 2 (2015): 211–225.
59. New Jersey Revised Statutes §26:6A-5 (2016).
60. In re Miranda Lawson (Richmond, Va Circuit Court, May 19, 2016).
61. In re Allen Callaway (Pondera County, Mont., September 2016).
62. Pierce v. Loma Linda University Medical Center (Bernardino County, CA, June 7, 2016) TRO.
63. Fonseca v. Kaiser (ED Cal April 28, 2016) TRO.
64. Stinson v. UC Davis (Placer County, CA. April 2016) TRO.
65. Hailu v. Prime Healthcare (Nev., November 2015).
66. A. Lewis, T. M. Pope, "Physician Power to Declare Death by Neurologic Criteria Threatened," *Neurocritical Care* 26, no. 3 (2017): 446–449.
67. L. O. Gostin, "Legal and Ethical Responsibilities following Brain Death: The McMath and Muñoz Cases," *Journal of the American Medical Association* 311, no. 9 (March 5, 2014): 903–904.
68. P. Smilevitch et. al., "Apnea Test for Brain Death Determination in a Patient on Extracorporeal Membrane Oxygenation," *Neurocritical Care* 19, no. 2 (October 2013): 215–217.
69. R. Muralidharan et al., "The Challenges with Brain Death Determination in Adult Patients on Extracorporeal Membrane Oxygenation," *Neurocritical Care* 14, no. 3 (June 2011): 423–426.
70. R. D. Truog, W. M. Robinson, "Role of Brain Death and the Dead-Donor Rule in the Ethics of Organ Transplantation," *Critical Care Medicine* 31, no. 9 (2003): 2391–2396.
71. R. M. Sade, "Brain Death, Cardiac Death, and the Dead Donor Rule," *Journal of South Carolina Medical Association* 107, no. 4 (2011): 146–149.
72. J. L. Bernat, "On Irreversibility as a Prerequisite for Brain Death Determination," *Advances in Experimental Medicine and Biology* 550 (2004): 161–167.
73. Gostin, "Legal and Ethical Responsibilities," 904.

CHAPTER 3 CIVIL LAW AND LIABILITY

1. J. I. Miller Jr., "The Complete Cardiothoracic Surgeon: Qualities of Excellence," *Annals of Thoracic Surgery* 78, no. 1 (July 2004): 2–8.
2. G. S. Kienle and H. Kiene, "Clinical Judgement and the Medical Profession," *Journal of Evaluation in Clinical Practice* 17, no. 1 (August 2011): 621–627.
3. Jones v. Chidester, 531 Pa. 31, 40, 610 A.2d 964 (1992).
4. Jones v. Chidester, 531 Pa. 31, 40, 610 A.2d 964 (1992).
5. B. Furrow et al., *Health Law*, 3rd ed. (St. Paul, MN: West, 1997).
6. Helling v. Carey 519 P.2d 981 (Wash. 1974).
7. David W. Louisell and Harold Williams, "Res Ipsa Loquitur—Its Future in Medical Malpractice Cases," *California Law Review* 48, no. 252 (1960).
8. Byrne v. Boadle, 2 H. & C. 722, 159 Eng. Rep. 299 (Exch. 1863).
9. Rudolf F. Binder, "*Res Ipsa Loquitur* in Medical Malpractice," *Cleveland-Marshall Law Review* 17, no. 218 (1968).

10. C. Heneghan, "Clinical and Medicolegal Aspects of Conscious Awareness during Anesthesia," *International Anesthesiology Clinics* 31, no. 4 (1993): 1–11.
11. Robert Kopple, "Medical Malpractice—*Res Ipsa Loquitur* and Informed Consent in Anesthesia Cases," *DePaul Law Review* 16, no. 432 (1967): 432–452.
12. Rowe v. Munye, 702 N.W.2d 729, 741 (2005).
13. Flood v. Smith, 126 Conn. 644, 647 (1940).
14. Hicks v. United States, 368 F.2d 626 (4th Cir. 1966).
15. N. Chesanow, "Malpractice: When to Settle a Suit and When to Fight," Medscape, September 25, 2013, accessed August 23, 2018, https://www.medscape.com/viewarticle/811323_3.
16. Ibid.
17. A. Y. Mahajan, D. H. Stacey, and V. Rao, "The National Practitioner Data Bank: Issues in Plastic Surgery," *Plastic and Reconstructive Surgery* 126, no. 6 (December 2010): 2252–2257.
18. New York Consolidated Laws, New York State Education Law § 6530 (2008) and § 6531 (2018), Definition of Professional Misconduct, https://www.health.ny.gov/professionals/office-based_surgery/law/6530.htm.

CHAPTER 4 LEGAL REASONING, LEGAL PROCESS, LEGAL PROOF

1. "All legislative Powers herein granted shall be vested in a Congress of the United States, which shall consist of a Senate and House of Representatives . . . ," U.S. Const. art. I.
2. Administrative Procedure Act, Pub. L. 79–404, 60 Stat. 237 (1946).
3. Lee Loevinger, "Standards of Proof in Science and Law," *Jurimetrics* 32 (1992): 323–344.
4. David H. Kaye, "Proof in Law and Science," *Jurimetrics* 32 (1992): 313.
5. Kaye, "Proof in Law and Science," 313.
6. B. A. Goldberg, "The Peer Review Privilege: A Law in Search of a Valid Policy," *American Journal of Law and Medicine* 10, no. 2 (1984): 151–167.
7. Healthcare Quality Improvement Act of 1986, 42 U.S.C. Section 11101 et seq. (1986).
8. K. M. Madison, "From HCQIA to the ACA. The Evolution of Reporting as a Quality Improvement Tool," *Journal of Legal Medicine* 33, no. 1 (2012): 63–92.
9. New York State Education Law § 6527.
10. New York Public Health Law Sections 2805 j–i.
11. New York Education Law §6527 Special provisions.
12. Michael Benson, Jordan Benson, and Mark Stein, "Hospital Quality Improvement: Are Peer Review Immunity, Privilege, and Confidentiality in the Public Interest?," *Northwestern Journal of Law and Social Policy* 11, no. 1 (2016).
13. Federal Rules of Civil Procedure, Title V. Disclosures and Discovery, Rule 26. Duty to Disclose; General Provisions Governing Discovery.
14. 2015 NY Slip Op 31369(U), 2015 N.Y. Misc. LEXIS 2653 (Sup. Ct. N.Y. Co. July 17, 2015).
15. Uppal v. Rosalind Franklin University of Medicine and Science, 2015 U.S. Dist. LEXIS 112705, at *9 (N.D. Ill. Aug. 26, 2015).
16. Federal Rules of Civil Procedure, Title V. 26(b)(1)(C)(3).
17. United States v. Nixon, 418 U.S. 683, 94 S. Ct. 3090, 41 L. Ed. 2d 1039 (1974).
18. Federal Rules of Evidence, Article IV. Relevance and Its Limits, Rule 402. General Admissibility of Relevant Evidence.
19. Federal Rules of Evidence, Article IV. Relevance and Its Limits, Rule 403. Excluding Relevant Evidence for Prejudice, Confusion, Waste of Time, or Other Reasons.
20. *Black's Law Dictionary* (8th ed. 2004).
21. Federal Rules of Civil Procedure, Title V. Disclosures and Discovery, Rule 37. Failure to Make Disclosures or to Cooperate in Discovery; Sanctions.

22. First Financial Security, Inc. v. Freedom Equity Group, LLC, No. 15-cv-1893-HRL, 2016 WL 5870218 (N.D. Cal. Oct. 7, 2016).
23. A. W. Wu, "Medical Error: The Second Victim. The Doctor Who Makes the Mistake Needs Help Too," *British Medical Journal* 320, no. 7237 (2000): 726–727.
24. S. D. Scott et al., "The Natural History of Recovery for the Health Care Provider 'Second Victim' after Adverse Patient Events," *Quality and Safety in Health Care* 18 (2009): 325–330.
25. M. Grissinger, "Too Many Abandon the 'Second Victims' of Medical Errors," *Pharmacy and Therapeutics* 39, no. 9 (2014): 591–592.
26. J. Aleccia, "Nurse's Suicide Highlights Twin Tragedies of Medical Errors," MSNBC.com, revised June 27, 2011, http://www.nbcnews.com/id/43529641/ns/health-health_care/t/nurses-suicide-highlights-twin-tragedies-medical-errors/#.W4HC1s5KjIU.
27. M. Rassin, T. Kanti, and D. Silner, "Chronology of Medication Errors by Nurses: Accumulation of Stresses and PTSD Symptoms," *Issues in Mental Health Nursing* 26, no. 8 (2005): 873–886.
28. A. D. Waterman et al., "The Emotional Impact of Medical Errors on Practicing Physicians in the United States and Canada," *The Joint Commission Journal on Quality and Patient Safety* 22 (2007): 467–476.
29. F. Gazoni et al., "The Impact of Perioperative Catastrophes on Anesthesiologists: Results of a National Survey," *Anesthesia and Analgesia* 113 (2012): 596–603.
30. S. Ullström et al., "Suffering in Silence: A Qualitative Study of Second Victims of Adverse Events," *British Medical Journal of Quality and Safety* (November 15, 2013). http://qualitysafety.bmj.com/content/early/2013/11/15/bmjqs-2013-002035#xref-ref-5-1.
31. C. M. Clancy, "Alleviating 'Second Victim' Syndrome: How We Should Handle Patient Harm," Agency for Healthcare Research and Quality Archive, accessed November 17, 2017, https://archive.ahrq.gov/news/newsroom/commentaries/second-victim-syndrome.html.
32. S. D. Scott et al., "Caring for Our Own: Deployment of a Second Victim Rapid Response System," *The Joint Commission Journal on Quality and Patient Safety* 36 (2010): 233–240.
33. J. Conway et al., *Respectful Management of Serious Clinical Adverse Events. Institute for Healthcare Improvement* (Cambridge, MA: Institute for Healthcare Improvement, 2010).
34. Medically Induced Trauma Support Services, accessed November 17, 2017, https://www.mitsstools.org/tool-kit-for-staff-support-for-healthcare-organizations.html.
35. J. Conway et al., *Respectful Management of Serious Clinical Adverse Events*, 2nd ed (Cambridge, MA: Institute for Healthcare Improvement, 2011), accessed October 12, 2018, www.ihi.org/knowledge/Pages/IHIWhitePapers/RespectfulManagementSeriousClinicalAEsWhitePaper.aspx.
36. C. Denham, "TRUST: The 5 Rights of the Second Victim," *Journal of Patient Safety* 3, no. 2 (June 2007): 107–119.
37. T. H. Gallagher, D. Studdert, and W. Levinson, "Disclosing Harmful Medical Errors to Patients," *New England Journal of Medicine* 356 (2007): 2713–2719.
38. A. A. White and T. H. Gallagher, "Medical Error and Disclosure," *Handbook of Clinical Neurology* 118 (2013): 107–117.
39. Joint Commission on the Accreditation of Healthcare Organizations, "Standard RI.2.90," in *Hospital Accreditation Standards* (Oak Brook, IL: Joint Commission Resources, 2005).
40. D. B. Raemer et al., "Rapid Learning of Adverse Medical Event Disclosure and Apology," *Journal of Patient Safety* 12, no. 3 (September 2016), 140–147.
41. N. Tavuchis, *Mea Culpa: A Sociology of Apology and Reconciliation* (Stanford: Stanford University Press, 1991):15–44.
42. T. H. Gallagher et al., "Patients' and Physicians' Attitudes Regarding the Disclosure of Medical Errors," *Journal of the American Medical Association* 289, no. 8 (February 26, 2003): 1001–1007.

43. J. K. Robbennolt, "Apologies and Medical Error," *Clinical Orthopaedics and Related Research* 467, no. 2 (February 2009): 376–382.
44. R. C. Boothman, S. J. Imhoff, and D. A. Campbell Jr., "Nurturing a Culture of Patient Safety and Achieving Lower Malpractice Risk through Disclosure: Lessons Learned and Future Directions," *Frontiers of Health Service Management* 28, no. 3 (Spring 2012): 13–28.
45. A. Kachalia et al., "Liability Claims and Costs before and after Implementation of a Medical Error Disclosure Program," *Annals of Internal Medicine* 153, no. 4 (August 17, 2010): 213–221.
46. S. Rice, "Hospitals Slow to Adopt Patient Apology Policies," *Modern Healthcare* 45, no. 33 (August 17, 2015): 16, 29–30.
47. N. MacDonald and A. Attaran, "Medical Errors, Apologies and Apology Laws," *Canadian Medical Association Journal* 180, no. 1 (January 6, 2009): 11, 13.
48. P. Browne, "Apologies, Medicine and the Law," *Journal of Law and Medicine* 16, no. 2 (October 2008): 200–208.
49. W. M. McDonnell and E. Guenther, "Narrative Review: Do State Laws Make It Easier to Say 'I'm sorry?'" *Annals of Internal Medicine* 149, no. 11 (December 2, 2008): 811–816.
50. A. C. Mastroianni et al., "The Flaws in State 'Apology' and 'Disclosure' Laws Dilute Their Intended Impact on Malpractice Suits," *Health Affairs (Millwood)* 29, no. 9 (September 2010): 1611–1619.
51. M. Waite, "To Tell the Truth: the Ethical and Legal Implications of Disclosure of Medical Error," *Health Law Journal* 13 (2005): 1–33.
52. J. S. Weissman et al., "Error Reporting and Disclosure Systems: Views from Hospital Leaders," *Journal of the American Medical Association* 293, no. 11 (March 16, 2005): 1359–1366.
53. L. L. Henry, "Disclosure of Medical Errors: Ethical Considerations for the Development of a Facility Policy and Organizational Culture Change," *Policy, Politics, and Nurse Practice* 6, no. 2 (May 2005): 127–134.

CHAPTER 5   REGULATORY LAW AND THE CLINICAL PRACTICE OF THE NEUROSCIENCES

1. U.S. Code, Title 44, Chapter 35, Subchapter I, § 3502.
2. Administrative Procedure Act, 5 U.S.C. § 551 et seq. and 5 U.S.C. § 701 et seq. (1946).
3. 5 U.S.C. §551(5) (2005).
4. 5 U.S.C. §551(4) (2005).
5. Chevron U.S.A., Inc. v. Natural Resources Defense Council, 467 U.S. 837 (1984).
6. Auer v. Robbins, 519 U.S. 452 (1997).
7. Skidmore v. Swift, 323 U.S. 134 (1944).
8. Chevron U.S.A. v. NRDC, 467 U.S. 837, 842–43 (1984).
9. Federal Register Act, 44 USC § 1501 et seq. (1935).
10. 21 U.S.C. §384(a)(3) (2005).
11. Controlled Substance Act (CSA) §101, 21 U.S.C. §801 et seq. (2005)
12. 21 U.S.C. §821 (2005).
13. Pure Food and Drugs Act, Pub. L. No. 59-384, Ch. 3915, 34 Stat. 768 (1906); 21 U.S.C. §§1–15 (1934). See S. 88, 59th Cong., 2d Sess. (1906), passed into law June 30, 1906. This Act was repealed in 1938 by U.S.C §329(a).
14. Pub. L. No. 75-717, 52 Stat. 1040 (1938) (codified, as amended, 21 U.S.C. §301 et seq.).
15. Pub. L. No. 82-215, 65 Stat. 648 (1951).
16. Pub. L. 108–173, 117 Stat. 2066 (2013).
17. 21 U.S.C. §§ 301 et seq.

18. 21 Code of Federal Regulations §314.2 (2006).
19. United States v. Park, 421 U.S. 658, 660 (1975).
20. "Citizen Petition Regarding the Food and Drug Administration's Policy on Promotion of Unapproved Uses of Approved Drugs and Devices; Request for Comments," *Federal Register* 59, no. 222 (November 18, 1994).
21. Shane M. Ward, "The First Amendment Inequity of the Food and Drug Administration's Regulation of Off-Label Drug Use Information on the Internet," *Food and Drug Law Journal* 56, no. 41 (2001).
22. "Clarification of When Products Made or Derived from Tobacco Are Regulated as Drugs, Devices, or Combination Products: Amendments to Regulations Regarding 'Intended Uses,'" *Federal Registry* 82, no. 5 (Jan 9, 2017): 2193–2217, *revising* 21 CFR § 201.128 and 21 CFR § 801.4.
23. Mazur v. Merck & Co., 964 F.2d 1348, 1356 (3d Cir. 1992).
24. Wyeth-Ayerst Lab. Co. v. Medrano, 28 S.W.3d 87, 91 (Tex. App.–Texarkana 2000, no writ).
25. Food and Drugs: Labeling, 21 Code of Federal Regulations §201 (2018).
26. A. S. Habib and T. J. Gan, "Food and Drug Administration Black Box Warning on the Perioperative Use of Droperidol: A Review of the Cases," *Anesthesia and Analgesia* 96 (2003): 1377–1379.
27. "About the Center for Drug Evaluation and Research," About FDA, Food and Drug Administration, accessed October 12, 2018, https://www.fda.gov/AboutFDA/CentersOffices/OfficeofMedicalProductsandTobacco/CDER/default.htm.
28. "About the Center for Biologics Evaluation and Research (CBER)," About FDA, Food and Drug Administration, accessed October 12, 2018, https://www.fda.gov/AboutFDA/CentersOffices/OfficeofMedicalProductsandTobacco/CBER/default.htm.
29. Medical Device Amendments, H.R.11124, 94th U.S. Congress (December 11, 1975).
30. Federal Food, Drug, and Cosmetics Act, Subchapter V, Drugs and Devices: State and Local Requirements Respecting Devices," U.S.C. §360k(a) (2006).
31. Riegel v. Medtronic, Inc., 552 U.S. 312, 330 (2008).
32. Federal Food, Drug, and Cosmetics Act, Subchapter V, Drugs and Devices: Classification of Devices Intended for Human Use, 21 U.S.C. 360c(a)(1)(C)(ii)(2006).
33. Federal Food, Drug, and Cosmetics Act, Subchapter H, Medical Device Reporting, 21 Code of Federal Regulations 803 (2018).
34. Federal Food, Drug, and Cosmetics Act, Subchapter H, Quality System Regulation, 21 Code of Federal Regulations 820.1(a)(1) (2018).
35. Christopher L. Thompson, "Imposing Strict Products Liability on Medical Care Providers," *Missouri Law Review* 60, no. 3 (Summer 1995): 711–730.
36. Health Insurance Portability and Accountability Act of 1996, Public Law 104-191, 110 Stat. 1936 (1996).
37. Bipartisan Budget Act of 2015, H.R.1314, 114th Congress (2015–2016); subsequently, Public Law No: 114-74.
38. Money and Finance: False Claims, 31 U.S.C. §§ 3729-3733 (2012).
39. Judiciary and Judicial Procedure: Fines, Penalties and Forfeitures; Mode of Recovery, 28 U.S.C. §2461 (1996).
40. Money and Finance: False Claims, 31 U.S.C. §3729 (2012).
41. Money and Finance: False Claims, 31 U.S.C. §§ 3729-3733 (2012).
42. Administrative Actions and Statistical Sampling for Overpayment Estimates: Use of Statistical Sampling for Overpayment Estimation, Program Integrity Manual, Pub. 100-08, Ch. 8.4.1.1. (2018), accessed October 12, 2018, https://cms.gov/Regulations-and-Guidance/Guidance/Manuals/downloads/pim83c08.pdf.
43. Centers for Medicare and Medicaid Services Ruling 86-1.

44. United States v. Aseracare, Inc. No.2:12-CV-245, 2014 U.S. Dist. LEXIS 167970 at *25 (N.D. Ala. Dec. 4, 2014).
45. Department of Health and Human Services, Office of Inspector General, *Medicare Payments for Surgical Debridement Services in 2004*, May 2007, last accessed December 17, 2017, https://www.oig.hhs.gov/oei/reports/oei-02-05-00390.pdf.
46. U.S. Department of Justice, Federal Bureau of Investigation, *Financial Crimes to the Public Report 2006*, 2006, accessed October 17, 2018, https://www.fbi.gov/file-repository/stats-services-publications-fcs_report2006-financial-crimes-report-to-the-public-2006-pdf/view.
47. U.S. Department of Health and Human Services, Centers for Medicare and Medicaid Services, *Pub 100-04 Medicare Claims Processing Centers for Medicare & Medicaid Services (CMS) Transmittal 2303 100.1.1—Evaluation and Management (E/M) Services*, September 14, 2011.
48. U.S. Congress, Senate, Subcommittee of the Committee on Appropriations, *Physicians at Teaching Hospitals. [PATH] Audits*, 105th Congress, 1st Session, 1998, accessed December 17, 2017, https://www.gpo.gov/fdsys/pkg/CHRG-105shrg46159/html/CHRG-105shrg46159.htm.
49. U.S. Government Accountability Office, *Report to the Chairman, Subcommittee on Health, Committee on Ways and Means, House of Representatives, Medicare: Concerns with Physicians at Teaching Hospitals (PATH) Audits*, July 1998.
50. David Johnston, "University Agrees to Pay in Settlement on Medicare," *The New York Times*, December 13, 1995, accessed December 17, 2017, http://www.nytimes.com/1995/12/13/us/university-agrees-to-pay-in-settlement-on-medicare.html.
51. U. S. Department of Health and Human Services, Centers for Medicare & Medicaid Services, "Medicare Program: Reporting and Returning of Overpayments. Final Rule," *Federal Register* 81, no. 29, (February 12, 2016): 7653–7684.
52. "A.G. Schneiderman Announces Joint State and Federal $2.95 Million Settlement with Hospitals in Mount Sinai Health System," Attorney General Barbara D. Underwood, last accessed October 12, 2018, https://ag.ny.gov/press-release/ag-schneiderman-announces-joint-state-and-federal-295-million-settlement-hospitals.
53. Patient Protection and Affordable Care Act, Pub. L. No. 111-148, 124 Stat. 119 (2010).
54. Money and Finance: Claims against the United States Government; Civil Actions for False Claims, 31 U.S.C. §3730(b)(1)(2102).
55. United States ex rel. Gear v. Emergency Medical Associates of Illinois, Inc., 2004 U.S. Dist. LEXIS 11729 (D. Ill. 2004).
56. "Justice Department Recovers Over $4.7 Billion from False Claims Act Cases in Fiscal Year 2016," *Justice News*, U.S. Department of Justice, accessed November 17, 2017, https://www.justice.gov/opa/pr/justice-department-recovers-over-47-billion-false-claims-act-cases-fiscal-year-2016.
57. U.S. Attorney's Office for the Northern District of Texas, U.S. Department of Justice, "Texas Dental Management Firm, 19 Affiliated Dental Practices, and Their Owners and Marketing Chief Agree to Pay $8.45 Million to Resolve Allegations of False Medicaid Claims for Pediatric Dental Services," January 9, 2017, updated January 11, 2017, https://www.justice.gov/usao-ndtx/pr/texas-dental-management-firm-19-affiliated-dental-practices-and-their-owners-and.
58. Pain Management Physician Resolves False Claims Act Allegations, U.S. Attorney's Office for the Eastern District of Kentucky, U.S. Department of Justice, February 1, 2017, accessed October 12, 2018, https://www.justice.gov/usao-edky/pr/pain-management-physician-resolves-false-claims-act-allegations.
59. Medicare Fee for Service Recovery Audit Program, CMS.gov, accessed November 17, 2017, https://www.cms.gov/Research-Statistics-Data-and-Systems/Monitoring-Programs/Medicare-FFS-Compliance-Programs/Recovery-Audit-Program.

60. Examination and Treatment for Emergency Medical Conditions and Women in Labor, 42 U.S.C. §1395dd (2005).
61. J. Zibulewsky, "The Emergency Medical Treatment and Active Labor Act (EMTALA): What It Is and What It Means for Physicians," *Proceeding (Baylor University Medical Center)* 14, no. 4 (Oct 2001): 339–346.
62. 42 Code of Federal Regulations § 489.24(b) (2011).
63. 42 Code of Federal Regulations § 489.24(a)(1)(i) (2011).
64. Morales v. Sociedad, 524 F.3d 54 (1st. Cir. 2008).
65. 42 Code of Federal Regulations § 489.24(a)(1)(i) (2011).
66. Medicare Program: Changes to the Hospital Inpatient Prospective Payment Systems and Fiscal Year 2009 Rates; Payments for Graduate Medical Education in Certain Emergency Situations; Changes to Disclosure of Physician Ownership in Hospitals and Physician Self-Referral Rules; Updates to the Long-Term Care Prospective Payment System; Updates to Certain IPPS-Excluded Hospitals; and Collection of information Regarding Financial Relationships between Hospitals 73, no. 161, 73 Fed. Reg. 48434-48659 (August 19, 2008).
67. 42 CFR Parts 413, 482, and 489, Medicare Program: Clarifying Policies Related to the Responsibilities of Medicare-Participating Hospitals in Treating Individuals with Emergency Medical Conditions; Final Rule 68, no. 174, Fed. Reg. 53221-53264 (September 9, 2003).
68. Limitation on Certain Physician Referrals, 42 U.S.C. § 1395nn (2011).
69. Provisions Relating to the Administration of Part A, 42 U.S.C. § 1395(h)(6) (2011); see also § 1395nn.
70. Section 1877 of the Social Security Act (42 U.S.C. § 1395nn).
71. Criminal Penalties for Acts Involving Federal Health Care Programs, 42 U.S.C. § 1320a-7b(b) (2011).
72. Ibid.
73. Criminal Penalties for Acts Involving Federal Health Care Programs, 42 U.S.C. § 1320a-7(a) (2011).
74. Criminal Penalties for Acts Involving Federal Health Care Programs, 42 U.S.C. § 1320a-7(b) (2011).
75. 4 Criminal Penalties for Acts Involving Federal Health Care Programs, 2 U.S.C § 1320a-7a(a)(7) (2011).
76. See Pub. L. 100-93, 101 Stat. 680 (1987) § 3.
77. U.S. v. Greber, 760 F.2d 68, 69 (3rd Cir. 1985), cert. denied, 474 U.S. 988 (1985).
78. Department of Health and Human Services, Office of the Inspector General, "Fraud Alert: Physician Compensation Arrangements May Result in Significant Liability," June 9, 2015, accessed December 20, 2017, https://www.oig.hhs.gov/compliance/alerts/guidance/Fraud_Alert_Physician_Compensation_06092015.pdf.
79. Department of Health and Human Services, Office of the Inspector General, "Fraud Alert: Physician Compensation Arrangements May Result in Significant Liability," June 9, 2015, last accessed December 20, 2017, https://www.oig.hhs.gov/compliance/alerts/guidance/Fraud_Alert_Physician_Compensation_06092015.pdf.
80. U.S. Department of Justice, Office of Public Affairs, "Significant False Claims Act Settlements and Judgments Fiscal Years 2009–2016," accessed November 17, 2017, https://www.justice.gov/opa/press-release/file/918366/download.
81. United States v. Campbell, 2011 U.S. Dist. LEXIS 1207 (Jan 2011).
82. "A.G. Schneiderman Announces Joint State and Federal $2.95 Million Settlement with Hospitals in Mount Sinai Health System," Attorney General Barbara D. Underwood, last accessed November 17, 2017, https://ag.ny.gov/press-release/ag-schneiderman-announces-joint-state-and-federal-295-million-settlement-hospitals.

CHAPTER 6 DIGITAL MEDICINE AND THE DATA REVOLUTION

1. *Business Dictionary*, s.v. "metadata," accessed December 8, 2017, http://www.businessdictionary.com/definition/metadata.html.
2. K. M. Lambert, P. Barry, and G. Stokes, "Risk Management and Legal Issues with the Use of Social Media in the Healthcare Setting," *Journal of Healthcare and Risk Management* 31, no. 4 (2012): 41–47.
3. B. Chauhan, R. George, and J. Coffin, "Social Media and You: What Every Physician Needs to Know," *The Journal of Medical Practice Management* 28, no. 3 (2012): 206–209.
4. J. M. Farnan et al., "Online Medical Professionalism: Patient and Public Relationships: Policy Statement from the American College of Physicians and the Federation of State Medical Boards," *Annals of Internal Medicine* 158, no. 8 (April 16, 2013): 620–627.
5. K. C. Chretien and T. Kind, "Social Media and Clinical Care: Ethical, Professional, and Social Implications," *Circulation* 127, no. 13 (2013): 1413–1421.
6. J. E. Szalados, "Digital Distraction and Legal Risk," in *Distracted Doctoring*, eds. P. J. Papadakos and S. Bertman (Switzerland: Springer, 2017), 201–218.
7. J. E. Szalados, "Digital Distraction and Legal Risk," in *Distracted Doctoring*, eds. P. J. Papadakos and S. Bertman (Switzerland: Springer, 2017), 201–218.
8. M. J. Kavanaugh, "Validation of the Intensive Care Unit Early Warning Dashboard: Quality Improvement Utilizing a Retrospective Case-Control Evaluation," *Telemedicine Journal & E-Health* 23, no. 2 (2017): 88–95.
9. K. L. Bagot, "Telemedicine Expedites Access to Optimal Acute Stroke Care," *Lancet* 388, no. 10046 (2016): 757–758.
10. K. E. Klein et al., "Teleneurocritical Care and Telestroke," *Critical Care Clinics* 31, no. 2 (2015): 197–224.
11. O. M. Panlaqui et al., "Outcomes of Telemedicine Intervention in a Regional Intensive Care Unit: A Before and After Study," *Anaesthesia and Intensive Care* 45, no. 5 (2017): 605–610.
12. P. L. Hoonakker, "Virtual Collaboration, Satisfaction, and Trust between Nurses in the Tele-ICU and ICUs: Results of a Multilevel Analysis," *Journal of Critical Care* 37 (2017): 224–229.
13. C. M. Lilly et al., "ICU Telemedicine Program Financial Outcomes," *Chest* 151, no. 2 (2017): 286–297.
14. *MLN Booklet: Telehealth Services* (Washington, DC: Centers for Medicare and Medicaid Services, February 2018), accessed December 18, 2017, https://www.cms.gov/Outreach-and-Education/Medicare-Learning-Network-MLN/MLNProducts/downloads/TelehealthSrvcsfctsht.pdf.
15. The National Telehealth Resource Policy Center, Center for Connected Health Policy, *State Telehealth Laws and Reimbursement Policies: A Comprehensive Scan of the 50 States and the District of Columbia* (Sacramento, CA: Public Health Institute Center for Connected Health Policy, 2017), accessed December 18, 2017, http://www.cchpca.org/sites/default/files/resources/50%20STATE%20PDF%20FILE%20APRIL%202017%20FINAL%20PASSWORD%20PROTECT.pdf.

CHAPTER 7 DEVELOPING AND LEADING A SUSTAINABLE HIGH-RELIABILITY, HIGH-PERFORMING UNIT

1. Thomas J. Peters and Robert H. Waterman Jr, *In Search of Excellence: Lessons from America's Best-Run Companies* (New York: Warner Books, 1982).

2. T. A. Atchison and J. S. Bujak JS, *Leading Transformational Change: The Physician-Executive Partnership* (Chicago: Health Administration Press, 2001).
3. K. E. Weick and K. M. Sutcliffe, "Mindfulness and the Quality of Organizational Attention," *Organization Science* 17, no. 4 (2006): 514–526.
4. J. Manion, *From Management to Leadership: Practical Strategies for Healthcare Leaders*, 2nd ed. (San Francisco: Jossey-Bass, 2005).
5. J. C. Collins, *Good to Great: Why Some Companies Make the Leap . . . and Others Don't* (UK: William Collins, 2001).
6. Jocko Willink and Leif Babin, *Extreme Ownership: How U.S. Navy SEALs Lead and Win* (New York: St. Martin's Press, 2015).
7. Ken Blanchard, Donald Carew, and Eunice Parisi-Carew, *One Minute Manager Builds High Performing Teams* (New York: HarperCollins, 2000).
8. Jon R. Katzenbach and Douglas K. Smith, *The Wisdom of Teams* (Brighton, MA: Harvard Business School Press, 1993).
9. Peter M. Senge, *The Fifth Discipline: The Art and Practice of the Learning Organization* (New York: Doubleday/Currency, 1990).
10. Paul M. Schyve, *Leadership in Healthcare Organizations: A Guide to Joint Commission Leadership Standards* (San Diego, CA: The Governance Institute, 2009), accessed December 17, 2017, https://www.jointcommission.org/assets/1/18/WP_Leadership_Standards.pdf.
11. D. Logan, H. Fischer-Wright, and J. King, *Tribal Leadership: Leveraging Natural Groups to Build a Thriving Organization* (New York: HarperCollins, 2008).
12. James M. Kouzes and Barry Z. Posner, *The Leadership Challenge* (San Francisco: Jossey-Bass, 2007).
13. E. C. Nelson et al., "Microsystems in Health Care: Part 1. Learning from High-Performing Front-Line Clinical Units," *The Joint Commission Journal on Quality Improvement* 28, no. 9 (September 28, 2002): 472–493.
14. A. R. Aitkenhead et al., "International Standards for Safety in the Intensive Care Unit," *Intensive Care Medicine* 19 (1993): 178–181.
15. E. F. M. Wijdicks, "Chapter 2: The First Neurointensive Care Units," in *Famous First Papers for the Neurointensivist* (New York: Springer Science+Business Media, 2013).
16. M. H. Weil, "The Society of Critical Care Medicine, Its History and Its Destiny," *Critical Care Medicine* 1 (1973): 1–4.
17. A. Grenvik and M. R. Pinsky, "Evolution of the Intensive Care Unit as a Clinical Center and Critical Care Medicine as a Discipline," *Critical Care Clinicians* 25 (2009): 239–250.
18. A. Grenvik et al., "Critical Care Medicine: Certification as a Multidisciplinary Subspecialty," *Critical Care Medicine* 9 (1981): 117–125.
19. E. F. Wijdicks, "The History of Neurocritical Care," *Handbook of Clinical Neurology* 140 (2017): 3–14.
20. E. F. M. Wijdicks, "A New Journal, A New Step, a New Energy," *Neurocritical Care* 1 (2004): 1.
21. M. Markandaya et al., "The Role of Neurocritical Care: A Brief Report on the Survey Results of Neurosciences and Critical Care Specialists," *Neurocritical Care* 16, no. 1 (2012): 72–81.
22. A. B. Nathens et al., "The Impact of an Intensivist-Model ICU on Trauma-Related Mortality," *Annals of Surgery* 244, no. 4 (2006): 545–554.
23. P. J. Pronovost et al., "The Organization of Intensive Care Unit Physician Services," *Critical Care Medicine* 35, no. 10 (October 2007): 2256–2261.
24. P. Pronovost et al., "Impact of the Leapfrog Group's Intensive Care Unit Physician Staffing Standard," *Journal of Critical Care* 22, no. 2 (2007): 89–96.

25. A. Parikh et al., "Quality Improvement and Cost Savings after Implementation of the Leapfrog Intensive Care Unit Physician Staffing Standard at a Community Teaching Hospital," *Critical Care Medicine* 40, no. 10 (2012): 2754–2759.
26. J. J. Brown and G. Sullivan, "Effect on ICU Mortality of a Full-Time Critical Care Specialist," *Chest* 96, no. 1 (1989): 127–129.
27. "Factsheet: ICU Physician Staffing," last revised April 1, 2016, http://www.leapfroggroup.org/sites/default/files/Files/IPS%20Fact%20Sheet.pdf.
28. D. C. Angus et al., "Epidemiology of Severe Sepsis in the United States: Analysis of Incidence, Outcome, and Associated Costs of Care," *Critical Care Medicine* 7, no. 29 (2001): 1303–1310.
29. Z. Fanari et al., "Impact of a Multidisciplinary Team Approach Including an Intensivist on the Outcomes of Critically Ill Patients in the Cardiac Care Unit," *Mayo Clinic Proceedings* 91, no. 12 (December 2016): 1727–1734.
30. S. S. Carson et al., "Effects of Organizational Change in the Medical Intensive Care Unit of a Teaching Hospital: A Comparison of 'Open' and 'Closed' Formats," *Journal of the American Medical Association* 276, no. 4 (1996): 322–328.
31. D. P. Baker et al., *Medical Teamwork and Patient Safety: The Evidence-Based Relation* (Washington, DC: American Institutes for Research, 2003).
32. A. K. Jain et al., "High-Performance Teams for Current and Future Physician Leaders: An Introduction," Journal of *Surgical Education* 65, no. 2 (2008): 145–150.
33. M. P. Young and J. D. Birkmeyer, "Potential Reduction in Mortality Rates Using an Intensivist Model to Manage Intensive Care Units," *Effective Clinical Practice* 3, no. 6 (2000): 284–289.
34. C. Manthous, A. M. Nembhard, and A. B. Hollingshead, "Building Effective Critical Care Teams," *Critical Care* 15, no. 4 (2011): 307, accessed December 17, 2017, https://ccforum.biomedcentral.com/articles/10.1186/cc10255.
35. R. J. Brilli et al., "Critical Care Delivery in the Intensive Care Unit: Defining Clinical Roles and the Best Practice Model," *Critical Care Medicine* 29, no. 10 (2001): 2007–2019.
36. M. M. Kim et al., "The Effect of Multidisciplinary Care Teams on Intensive Care Unit Mortality," *Archives of Internal Medicine* 170, no.4 (2010): 369–376.
37. A. Marra et al., "The ABCDEF Bundle in Critical Care," *Critical Care Clinicians* 33, no. 2 (April 2017): 225–243.
38. The Joint Commission, "Behaviors That Undermine a Culture of Safety," *Sentinel Event Alert* 40, no. 3 (July 9, 2008): 1–3.
39. K. E. Weick, K. M. Sutcliffe, and D. Obstfeld, "Organizing for High Reliability: Processes of Collective Mindfulness," in *Research in Organizational Behavior*, eds. R. I. Sutton and B. M. Staw (Stamford, CT: JAI Press, 1999), 81–123.
40. K. E. Weick and K. M. Sutcliffe, *Managing the Unexpected* 2nd ed. (San Francisco: Jossey-Bass, 2007).
41. "Patient Safety Primer: High Reliability," Patient Safety Network, Agency for Healthcare Research and Quality, last accessed November 17, 2017, https://psnet.ahrq.gov/primers/primer/31/high-reliability.
42. J. L. Sullivan et al., "Applying the High Reliability Health Care Maturity Model to Assess Hospital Performance: A VA Case Study," *The Joint Commission Journal on Quality and Patient Safety* 42, no. 9 (September 2016): 389–411.
43. N. A. Halpern, S. M. Pastores, and R. J. Greenstein, "Critical Care Medicine in the United States 1985–2000: An Analysis of Bed Numbers, Use, and Costs," *Critical Care Medicine* 32, no. 6 (2004): 1254–1259.

44. M. K. Christianson et al., "Becoming a High Reliability Organization," *Critical Care* 15, no. 6 (2011): 314, accessed November 17, 2017, https://www.ncbi.nlm.nih.gov/pmc/articles/PMC3388695/.
45. M. R. Chassin and J. M. Loeb, "High-Reliability Health Care: Getting There from Here," *Milbank Quarterly* 91, no 3 (Sep 2013): 459–490.
46. Institute of Medicine, Committee on Quality of Health Care in America, "Foreword," in *Crossing the Quality Chasm: A New Health System for the 21st Century* (Washington, DC: National Academies Press, 2001).
47. A. Donabedian, "Evaluating the Quality of Medical Care," *Milbank Memorial Fund Quarterly* 44, no. 3 (July 1966): Supplemental 166–206.
48. J. M. Luce, A. B. Bindman, and P. R. Lee, "A Brief History of Health Care Quality Assessment and Improvement in the United States," *The Western Journal of Medicine* 160, no. 3 (March 1994): 263–268.
49. B. J. Gagel, "Health Care Quality Improvement Program: A New Approach," *Health Care Financial Review* 16, no. 4 (Summer 1995): 15–23.
50. S. F. Khuri, "The NSQIP: A New Frontier in Surgery," *Surgery* 138 (2005): 837–843.
51. L. T. Kohn et al., Institute of Medicine, *To Err is Human: Building a Safer Health System* (Washington, DC: National Academies Press, 2000).
52. Institute of Medicine, Committee on Quality of Health Care in America, "Foreword," in *Crossing the Quality Chasm: A New Health System for the 21st Century* (Washington, DC: National Academies Press, 2001).
53. The Patient Protection and Affordable Care Act, Public Law 111-148, 42 U.S.C. 18003 (2010).
54. "Final Rule, Centers for Medicare and Medicaid Services (CMS), HHS. Medicaid Program; Payment Adjustment for Provider-Preventable Conditions Including Health Care-Acquired Conditions," *Federal Register* 76, no. 108 (Jun 6, 2011): 32816–32838.
55. Department of Health and Human Services, Centers for Medicare and Medicaid Services, "Medicare Program; Payment Policies under the Physician Fee Schedule, Five-Year Review of Work Relative Value Units, Clinical Laboratory Fee Schedule: Signature on Requisition, and Other Revisions to Part B for CY 2012. Final Rule with Comment Period," *Federal Register* 76, no. 228 (Nov 28, 2011): 73026–73474.
56. "Find and Compare Doctors, Hospitals and Other Providers," Medicare.gov, accessed October 12, 2018, https://www.medicare.gov/forms-help-and-resources/find-doctors-hospitals-and-facilities/quality-care-finder.html.
57. W. E. Deming, *Elementary Principles of the Statistical Control of Quality* (Tokyo: Nippon Kagaku, Gijutsu, Renmei, 1952).
58. Masaaki Imai, *Kaizen: The Key to Japan's Competitive Success* (New York: Random House, 1986).
59. Terence T. Burton, "Is This a Six Sigma, Lean or Kaizen Project?," Six Sigma, accessed December 8, 2017, https://www.isixsigma.com/new-to-six-sigma/how-is-six-sigma-different/six-sigma-lean-or-kaizen-project/.
60. M. A. Makary, "Medical Error: The Third Leading Cause of Death in the US," *British Medical Journal* 352 (2016): i2139.
61. E. D. Grober and J. M. A. Bohnen, "Defining Medical Error," *Canadian Journal of Surgery* 48, no. 1 (Feb 2005): 39–44.
62. "Agenda for Research and Development in Patient Safety," National Patient Safety Foundation, accessed October 12, 2018, https://cdn.ymaws.com/www.npsf.org/resource/collection/4B2E552F-48FA-4DCF-8BD8-574EE15EFD99/Agenda_for_RD_in_Patient_Safety.pdf.
63. L. L. Leape, "Error in Medicine," *Journal of the American Medical Association* 272, no. 23 (1994): 1851–1857.

64. J. Reason, *Human Error* (Cambridge, MA: Cambridge University Press, 1990).
65. J. T. Reason, "Understanding Adverse Events: The Human Factor," in *Clinical Risk Management: Enhancing Patient Safety*, ed. C. Vincent (London: BMJ Publishing Group, 2001), 9–30.
66. T. A. Brennan et al., "Incidence of Adverse Events and Negligence in Hospitalized Patients. Results of the Harvard Medical Practice Study I," *New England Journal of Medicine* 324, no. 6 (1991): 370–376.
67. L. L. Leape et al., "The Nature of Adverse Events in Hospitalized Patients. Results of the Harvard Medical Practice Study II," *New England Journal of Medicine* 324, no. 6 (Feb 7, 1991): 377–384.
68. R. M. Wilson et al., "The Quality in Australian Health Care Study," *Medical Journal of Australia* 163, no. 9 (1995): 458–471.
69. J. Reason, *Managing the Risks of Organizational Accidents* (Aldershot, UK: Ashgate, 1997).
70. P. Barach and S. D. Small, "Reporting and Preventing Medical Mishaps: Lessons from Non-Medical Near Miss Reporting Systems," *British Medical Journal* 320, no. 7237 (2000): 759–763.
71. G. E. Cooper, M. D. White, and J. K. Lauber, eds., *Resource management on the Flightdeck: Proceedings of a NASA/Industry Workshop (NASA CP-2120)* (Moffett Field, CA: NASA-Ames Research Center, 1980).
72. R. L. Helmreich and H. C. Foushee, "Why Crew Resource Management? Empirical and Theoretical Bases of Human Factors Training in Aviation," in *Cockpit Resource Management*, eds. E. Weiner, B. Kanki, and R. Helmreich (San Diego, CA: Academic Press, 1993), 3–45.
73. Department of the Air Force, Air Force Standards Agency. *Crew Resource Management: Basic Concepts* (Dec 1998), accessed October 17, 2018, https://webapp1.dlib.indiana.edu/virtual_disk_library/index.cgi/821003/FID177/pubs/af/atc/at-m-06a/at-m-06a.pdf.
74. Ibid.
75. H. B. King et al., "TeamSTEPPS™: Team Strategies and Tools to Enhance Performance and Patient Safety," in *Advances in Patient Safety: New Directions and Alternative Approaches (Vol. 3: Performance and Tools)*, ed. K. Henriksen et al. (Rockville, MD: Agency for Healthcare Research and Quality, 2008).
76. S. M. Berenholtz et al., "Qualitative Review of Intensive Care Unit Quality Indicators," *Journal of Critical Care* 17, no. 1 (Mar 2002): 1–12.
77. M. de Vos et al., "Quality Measurement at Intensive Care Units: Which Indicators Should We Use?," *Journal of Critical Care* 22, no. 4 (Dec 2007): 267–274.
78. J. R. Curtis et al., "Intensive Care Unit Quality Improvement: A 'How-To' Guide for the Interdisciplinary Team," *Critical Care Medicine* 34, no. 1 (2006): 211–218.
79. S. S. Magill et al., "Developing a New, National Approach to Surveillance for Ventilator-Associated Events," *American Journal of Critical Care* 22, no. 6 (Nov 2013): 469–473.
80. P. Pronovost et al., "An Intervention to Decrease Catheter-Related Bloodstream Infections in the ICU," *New England Journal of Medicine* 355, no. 26 (2006): 2725–2732.
81. M. M. Levy et al., "Association between Critical Care Physician Management and Patient Mortality in the Intensive Care Unit," *Annals of Internal Medicine* 148, no. 11 (2008): 801–809.
82. J. D. Burns et al., "The Effect of a Neurocritical Care Service without a Dedicated Neuro-ICU on Quality of Care in Intracerebral Hemorrhage," *Neurocritical Care* 18, no. 3 (2013): 305–312.
83. J. I. Suarez et al., "Length of Stay and Mortality in Neurocritically Ill Patients: Impact of a Specialized Neurocritical Care Team," *Critical Care Medicine* 32, no. 11 (2004): 2311–2317.
84. P. N. Varelas et al., "The Impact of a Neurointensivist-Led Team on a Semiclosed Neurosciences Intensive Care Unit," *Critical Care Medicine* 32, no. 11 (2004): 2191–2198.

85. M. N. Diringer and D. F. Edwards, "Admission to a Neurologic/Neurosurgical Intensive Care Unit Is Associated with Reduced Mortality Rate after Intracerebral Hemorrhage," *Critical Care Medicine* 29, no. 3 (2001): 635–640.
86. Y. Sarpong, P. Nattanmai, and G. Schelp, "Improvement in Quality Metrics Outcomes and Patient and Family Satisfaction in a Neurosciences Intensive Care Unit after Creation of a Dedicated Neurocritical Care Team," *Critical Care Research and Practice* 2017 (October 8, 2017), accessed October 12, 2018, https://doi.org/10.1155/2017/6394105.

CHAPTER 8 NEUROLAW AND THE INTEGRATION OF NEUROSCIENCE, ETHICS, AND THE LAW

1. J. Sherrod Taylor, J. Anderson Harp, and Tyron Elliott, "Neuropsychologists and Neurolawyers," *Neuropsychology* 5, no. 4 (October 1991): 293–305.
2. M. S. Pardo and D. Patterson, *Minds, Brains, and Law: The Conceptual Foundations of Law and Neuroscience* (Oxford: Oxford University Press, 2013), 23–24.
3. Wikipedia, s.v. "neurolaw," last accessed November 26, 2017, https://en.wikipedia.org/wiki/Neurolaw.
4. N. Shafi, "Neuroscience and Law: The Evidentiary Value of Brain Imaging," *Graduate Student Journal of Psychology* 11 (2009): 27–39.
5. S. K. Robbins and C. F. Craver, "No Nonsense Neuro-Law," *Neuroethics* 4, no. 3 (November 2011): 195–203, accessed October 12, 2018, https://doi.org/10.1007/s12152-010-9085-1.
6. "Model Penal Code—Selected Provisions," accessed December 16, 2017, http://www1.law.umkc.edu/suni/crimLaw/MPC_Provisions/model_penal_code_default_rules.htm.
7. S. A. Tovino, "Functional Neuroimaging and the Law: Trends and Directions for Future Scholarship," *American Journal of Bioethics* 7, no. 9 (2007): 44–56.
8. G. M. Gkotsi, V. Moulin, and J. Gasser, "Neuroscience in the Courtroom: From Responsibility to Dangerousness, Ethical Issues Raised by the new French Law," *Encephale* 41, no. 5 (October 2015): 385–393.
9. D. M. Eagleman, "The Brain on Trial," *Atlantic*, July 2011, accessed October 12, 2018, https://www.theatlantic.com/magazine/archive/2011/07/the-brain-on-trial/308520/.
10. S. Choudhury, S. K. Nagel, and J. Slaby, "Critical Neuroscience: Linking Neuroscience and Society through Critical Practice," *BioSocieties* 4 (2009): 61–77, https://doi.org/10.1017/S1745855209006437.
11. M. E. Raichle, "Functional Brain Imaging and Human Brain Function," *Journal of Neuroscience* 23, no. 10 (2003): 3959–3962.
12. B. Garland and P. W. Glimcher, "Cognitive Neuroscience and the Law," *Current Opinion in Neurobiology* 16, no. 2 (April 2006): 130–134.
13. J. P. Rosenfeld et al., "A Modified, Event-Related Potential-Based Guilty Knowledge Test," *International Journal of Neuroscience* 42, no. 1–2 (September 1988): 157–161.
14. J. H. Ko, C. C. Tang, and D. Eidelberg, "Brain Stimulation and Functional Imaging with fMRI and PET," *Handbook of Clinical Neurology* 116 (2013): 77–95.
15. M. M. Monti et al., "Willful Modulation of Brain Activity in Disorders of Consciousness," *New England Journal of Medicine* 362 (2010): 579–589.
16. M. Boly et al., "When Thoughts Become Action: An fMRI Paradigm to Study Volitional Brain Activity in Non-Communicative Brain Injured Patients," *Neuroimage* 36 (2007): 979–992.
17. M. E. Raichle, "Neuroscience: The Brain's Dark Energy," *Science* 314 (2006): 1249–1250.
18. A. E. Cavanna and M. R. Trimble, "The Precuneus: A Review of Its Functional Anatomy and Behavioural Correlates," *Brain* 129, no. 3 (2006): 564–583.

19. A. Vanhaudenhuyse et al., "Default Network Connectivity Reflects the Level of Consciousness in Non-Communicative Brain-Damaged Patients," *Brain* 133 (2010): 161–171.
20. A. Downes and N. Pouratian, "Advanced Neuroimaging Techniques for Central Neuromodulation," *Neurosurgery Clinics of North America* 25, no. 1 (2014): 173–185.
21. R. A. Robison et al., "Surgery of the Mind, Mood, and Conscious State: An Idea in Evolution," *World Neurosurgery* 80, no. 3–4 (2013): S2–S26.
22. L. A. Farwell, "Brain Fingerprinting: A Comprehensive Tutorial Review of Detection of Concealed Information with Event-Related Brain Potentials," *Cognitive Neurodynamics* 6, no. 2 (April 6, 2012): 115–154, https://doi.org/10.1007/s11571-012-9192-2.
23. D. Mobbs et al., "Law, Responsibility, and the Brain," *PLoS Biology* 5 no. 4 (April 2007): e103, https://doi.org/10.1371/journal.pbio.0050103.
24. M. Minsky, *The Society of Mind* (New York: Simon and Schuster, 1986), 339.
25. B. Libet et al., "Time of Conscious Intention to Act in Relation to Onset of Cerebral Activity (Readiness Potential): The Unconscious Initiation of a Freely Voluntary Act," *Brain* 106 (1983): 623–642.
26. N. S. Pandya et al., "Epilepsy and Homicide," *Neuropsychiatric Disease and Treatment* 9 (2013): 667–673, https://doi.org/10.2147/NDT.S45370.
27. S. Eisenschenk, H. Krop, and O. Devinsky, "Homicide during Postictal Psychosis," *Epilepsy Behavior Case Reports* 2 (2014): 118–120.
28. Tarasoff v. Regents of the University of California, 17 Cal. 3d 425, 551 P.2d 334, 131 Cal. Rptr. 14 (Cal. 1976).
29. Ewing v. Goldstein (120 Cal. App. 4th 807 [2004]) and Ewing v. Northridge Hospital Medical Center (120 Cal. App. 4th 1289 [2004]).
30. J. Grafman et al., "Frontal Lobe Injuries, Violence, and Aggression: A Report of the Vietnam Head Injury Study," *Neurology* 46, no. 5 (1996): 1231–1238.
31. I. Cristofori et al., "Brain Regions Influencing Implicit Violent Attitudes: A Lesion-Mapping Study," *Journal of Neuroscience* 36, no. 9 (March 2, 2016): 2757–2768, https://doi.org/10.1523/JNEUROSCI.2975-15.2016.
32. M. C. Brower and B. H. Price, "Neuropsychiatry of Frontal Lobe Dysfunction in Violent and Criminal Behaviour: A Critical Review," *Journal of Neurology, Neurosurgery, and Psychiatry* 71, no. 6 (December 2001): 720–726.
33. S. L. Risacher and A. J. Saykin, "Neuroimaging and Other Biomarkers for Alzheimer's Disease: The Changing Landscape of Early Detection," *Annual Review of Clinical Psychology* 9 (2013): 621–648.
34. Health Quality Ontario, "Functional Brain Imaging: An Evidence-Based Analysis," *Ontario Health Technology Assessment Series* 6, no. 22 (2006): 1–79.
35. M. W. Weiner et al., "The Alzheimer's Disease Neuroimaging Initiative: A Review of Papers Published since Its Inception," *Alzheimer's & Dementia* 9, no. 5 (September 2013): e111–e194, https://doi.org/10.1016/j.jalz.2013.05.1769.
36. J. Preston et al., "The Legal Implications of Detecting Alzheimer's Disease Earlier," *American Medical Association Journal of Ethics* 18, no. 12 (2016): 1207–1217.
37. R. Adolphs, J. Gläscher, and D. Tranel, "Searching for the Neural Causes of Criminal Behavior," *Proceedings of the National Academy of Sciences of the United States of America*, December 29, 2017, https://doi.org/10.1073/pnas.1720442115.
38. M. Liljegren et al., "Criminal Behavior in Frontotemporal Dementia and Alzheimer Disease," *Journal of the American Medical Association Neurology* 72, no. 3 (March 2015): 295–300.
39. M. R. Lovell et al., "Does Loss of Consciousness Predict Neuropsychological Decrements after Concussion?," *Clinical Journal of Sports Medicine* 9 (1999): 193–198.

40. D. Erlanger et al., "Symptom-Based Assessment of the Severity of a Concussion," *Journal of Neurosurgery* 98 (2003): 477–484.
41. R. C. Cantu, "Posttraumatic Retrograde and Anterograde Amnesia: Pathophysiology and Implications in Grading and Safe Return to Play," *Journal of Athletic Training* 36 (2001): 244–248.
42. C. Giza and D. Hovda, "The New Neurometabolic Cascade of Concussion," *Neurosurgery* 75 (2014): 524–533.
43. A. H. Ropper and K. C. Gorson, "Clinical Practice: Concussion," *New England Journal Medicine* 356 (2007): 166–172.
44. J. Halford et al., "New Astroglial Injury-Defined Biomarkers for Neurotrauma Assessment," *Journal of Cerebral Blood Flow & Metabolism* 37, no. 10 (2017): 3278–3299.
45. L. M. Lewis et al., "Utility of Serum Biomarkers in the Diagnosis and Stratification of Mild Traumatic Brain Injury," *Academic Emergency Medicine* 24, no. 6 (2017): 710–720.
46. Arthur L. Caplan & Lee H. Igel, "Is Saliva Test to Diagnose Concussions in English Rugby Worth a Spit?," *Forbes*, last accessed December 18, 2017, https://www.forbes.com/sites/leeigel/2017/09/01/is-saliva-test-to-diagnose-concussions-in-english-rugby-worth-a-spit/#2ff553254490.
47. R. Sharma et al., "A Blood-Based Biomarker Panel to Risk-Stratify Mild Traumatic Brain Injury," *PLoS ONE* [Electronic Resource] 12, no. 3 (2017): e0173798, accessed October 12, 2018, https://doi.org/10.1371/journal.pone.0173798.
48. H. L. Parker, "Traumatic Encephalopathy ("Punch Drunk") of Professional Pugilists," *Journal of Neurology and Psychopathology* 15 (1934): 20–28.
49. J. Millspaugh, "Dementia Pugilistica," *United States Naval Medical Bulletin* 35 (1937): 297–303.
50. M. Critchley, "Punch-Drunk Syndromes: The Chronic Traumatic Encephalopathy of Boxers," in *Hommage à Clovis Vincent*, ed. C. Vincent (Paris: Maloine, 1949).
51. B. I. Omalu et al., "Chronic Traumatic Encephalopathy in a National Football League Player," *Neurosurgery* 57 (2005): 128–134.
52. P. H. Montenigro et al., "Clinical Subtypes of Chronic Traumatic Encephalopathy: Literature Review and Proposed Research Diagnostic Criteria for Traumatic Encephalopathy Syndrome," *Alzheimer's Research and Therapy* 6 (2014): 1–17.
53. T. A. West and D. W. Marion, "Current Recommendations for the Diagnosis and Treatment of Concussion in Sport: A Comparison of Three New Guidelines," *Journal of Neurotrauma* 31, no. 2 (January 15, 2014): 159–168.
54. P. McCrory et al., "What Is the Evidence for Chronic Concussion-Related Changes in Retired Athletes: Behavioural, Pathological and Clinical Outcomes?," *British Journal of Sports Medicine* 47 (2013): 327–330.
55. K. Perrine et al., "The Current Status of Research on Chronic Traumatic Encephalopathy," *World Neurosurgery* 102 (2017): 533–544.
56. B. Omalu et al, "Emerging Histomorphologic Phenotypes of Chronic Traumatic Encephalopathy in American Athletes," *Neurosurgery* 69 (2011): 173–183.
57. Miranda v. Arizona, 384 U.S. 436, 444, 86 S. Ct. 1602, 16 L.Ed.2d 694 (1966).
58. People v. May, 859 P.2d 879, 883 (Colo. 1993); see also People v. Hopkins, 774 P.2d 849, 851 (Colo. 1989).
59. T. Grisso, *Instruments for Assessing Understanding and Appreciation of Miranda Rights* (Sarasota, FL: Professional Resource Press, 1998).
60. R. Rogers et al., "An Analysis of Miranda Warnings and Waivers: Comprehension and Coverage," *Law and Human Behavior* 31, no. 2 (2007): 177–192.
61. People v. Platt, 81 P.3d 1060, 1065–66 (Colo. 2004).

62. Colorado v. Jewell, No. 07SA319 (February 04, 2008).
63. B. E. Leonard et al., "Methylphenidate: A Review of Its Neuropharmacological, Neuropsychological and Adverse Clinical Effects," *Human Psychopharmacology* 19, no. 3 (2004): 151–180.
64. F. A. López, "ADHD: New Pharmacological Treatments on the Horizon," *Journal of Developmental and Behavioral Pediatrics* 27 (2006): 410–416.
65. M. R. Farlow and J. L. Cummings, "Effective Pharmacologic Management of Alzheimer's Disease," *American Journal of Medicine* 120 (2007): 388–397.
66. P. Frati et al., "Smart Drugs and Synthetic Androgens for Cognitive and Physical Enhancement: Revolving Doors of Cosmetic Neurology," *Current Neuropharmacology* 13, no. 1 (2015): 5–11.
67. British Medical Association, "Boosting Your Brainpower: Ethical Aspects of Cognitive Enhancements: A Discussion Paper from the British Medical Association," British Medical Association, November 2007, accessed December 17, 2017, http://enhancingresponsibility.com/wp-content/uploads/2014/01/Boosting_brainpower_tcm41-147266.pdf.
68. S. M. Outram, "The Use of Methylphenidate among Students: The Future of Enhancement?," *Journal of Medical Ethics* 36, no. 4 (2010): 198–202.
69. A. Estrada et al., "Modafinil as a Replacement for Dextroamphetamine for Sustaining Alertness in Military Helicopter Pilots," *Aviation, Space, and Environmental Medicine* 83, no. 6 (2012): 556–564.
70. V. Cakic, "Smart Drugs for Cognitive Enhancement: Ethical and Pragmatic Considerations in the Era of Cosmetic Neurology," *Journal of Medical Ethics* 35, no. 10 (October 2009): 611–615.
71. H. Maslen, N. Faulmüller, and J. Savulescu, "Pharmacological Cognitive Enhancement—How Neuroscientific Research Could Advance Ethical Debate," *Frontiers in Systems Neuroscience* 8 (2014): 107, https://doi.org/10.3389/fnsys.2014.00107.
72. R. Goodman, "Cognitive Enhancement, Cheating, and Accomplishment," *Kennedy Institute of Ethics Journal* 20, no. 2 (2010): 145–160.
73. W. P. Cheshire and J. C. Hutchins, "Professionalism in Court: The Neurologist as Expert Witness," *Neurology Clinical Practice* 4, no. 4 (August 2014): 335–341, https://doi.org/10.1212/CPJ.0000000000000041.
74. *Black's Law Dictionary*, 9th ed., ed. B. A. Garner (New York: Thomas West, 2009).
75. Frye v. United States, 130 S. Ct. 307 (1923).
76. Daubert v. Merrell Dow Pharmaceuticals, 509 U.S. 579 (1993).
77. Frye v. United States, 293 F 1013 (DC Cir 1923).
78. Kumho Tire Co. v. Carmichael, 119 S. Ct. 1167 (1999).
79. C. H. Klee and H. J. Friedman, "Neurolitigation: A Perspective on the Elements of Expert Testimony for Extending the Daubert Challenge," *NeuroRehabilitation* 16, no. 2 (2001): 79–85.
80. United States v. Semrau, No. 11-5396 (62nd Circuit Court of Appeals of the United States, 2012).

INDEX

Accountable Care Organizations, 124
Acute Physiology And Chronic Health Evaluation (APACHE), 128
Administrative Procedure Act (APA), 63, 81
advance directives, 8–9, 29, 30. *See also* end-of-life decisions
adverse events, 50, 86, 106, 114; definitions of, 78, 126; disclosure of, 20, 78–79; effects on health care professionals of, 77–78; with medical devices, 88
Affordable Care Act (2010), 91, 96, 97, 102, 124
Agency for Healthcare Research and Quality (AHRQ), 63, 83, 123–124
alcohol use, 57, 135, 136, 139–140
Alzheimer's disease, 22, 27; diagnosis of, 134, 136; treatment of, 140. *See also* dementia
American Academy of Neurology (AAN): on brain death, 37; on sports-related concussions, 137
American Association of Critical Care Nurses, 119, 121
American Association of Neurological Surgeons (AANS), 6
American Bar Association (ABA), 6, 35
American College of Critical Care, 119
American College of Physicians, 79
American College of Surgeons, 124
American Medical Association (AMA), 5, 6, 113; on brain death, 35; on disclosing medical errors, 79
American Medical Society for Sports Medicine, 137
American Recovery and Reinvestment Act (2009), 90
American Thoracic Society, 25
amnesia, 137
amphetamines, 57, 141
amyotrophic lateral sclerosis (ALS), 28
anencephaly, 29
Anti-Kickback Statute (AKS), 83, 101–103
antisocial behavior, 132, 135
aphasia, 136

apnea test, 38, 39
Aquinas, Thomas, 21
Aristotle, 3, 23, 25–26
Arizona Study of Aging and Neurodegenerative Disorders (AZSAND), 13–14
artificial intelligence (AI), 105–106
assisted suicide, 8, 15–18, 21–22, 30–31
atrial fibrillation, 104–105
attention-deficit/hyperactivity disorder (ADHD), 22, 140
attorney-client privilege, 68
Auer v. Robbins (1997), 82
autonomy, 78; assisted suicide and, 17; beneficence and, 20, 31; biomedical research and, 9–15; informed consent and, 7–8; paternalism versus, 7, 24; respect for, 7–15; right to choose and, 34

Baby K case, 29
Balance Error Scoring System, 138
Banner Sun Health Research Institute, 13–14
Barber v. Superior Court (1983), 16–17
Barthel Index, 27
Beauchamp, Tom L., 6, 15
Beecher, Henry, 35
Belmont Report (1979), 12
beneficence principle, 6, 15–20, 31, 78
Bentham, Jeremy, 3, 23
Best Evidence Rule, 74–75
Best Interests test, 19
blood pressure monitoring, 104–105, 112
Bouvia v. Superior Court (1986), 16
boxing injuries, 138
Brain and Body Donation Program (BBDP), 13–14
brain death, 8, 17, 35–40
brain fingerprinting, 135
brain injury, 132–137. *See also* traumatic brain injury
Breach Notification Rule, 91

Callaway, Allen, 38
Cardozo, Benjamin, 8

catheter-related urinary tract infections (CAUTIs), 128–129
cell line research, 13–14
cellphones, 104–105
Centers for Disease Control and Prevention (CDC), 63, 83
Centers for Medicare and Medicaid Services (CMS), 63, 83, 123; consumer websites of, 124; false claims to, 92–103; on informed consent, 9; "patient dumping" and, 100; Teaching Rule of, 96
cerebellar disorders, 138
cerebral palsy, 16
cerebrovascular accidents (CVAs). See strokes
cervical cancer, 13
Chevron U.S.A., Inc. v. Natural Resources Defense Council (1984), 82
Childress, James F., 6, 15
chronic traumatic encephalopathy (CTE), 138–139
claims-made liability policies, 60
clinical assistant professor (CAP) agreements, 103
Code of Federal Regulations (CFR), 63
Code of Medical Ethics, 5
codes of conduct, 3–6, 14
cognitive enhancement, 22, 133, 140–141
Compassion in Dying (organization), 17
competency, 75, 136; determination of, 19; treatment refusal and, 8–9, 16, 17, 31
computed tomography (CT), 73, 101, 133, 137, 138
concussion, 133, 137–140
conflicts of interest, 68
consent, implied, 18. *See also* informed consent
consequentialism, 23
Constitution, U.S., 2, 62, 132; Fifth Amendment of, 139; Fourteenth Amendment of, 8, 17
Consumer Assessment of Healthcare Providers and Systems, 124
contracts, 65, 132
Controlled Substances Act (2005), 83
"cooperation clause," of malpractice insurance, 79
Council for the International Organizations of Medical Sciences (CIOMS), 11

credentialing, 115
Crew Resource Management (CRM), 127
criminal behavior, 132, 135, 136
critical care nursing, 119
Cruzan v. Director, Missouri Department of Health (1990), 8, 15–16

Dandy, Walter, 119
Data Monitoring Committees (DMCs), 14
data safety monitoring boards (DSMBs), 14
Daubert v. Merrell Dow Pharmaceuticals (1993), 142
Dead Donor Rule (DDR), 39
death determined by neurological criteria (DDNC), 37–39
Death with Dignity Act (DWDA), 18
decision-making: Crew Resource Management and, 127–128; informed, 9; prognostication and, 32; shared, 117
decubitus ulcers, 128
deep brain stimulation (DBS), 22
default mode network (DMN), of brain function, 134
Deficit Reduction Act (2005), 92, 94
dementia, 22, 24, 27, 132–136, 140
Deming, W. E., 125
Denham, C., 78
Department of Health and Human Servics (DHHS), 63, 82–83, 95–96
depositions, 69, 75
digital medicine, 104–115
disclosure, of medical errors, 20, 69–70, 78–79
discovery process, 69–71, 111
discrimination, 24
distributive justice, 23, 28, 39, 41
Donabedian, Avedis, 123
do-not-resuscitate (DNR) orders, 33, 34
double effect principle, 22; palliative sedation and, 30–31
Drug Enforcement Administration (DEA), 63, 83
Drug Quality Safety and Security Act, 84
drug regulations, 63, 83–89
due process, 8, 17, 56, 64, 67
duty, 40–42, 110; breach of, 44, 45, 111; ethical, 3, 15; fiduciary, 14–15, 20, 78
dysarthria, 138

Index

Eggshell Plaintiff Rule, 49
electroencephalography (EEG), 133, 135
electronic medical record (EMR). *See under* medical records
Emergency Medical Treatment and Active Labor Act (2005), 99–100
end-of-life decisions, 29–31, 76, 119, 130; advance directives for, 8–9, 29, 30; DNR orders and, 33, 34; right to die and, 8, 15–18
English Common Law, 42, 63
entitlements, 24
epilepsy, 112, 135
errors. *See* medical errors
ethics, 2–6, 45, 79, 90, 130–131; Aristotelian, 26; biomedical, 6–7, 11–14, 18–20; Hippocratic, 11, 28, 31; normative, 3
ethics committees, 5–7, 11, 29–30
euthanasia, 15–18; palliative sedation and, 21–22, 30–31
event-related potentials (ERPs), 133, 135
evidence: accumulation of, 69; admissibility of, 72–75; electronic, 70, 74; expert, 142; facts and, 65–67, 72–73; preponderance of, 76; rules of, 64, 73; spoliation of, 73–74; testimonial, 75; types of, 70
Ewing v. Goldstein (2004), 135
examination before trial (EBT), 75
expert witnesses, 6, 69, 131–132, 141–142
extracorporeal membrane oxygenation (ECMO), 33, 39
extrapyramidal disorders, 138

facts: evidence and, 65–66, 72–73; legal versus scientific, 65–66, 142
failure to warn, 89
false claims, 108. *See also* Federal False Claims Act
FDA Safety and Innovation Act (2012), 84
Federal Civil Penalties Inflation Adjustment Act (1990), 92
Federal Drug Administration (FDA): drug approval by, 83–86; medical devices approval by, 86–89
Federal False Claims Act (FFCA), 72, 92–97, 102, 108, 115
Federal Food, Drug, and Cosmetic Act (FFDCA), 83–84, 86–87
Federal Rules of Civil Procedure (FRCP), 70–71, 74

Federal Rules of Evidence (FRE), 73
Federal Tort Claims Act, 44
feeding tubes, 8, 16, 27–30
Fifth Amendment rights, 139
First Financial Security v. Freedom Equity (2016), 74
Food and Drug Administration (FDA), 63; medical device regulation by, 86–89; pharmaceutical regulation by, 83–86
football brain injuries, 138
Fourteenth Amendment. *See* Constitution, U.S.
fraud, 72, 92–98, 101
Frye v. United States (2009), 142
functional magnetic resonance imaging (fMRI), 133–134, 142
futile treatments. *See* medical futility

General Practitioner Assessment of Cognition, 27
Geneva Convention (1864), 24
Glasgow Coma Scale, 34, 137
GlaxoSmithKline, 103
glucose monitoring, 105
Gonzales v. Oregon (2006), 17
Good Manufacturing Procedures (GMPs), 85
Gostin, L. O., 39–40
Goulon, M., 35
Graduate Medical Education (GME), 95
guilt, proof of, 76

head injury, 132, 133, 136–139. *See also* traumatic brain injury
Healthcare Common Procedure Coding System (HCPCS), 113
Healthcare Effectiveness Data and Information Set, 124
Health Care Financing Administration (HCFA), 9, 124
Health Care Fraud and Abuse Control Program, 93
Health Care Fraud Prevention and Enforcement Action Team, 101
Healthcare Integrity and Protection Data Bank (HIPDB), 52
Health Care Quality Improvement Act (HCQIA), 69
Health Information Technology for Economic and Clinical Health Act (HITECH), 74, 90–91, 108, 109, 115

Index

Health Insurance Portability and Accountability Act (HIPPA), 12, 52, 90, 91; electronic medical records and, 74, 105, 107–109, 115
Health Resources and Services Administration (HRSA), 83
healthy lifestyle management, 104, 105
Heller v. Doe, 19
Helling v. Carey (1974), 48
Helsinki, Declaration of (1964), 11
heroic interventions, 130; advance directives for, 8–9, 29–31; prognostication and, 32–35
Hicks v. United States (1966), 49
High Reliability Health Care Maturity (HRHCM) model, 122
high-reliability organizations (HROs), 121–123
Hippocratic ethics, 11, 28, 31
Hippocratic Oath, 4, 45; assisted suicide and, 17; beneficence in, 15; on nonmaleficence, 20
Hurst, S. A., 7

incident reports, 69–70
informed consent, 2, 7–15; implied versus, 18; malpractice law and, 51–52; Nuremberg Code and, 9–11; requirements for, 13, 140
In re Allen Callaway (2016), 38
In re Helen Wanglie (1991), 29
In re Miranda Lawson (2016), 38
insanity defense, 133, 135
Institute of Medicine (IOM), 21, 123, 126
institutional review board (IRB), 13
insurance, liability, 46, 56–61, 67–68, 79
intensive care units (ICUs), 118–121; quality measures of, 128–129; telemedicine and, 112–113; triage algorithm for, 25, 40–41. *See also* neurocritical care units
intent, 135; negligence and, 43–44, 131–132
International Bioethics Committee (IBC), 11
International Conference on Concussion in Sport, 137
Intracerebral Hemorrhage (ICH) score, 34. *See also* strokes
intracranial hemorrhage, 112. *See also* traumatic brain injury
investigational new drug (IND), 84–85

Jewell case (2008), 139–140
Joint Commission on Accreditation of Healthcare Organizations (JCAHO), 69; on disclosing medical errors, 79; on leadership standards, 118; on Sterile Cockpit Rule, 111
Jones v. Chidester (1992), 48
justice, 2, 6, 23–25; distributive, 23, 28, 39, 41; torts and, 42; types of, 23
justifiable reliance principle, 45

Kaizen method, 125
Kant, Immanuel, 3
Kennedy, Anthony McLeod, Justice, 19
Kumho Tire Company v. Carmichael (1999), 142

Lacks, Henrietta, 13
Lasagna, Louis, 4
Lawson, Miranda, 38
leadership, 116–118, 122–123, 127–128, 143
Leape, Lucian, 126
Leapfrog Group, 120
learned intermediary doctrine, 86
learning organizations, 117, 121–122
legal system, 63–64
Lewy body dementia, 14, 27
liability, 42–50, 78–79; criminal, 135; immunity from, 53; malpractice insurance for, 46, 56–61, 67–68, 79; product, 42, 88–89; theories of, 14; for torts, 42–43, 46, 114
lie detector machines, 133, 135
limitations, statute of, 68
living wills, 8–9, 29, 30
Locality Rule, 37
locked-in syndrome, 130, 134
loss of chance doctrine (LOCD), 49–50

magnetic resonance imaging (MRI), 100–101, 133–134, 137, 142
magnetic resonance spectroscopy (MRS), 133
magnetoencephalography (MEG), 133
Maimonides, Moses, 5
malpractice, 42–61; damages for, 50; determination of, 43–47; guilty verdict for, 52–53; legal risks of, 53–56; liability insurance for, 46, 56–61, 67–68, 79; Locality Rule in, 37; National Practitioner

Databank of, 54–55; negligence and, 43–44, 77; prevention of, 69–70, 78; professional misconduct and, 57–59
MB2 Dental Solutions, 98
McCarran-Ferguson Act (1945), 56
Medicaid Drug Rebate Program, 103
Medicaid Integrity Program (MIP), 94
Medical Device Amendments Act (1976), 86–87
medical devices, regulation of, 86–89
medical errors, 126–127; definitions of, 126; disclosure of, 20, 69–70, 78–79; incident reports of, 69–70; Institute of Medicine on, 21; mortality from, 126; Osler on, 77. *See also* negligence
medical futility, 28–30, 33. *See also* withholding treatment
Medical Judgment Rule, 47–48
Medically Induced Trauma Support Services, 78
medical records, 37–38, 50–51; electronic, 74, 90–91, 106–111, 115; as legal evidence, 70, 73; triage decisions in, 41
Medicare and Medicaid Patient and Program Protection Act (1987), 102
Medicare/Medicaid. *See* Centers for Medicare and Medicaid Services
Medicare Modernization Act (2003), 84
MedWatch, 86
mens rea, 131–132, 135, 136
methylphenidate (Ritalin), 141
Mill, John Stuart, 2, 3, 23
Miranda warning, 133, 139–140
misconduct, professional, 57–59
modafinil, 141
Model Code of Ethics, 14
Model Penal Code, 131
Mollaret, P., 35
moral philosophy, 3
morality, 1–2, 15, 25, 45, 130–131
Mount Sinai School of Medicine Brain Bank (MSSM-BB), 14
multidisciplinary team model of critical care, 120–122

National Bioethics Advisory Commission, 13, 14
National Committee for Quality Assurance (NCQA), 124

National Healthcare Antifraud Association, 93–94
National Institute of Mental Health (NIMH) Brain Collection, 14
National Institutes of Health (NIH), 83
National Pain Care, Inc., 98
National Patient Safety Foundation, 126
National Practitioner Data Bank (NPDB), 52–55, 68, 97
National Quality Strategy, 124
National Surgery Quality Improvement Project, 124
National Telehealth Policy Resource Center, 114
Natural Death Act (1979), 17
negligence, 21, 42–45; definition of, 42; intent and, 43–44, 131–132; Locality Rule and, 37; loss of chance doctrine and, 49; malpractice law and, 43–44, 77; medical devices and, 89. *See also* medical errors; torts
Neurocritical Care Society, 5–6, 120
neurocritical care units, 33, 34, 119–121, 128–129, 143. *See also* intensive care units
"neurolaw," 131–133
Neurological Devices Panel, 89
neuropharmacology, 140–141
New York Public Health Law (NY PHL), 69
nihilism, clinical, 34, 35
nonmaleficence principle, 6, 15, 20–23, 28, 39, 78
nootropic drugs, 140–141
Nuremberg Code, 5, 9–12

oath, 3–5; examination under, 75; Hippocratic, 4, 15, 17, 20, 45
occurrence liability policies, 60
Office for Civil Rights (OCR), 91
Office of Human Research Protections (OHRP), 14
Office of the Inspector General (OIG), 83, 92, 94, 97, 102
Offices of the Medicaid Inspector General (OMIGs), 94
off-label drug use, 85
one purpose test, 102
opiates, 31
organ procurement, 18; Dead Donor Rule for, 39; tissue banks and, 12–15
Osler, William, 21, 77
over-the-counter (OTC) drugs, 83

pain management, 31, 98
palliative care, 21–22, 28–31
Paré, Ambroise, 31
parens patriae doctrine, 19
Parkinson's disease, 14, 140
paternalism, 7, 24. *See also* autonomy
Patient-Centered Outcomes Research Institute, 124
Patient Protection and Accountable Care Act (PPACA). *See* Affordable Care Act
patient-provider relationship, 40, 45, 47, 114
Patient Self-Determination Act (PSDA), 8–9
Pederson v. Dumouchel (1967), 37
peer review, 69–70, 123
People v. Jewell (2008), 139–140
People v. Platt (2004), 139
Percival, Thomas, 5
persistent vegetative state (PVS), 8, 17. *See also* brain death
persuasion, burden of, 76
Peters, Tom, 116
Physicians at Teaching Hospitals (PATH) program, 95–96
Physician's Oath, 5
Physician Self-Referral Law, 83, 100–101
Plato, 3
Platt case (2004), 139
polygraph machines, 133, 135
positron emission tomography (PET), 133–134, 136
postconcussion syndrome (PCS), 138
post-traumatic stress disorder (PTSD), 77
privacy, 4, 11–12, 42, 90–91, 106–109
procedural law, 64
professional judgment rule, 47–48
professional standards review organizations (PSROs), 123
prognostication, 16, 32–35, 41
proof: burden of, 75–76; legal versus scientific, 66–67, 142. *See also* evidence
provider-patient relationship, 40, 45, 47, 114
psychopharmacology, 140
P300 Memory and Encoding Related Multifacted Electroencephalographic Response (P300-MEMER), 135

quality assurance reviews, 21, 69–70
quality improvement programs, 123–125, 128–129
quality of life issues, 16, 27–28
qui tam lawsuits, 97–98, 103
Quinlan, Karen Ann, 15–16

Rapid Cycle Performance Improvement (RCPI), 125
Reason, James, 126
reasonable doubt, 76
reasonably prudent person standard, 42–44, 66
Recovery Audit Contractors (RACs), 98
refusal of treatment. *See* treatment refusal
regulatory law, 81–103
Rehnquist, William, 8
religious beliefs, 3, 37–38
renal failure, 120
Research on Adverse Drug Events and Reports (RADAR), 86
res ipsa loquitur doctrine, 43, 48
Respectable Minority Rule, 48
"Respectful Management of Serious Clinical Adverse Events," 78
Riegel v. Medtronic, Inc. (2008), 86–87
right to die, 8, 15–18
Robust Process Improvement, 122
rulemaking process, 81–82

safe harbor provisions, 79, 102
safety culture, 122, 126, 143
Scalia, Antonin, 17
sedation, palliative, 21–22, 30–31
seizure disorders, 112, 135
self-fulfilling prophecies, 34–35
Senge, Peter M., 117
sepsis, 120
single-photon emission computed tomography (SPECT), 133
situational awareness, 127
Six Sigma program, 125
Skidmore v. Swift (1944), 82
smartphones, 104–105
social media, 109
Society of Critical Care Medicine, 25, 119, 121
Stamos v. Davies (1985), 20
Stark law (2011), 83, 100–101
Sterile Cockpit Rule, 111
strokes, 28, 105; hemorrhagic, 28, 34; ischemic, 50, 112; treatment of, 140

Suarez, J. I., 129
subpoenas, 71–72
"Substituted Judgment" test, 19
suicide, 77; physician-assisted, 8, 15–18, 21–22, 30–31; prevention of, 16
summons, 67
systems theory, 118

Tarasoff v. Regents of University of California (1976), 135
Tax Relief and Health Care Act (2006), 98
Taylor, Sherrod J., 131
teamwork, 116–122; resource management and, 127–128
technology-forcing regulations, 130–131
telecritical care, 112–115
telehealth, 104–105
teleneurology, 111–115
Tenet Healthcare Corp., 103
testimonial evidence, 75
Thin Skull Rule, 49
tissue banks, 12–15. *See also* organ procurement
tissue plasminogen activator (tPA), 50, 112
Title IV, 53
torts, 14, 21, 23, 42–46; damages for, 50; evidence of, 49, 73, 134; liability for, 42–43, 46, 114; types of, 42
Total Quality Management (TQM), 125
Tourette's syndrome, 132
Toyota Corporation, 125
traumatic brain injury (TBI), 27–28, 32–35, 132–133, 136–140
traumatic encephalopathy syndrome, 139
treatment refusal, 7–8, 15–17, 29–30, 32, 34. *See also* withholding treatment
triage, 24–25; algorithm for, 24, 40–41
"two schools of thought doctrine," 48

UNESCO International Bioethics Committee, 11
Uniform Anatomical Gift Act (UAGA), 13
Uniform Brain Death Act (UBDA), 35, 37
Uniform Determination of Death Act (UDDA), 35, 37, 38
United Council of Neurological Subspecialties, 120
United States Code (USC), 63
United States v. Aseracare, Inc. (2014), 93
United States v. Campbell (2011), 103
United States v. Greber (1985), 102
United States v. McClatchey (2000), 103
United States v. Semrau (2012), 142
Universal Declaration of Human Rights (1948), 24
urinary catheters, 128–129
utility principle, 15; allocating resources by, 41; beneficence and, 18–19, 20
utilization review programs, 123

Vacco v. Quill (1997), 17
value-based care, 104
value-based purchasing (VBP), 124
Veterans Administration (VA), 44, 97, 124

Wanglie, Helen, 29
Washington v. Glucksberg (1997), 17, 21
whistleblower lawsuits, 97–98, 103
Wiley Act (1906), 83
Windsor, Robert, 98
withholding treatment, 27–30; demanding treatment versus, 38–39; DNR orders and, 33, 34. *See also* medical futility; treatment refusal
witnesses: competency of, 75; expert, 6, 69, 131–132, 141–142
World Medical Association, 11, 5

ABOUT THE AUTHOR

JAMES E. SZALADOS, MD, MBA, MHA, Esq. has over thirty years of training and clinical experience in medicine and over a decade of experience as an attorney. Dr. Szalados has earned the distinction of fellowship in the Societies of Critical Care Medicine, Neurocritical Care; and the American Colleges of Chest Physicians, Legal Medicine, and the American College of Healthcare Executives. The author of dozens of articles and chapters on diverse aspects of health care law, Dr. Szalados is also a professional speaker and educator who regularly participates in the education of administrators, attorneys, and physicians on medical-legal matters.